THE FUTURE OF RETAIL BANKING

Also by Joseph A. DiVanna:

Redefining Financial Services: The New Renaissance in Value Propositions

Thinking Beyond Technology: Creating New Value in Business

Synconomy: Adding Value in a World of Continuously Connected Business

THE FUTURE OF RETAIL BANKING

Delivering value to global customers

Joseph A. DiVanna

First published 2004 by
PALGRAVE MACMILLAN
Houndmills, Basingstoke, Hampshire RG21 6XS and
175 Fifth Avenue, New York, N.Y. 10010
Companies and representatives throughout the world

PALGRAVE MACMILLAN is the global academic imprint of the Palgrave Macmillan division of St. Martin's Press, LLC and of Palgrave Macmillan Ltd. Macmillan® is a registered trademark in the United States, United Kingdom and other countries. Palgrave is a registered trademark in the European Union and other countries.

ISBN 1–4039–1126–6

This book is printed on paper suitable for recycling and made from fully managed and sustained forest sources.

A catalogue record for this book is available from the British Library.

Library of Congress Cataloging-in-Publication Data

DiVanna, Joseph A.
The future of retail banking : delivering value to global customers / Joseph A. DiVanna.
p. cm.
Includes bibliographical references and index.
ISBN 1–4039–1126–6
1. Banks and banking. 2. Financial services industry. 3. Customer services—Management. 4. Value. I. Title.

HG1601.D58 2003
332.1'2'068—dc22 2003060964

Editing and origination by Aardvark Editorial, Mendham, Suffolk

10 9 8 7 6 5 4 3 2 1
13 12 11 10 09 08 07 06 05 04

Printed and bound in Great Britain by
Creative Print & Design (Wales), Ebbw Vale

To my wife Isabel, who is always there when I need a push.

To my siblings Lori, Tony and Michael who, having sprung from the same household, adopted very dissimilar approaches to money, investment and banking, each defining their happiness in more than simple financial terms.

CONTENTS

List of Figures

PREFACE

This book is not designed as a prediction of the future, but rather as a reflection on how banks from many different parts of the world are preparing for the future. As a reader, you will notice the number of smaller banks, regional banks and lesser-known financial services companies from all parts of the world referenced in this text; this is not to demonstrate a superior capability, product or offering but to illustrate the diversity in the global tapestry of retail banking. I used these institutions to illustrate banking services because, as a reader, I myself think that many of the more traditional examples of large international banks have been overused by other authors in the last few years. However, many of these firms do indeed have valuable lessons to teach large and small banks.

The intention of this book is to stimulate an understanding of the metamorphosis that is happening within the retail banking industry at this time. One must consider while reading this book that the traditional operations of banking have to be reconsidered, rethought and revitalized not only because technology makes new services and products possible, but also because of the new opportunities that technology brings in terms of value to customers and shareholders. Because I believe that more lessons may be learned from the mistakes that companies make than from their successful stories, I have examined several case studies of financial services blunders. To preserve companies' confidentiality, I have omitted their identities in the case of blunders, whereas I identified them by name and product name in the case of good examples of products, services and the application of technology.

JOSEPH A. DIVANNA II

Acknowledgements

It would take a book in its own right to acknowledge all the people who have shared ideas, expressed opinions and engaged in the arguments that have shaped the contents of this book. First and foremost, I would like to thank my wife Isabel for her continual willingness to read the iterative versions of this book during its development and her patience with my sometimes avant-garde approach to writing.

To my many colleagues in the financial services industry, I offer my most heartfelt thanks for the many energetic and sometimes heated debates on the future of retail banking. I would like to thank my many clients for giving me the privilege of spending time with their organizations and allowing me to have an inside view to their operations. The list is quite long, so I would like to express my thanks to those who have contributed to the preparation of this book in a special way through our lively discussions: Jean Louis de la Salle, from Lexmark France; Martin Dolan and Daragh O'Byrne from Misys International Banking Systems; Bill Postgate from ePayCom; Wendy Martin and the staff of the Bank Card Business School of Visa International; Jeff Bartman, Roy Frangione, Vic Lund and Boxley Llewellyn from IBM; Mark Sievewright, John Stone and Jim Eckenrode from TowerGroup; Ralph Richards from UBS; Gil Trottino from BMC Software; Jiri Necas from Hewlett-Packard; Sriram Padmanabhan from the Standard Chartered Bank; and Jay Rogers from The Valance Group.

My most special thanks to Professor Pat Bateson, Provost of King's College, Cambridge, and the fellows of King's College for permitting me to continue my research into the practices, techniques and behaviours of the medieval masons, which has led me to develop a greater understanding of the medieval economy. I would also like to thank my publisher Stephen Rutt at Palgrave Macmillan, for his continual support, unending patience during the development of the manuscript and willingness to take my ideas and provide me with a platform for my views on business in this new century. The production of this book would not be possible without the hard work of the staff of Palgrave Macmillan: Sanphy Thomas, Jacky Kippenberger, Fionnuala Kennedy and Anna Van Boxel.

A special acknowledgement and thank you to Janice Nagourney of Thought Leaders International in Paris for her tireless work in orchestrating my speaking engagements and providing me with global forums to share my perspectives on doing business in the new century. I would also like to thank the countless people who have taken time from their business schedules to attend my lectures and share their global perspectives with me; it is indeed a rare privilege to be welcomed by so many people.

Once again, I would like to thank Richard Buckminster Fuller for his influence on my life and his ability to shape my approach to research which I hope to pass on to a new generation of students and young people.

INTRODUCTION

In the 1990s, amidst the hype generated by the computer industry, the future of retail banking seemed paved with technology, only to find an abrupt reversal in attitude towards spending on technology in the aftermath of the dot-com meltdown. By the year 2000, retail banking began to experience aftershocks from their technological enthusiasm as banks realized that many customer segments depended on the services found in branches. A larger than expected percentage of customers, including those who were already using the Internet, valued branches as complementary to the more sophisticated Internet offerings. The industry has realized that the potential cost savings of closing branches based solely on projected Internet growth rates may have been overstated. Banks soon noticed that, surprisingly, customers valued the branches, which launched many institutions into a process of chasing the needs of customers rather than leading customers to value.

Some banks adopted an approach which focused on servicing specific market segments such as the wealthy, while other organizations opted to match banking products to various demographic profiles. The byproduct of these two efforts to refocus has rekindled a fascination with a continuous and often maniacal search for the relentless reduction of operating costs, in many cases at the expense of missing critical investment opportunities to enhance the long-term performance of the institution. As we will see, the future of retail banking is neither technological nor is it simply embracing customers ever-changing needs. The future of retail banking is a complex task of transforming traditional banking institutions into agile organizations that deliver financial services to facilitate a rising set of emerging global lifestyles. Institutions will be challenged to optimize the cost of services predicated on embracing new corporate structures that are competent in sensing changes in the marketplace, dynamically reconfiguring products, aligning services to global customer needs and enabling a new era of global business transactions and individual financial management.

The original intention of this book was to explore how various financial institutions across the globe were developing visions of the retail branch of the future. However, during the research it became apparent that the visions for activities within a branch are just a diversion to the radical changes needed for retail banks to compete in the global economy. The branch is only the tip of the financial services iceberg, an icon representing only the first in a series of changes needed to realign the lines of business within the institution with sustainable long-term profitability. The future of retail banking centres on generating value for customers while providing consistent returns for shareholders in fundamentally different ways than those of previous generations of banking institutions.

Achieving a balance between high-tech customer service and lower operating costs is not a new goal for banks. In fact, it has been the driving force behind banking organizations from their beginning to the present day. What is different, however, are the new levels of services and higher degrees of product sophistication necessary to attract and retain customers while optimizing profits. Reaching these objectives is not as easy as it used to be, because, in the past, banks were sheltered from competition to some degree by legislation. Many of the laws controlling the conduct of today's retail banks were created in direct response to failures that occurred in the banking system or economic catastrophes of the past. As world governments rewrite banking legislation, they create opportunities for retail banks to explore new avenues to customers and introduce new products that more closely reflect the changing needs of their customers. However, this also creates opportunities for organizations that were previously considered non-financial institutions to become competitors.

In order to arrive at the future state of banking, a financial services organization will typically have to make the transition in three major steps or phases: thinking ahead, preparing to transform the organization and, finally, competing in the new competitive marketplace. Obviously, many institutions have already begun the journey, some having achieved successes in all three steps. Chapter 1 takes a historical view of intermediaries that have provided banking services to establish the fundamentals of the retail banking value proposition. Chapter 2 examines what is happening now with products, services and customer behaviour and other external factors. In Chapter 3, we begin to look at how external factors are reshaping the nature of retail banking and the influence these factors have on altering the structure of the organization. The focus of Chapter 4 is the relativity of the external factors and the changes occurring within financial services companies against the firm's value proposition and market disciplines. Chapter 5 proposes several scenarios of operating states which culminate in the development of operating synergies within the firm and the evolution of the organization into a node on a network of value.

The saying 'a journey of a thousand miles begins by taking the initial step'[1] has been attributed to the sixth-century Chinese philosopher Lao Tzu. The first step in our journey to the future of retail banking is an examination of where banking has come from. I do not intend to conduct a nostalgic look at the past, but a look at value propositions of earlier banking organizations provides a foundation on which to develop future value propositions. We will start by investigating financial institutions of the past and analysing how much the value proposition of banks has changed over the years. With the start of the twenty-first century, technological advances coupled with changing global lifestyles are now forcing a fundamental change in the value proposition for retail and commercial banking services providers.

Chapter 2 will focus on thinking ahead by developing an understanding of the future state of the competitive marketplace based on the visions of banks and technology companies found in all geographies. Technological advances in currency and payment systems will again alter the way in which people approach banking as a mechanism to facilitate their lifestyles. We shall discuss globalization, disintermediation, technical innovation, cultural, demographic and other social factors that will influence customer behaviours, as attitudes towards money, savings and investment adjust to meet the needs of evolving lifestyles.

Chapter 3 discusses how these external factors are reshaping banking products, altering the structure of the financial services organizations, the lines of business the institutions offer, the sources of revenue and, ultimately, the channels to market. More importantly, this chapter links these factors to changing customer behaviour and offers methods of qualitative and quantitative measurement.

Chapter 4 considers the reality of bringing a fundamental change to the retail banking institution by reviewing the strategic initiatives of organizations by placing them into a context of the value disciplines.[2] In this chapter, we also look at the emerging cooperative landscape of the changing financial services marketplace and seek to offer insight into establishing relationships with external entities that are based on partnerships, associations and affiliations.

Chapter 5, 'Synergistic Banking', examines new areas of thinking that are taking financial institutions beyond the boundaries of traditional retail banking design. Co-opetition, collaboration and other approaches are reviewed as retail banks in all parts of the world continue to experiment, with good and bad results. The conclusion offers a framework to consider

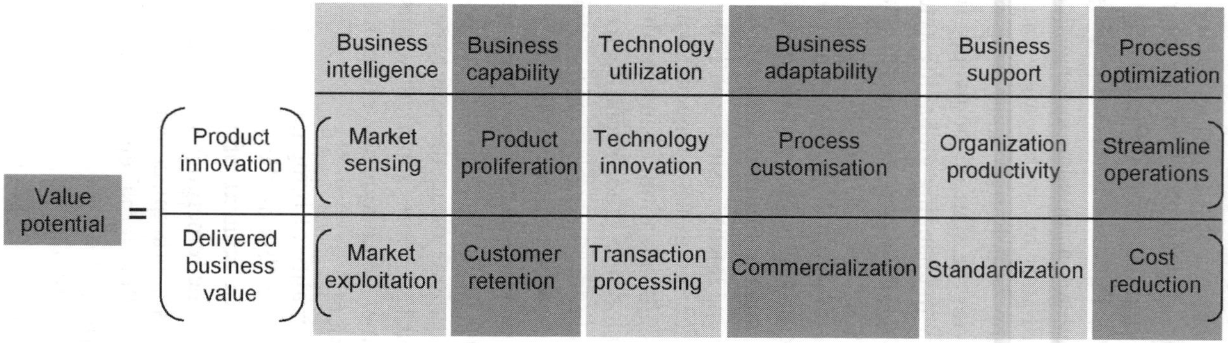

Value potential =	Business intelligence	Business capability	Technology utilization	Business adaptability	Business support	Process optimization
Product innovation	Market sensing	Product proliferation	Technology innovation	Process customisation	Organization productivity	Streamline operations
Delivered business value	Market exploitation	Customer retention	Transaction processing	Commercialization	Standardization	Cost reduction

Figure 0.1 The value potential model

value generation, which provides a method for institutions to make the transition into the future.

Retail banks, as any global business, have an untapped potential to generate value. This potential is found when thinking about the lines of business in a new way. In order to rethink the traditional lines of business, managers in the retail banking industry may consider the framework depicted in Figure 0.1.

In Figure 0.1, the firm's potential to add value is a product of the firm's ability to harness resources and technology through innovation over the competencies within the organization to focus on strategic initiatives which drive value. It can be said that retail banks, equipped with identical resources of people, technology and funding, will deliver inherently different results due to differences in skills, attitude, motivations and competencies that are brought together to form the core competencies of the firm. Many of the observations found in this book are a direct result of an ongoing survey of the financial services industry conducted by Maris Strategies Ltd using this value framework. The primary use of the survey is for banks to self-diagnose areas within the company which need improvement, that is, demonstrate gaps in capabilities. Because of the confidential data regarding the institution's capabilities, the detailed data and names of banks are not revealed in this book. The data supplied is merely used to categorize and identify anomalies and global trends in banking business processes, the applied use of technology and organizational structures. Any retail bank is invited to participate in the survey; details can be found at http://www.marisstrategies.com/future-of-banking/.

Notes

1 Lao Tzu, trans. T. C. Lau, *Tao Te Ching*, in Andrews, Biggs, Siedal et al. *The Columbia World of Quotations*, New York: Columbia University Press, 1996.

2 M. Treacy and F. Wiersema, *The Discipline of Market Leaders*, Reading, MA: Perseus Books, 1997.

CHAPTER 1

The Nature of Banking and its Future

It can be argued that since the time of the medieval Florentine bankers, the nature of banking and general services used to facilitate commerce has changed very little. Technology is often credited with revolutionizing the banking industry; in reality, technology has been used, for the most part, to pour old wine into new bottles. Each new generation of technology is applied to the legacy of banking services to automate labour-intensive processes, accelerate the speed of transactions, attract new customers, authenticate parties in a transaction, augment profit margins and a host of other traditional banking measurements. Technology has led to a greater sophistication of banking and investment products, making them more complex and harder to understand by potential customers, in many cases resulting in having to educate customers before they will subscribe to new banking products. Paradoxically, although the cost of operating technology-driven products continues to reduce through commoditization, a portion of this saving is lost by the increase in the cost of sales because of the additional education and longer sales cycle. This interrelationship between technology, cost, customer and sales leads institutions to compare the task of providing banking services to the activities of manufacturing companies.

Banks are unlike manufacturing companies, commodity goods providers or retailers because they do not supply products to customers, they provide a service to the general public and business while acting as a means of public trust. Thus, a bank is not merely a business; it is the establishment and maintenance of a relationship, which facilitates interactions between members of society and international business entities governed by laws and rules that span geopolitical boundaries. The relationship between financial institutions is regulated by (in most cases) the public it serves and is continually changing, as observed by Gregory in 1936 and still true today:

> Economic structures obey laws of their own; beneath all the infinite variety of form the student of banking observes, at all times and in all places, a fundamental pattern which is the response of the banking structure to the function which it has to carry out … that if the scale of the banking structure is 'out of line' with general economic development, radical changes in the existing banking order will sooner or later take place, the pace of alteration depending upon the degree to which the necessity of change is recognized by public opinion.[1]

A recent example of the interdependent relationship can be seen in actions such as the changes regarding ATM fees brought about by public pressure, the Basel II accord (which provides guidance to banks on their capital requirements, supervisory reviews and disclosure), and a host of new regulations devised to thwart terrorism and money laundering. The continual updating of legislation and regulations reflects many factors, which include but are not restricted to changing economic conditions, social attitudes, culture and religion. Understanding the shift in social attitudes towards banking, for example, must therefore be an integral part of a retail bank's competitive strategy. In order to remain competitive, financial services companies engaged in retail and corporate banking activities must not simply react to regulatory or social changes on the horizon; instead they must take proactive measures that anticipate or in some cases diffuse the need to institute new regulations.

An organization's ability to adapt to changes such as evolving regulations, consumer attitudes, economic or demographic trends and other elements determines its long-term viability and is its most vital feature. The process of adaptation, which today is used synonymously with 'business transformation' is increasingly the key factor that will separate the leaders in the financial services industry and those that will fall under competitive pressures. Traditional and non-traditional banking services providers are constantly being absorbed or eliminated altogether. Often financial institutions, like their non-banking counterparts, misunderstand the influence and complexity of these external factors on the internal business processes of the firm. The lack of recognition of this causal relationship creates within the firm an organizational behaviour in which the firm typically does not take pre-emptive actions, opting to wait until the changes in the external factors are perceived as a competitive threat, and then being surprised when they are suddenly, sometimes in a matter of months, put out of business.

Why is the nature of retail banking changing?

Retail banking institutions periodically forget the cyclical nature of socioeconomic life when developing strategic initiatives and/or creating new banking products. In the post-dot-com era, the significant factor that banking services must incorporate into a competitive strategic context is that of changing consumer/cultural tastes as a result of globalization and technological disintermediation. Years of cost cutting, mergers and other internally focused activities targeted to increase shareholder value have acted to commoditize banking products to the point where there is little perceived differentiation between financial services providers with local, regional and national markets. In banks operating in the international markets, clear lines of demarcation in capabilities exist, as demonstrated by the availability of transnational banking products such as foreign exchange, international cash management and other services that facilitate cross-border banking and commerce services. Unfortunately, a large number of customers have now become shoppers and view banking services as single commoditized products, rather than mechanisms to facilitate a total relationship of services. The new challenge for retail banks is to educate customers on the advantages of maintaining a total relationship with the institution, understanding how the bank tailors services to meet the clients' individual financial needs, incorporating cultural, social, lifestyle and life events into a cohesive structure that results in overall wealth generation. Banks are addressing this change by consciously rebranding their products in two ways, for example the Hong Kong and Shanghai Banking Corporation's (HSBC) motto 'the world's local bank',[2] or by catering to a market subsegment by introducing narrowly focused services such as Islamic banking.

In the early 1990s, Catherine Smith noted the importance of demographic change (birth rate, inheritance, changes in personal wealth) in the demand for increased small business services, augmented consumer awareness and more globally focused regulation.[3] These factors must be viewed in the context of how they can be applied to retail banking strategies because they will continue to drive competitive change in the retail banking environment. Firstly, these factors must be divided into subsegments in order to develop comprehensive strategies that are measurable; secondly, they must be viewed in the context of the geographic and cultural markets they serve. For example, it is naive to think that married men aged 25 to 35 in rural India have the same banking behaviour as their counterparts in midtown Manhattan.

Retail banking customers are changing their banking habits. This is not a sudden, abrupt alteration of a social attitude towards savings, spending and investment, but the product of changing lifestyles such as the rise of single-family households in Western society. As people in all parts of the world embrace (or reject) the process of globalization, their attitude towards banking services, goals and aspirations will continue to be centred on the individual. Technology has been a tremendous agent of influence in changing retail customer behaviour, making the average banking customer more and more technology-astute and willing to adopt new, technologically driven banking products. A perfect example is the rise of Internet banking, cheaper than telephone banking and more convenient than branch banking. Typically, technology has been regarded as a cost reducer and latterly as a revenue generator. However, technology's ability to commoditize banking products and services is a double-edged sword, in that it continues to lower operating cost per transaction but it also enables non-banking competitors rapidly to enter the market. That said, technology is also creating a condition in which the competitive market of the traditional retail bank is no longer bound by geography. Financial services organizations and retail banks can now offer products and services both globally and domestically.

A byproduct of the process of globalization and technological advance is the increasing number of individuals who view themselves as global citizens or *cosmocrats*.[4] These individuals have an economic freedom that allows them to reside in more than one country or have interests in multiple sovereign states; they require services such as multi-currency savings and current (checking) accounts, and look for investments that offer transnational opportunities. In many cases, their income is generated from sources in several nation states and is not confined to a single tax authority. Although this group is a small but growing market segment, it identifies the need to rethink several traditional banking products and services.

The majority of customers in Western nations subscribe to more than one banking product to support their lifestyle. In the past, customers would hold all their banking accounts within one institution. In the last two decades, the commoditization of banking products, based on competitive interest rates, lower account fees and other incentives engineered to acquire new customers, has resulted in customers shopping around to find the best products to facilitate their individual lifestyles. Unfortunately, for most retail banks this has led to customers holding accounts in multiple institutions. Individuals faced with having to combine accounts manually turned to technologies such as the Internet as a mechanism to perform account aggregation services, which we will discuss later in this chapter.

Technological account aggregation raises an important question for retail bankers: how to give customers a wider choice of products without adding costs? Each additional account increases the cost of administration that over time lowers profits. A more fundamental question is: why do customers need so many accounts? Is there a more comprehensive set of services that will reduce the complexity of banking products? Customers open savings and current accounts, money market and other short-term instruments not out of desire, but out of need. Savings and investment accounts represent the consumers' quest to achieve higher interest for short-term funds. Customers are looking for a universal account with graduated interest rates and flexibility, enabling them to use the account for debit and credit transactions while acting as a holding tank for unused funds.

The new challenge for retail banks is to use technology to leverage the relationship with the customer to provide them with an alternative to account shopping. As traditional retail banking products continue to be commoditized, financial services offerings must be extended beyond the limitations of traditional banking products in two ways: by value added as an intermediary providing access to other institutions; and by consolidating the customer relationship within the bank's product offerings.

One area often overlooked, or in some geographies hindered by regulations, is that banking products are processed and administered by often disassociated computer applications, resulting in the replication of customer information (name, address, phone number, date of birth) in multiple systems. Financial institutions are struggling with multiple legacy computer systems, where customer information may be retained for each account opened, resulting in additional administrative cost. It could be argued that it is more cost effective to administer one universal account, with graduated rates incrementally matching accumulated daily balances, than multiple accounts.

Changing consumer demand coupled with financial incentives to reduce cost will continue to reshape retail banking product offerings. For most institutions, this will result in a need to map savings and investment products directly onto market subsegments to develop a sense of product efficacy and market penetration. Retail product managers will need to embrace a philosophy of managing a product life cycle in which, as the underlying lifestyles change the demand for banking products, the products themselves will need to be either modified or retired. Therefore, organizations that offer retail banking products and services will need to develop a topology of products, as illustrated in the Figure 1.1.

The topology of retail banking consists of three fundamental components: *partnerships*, *centralizing functions* and *distribution channels*. These

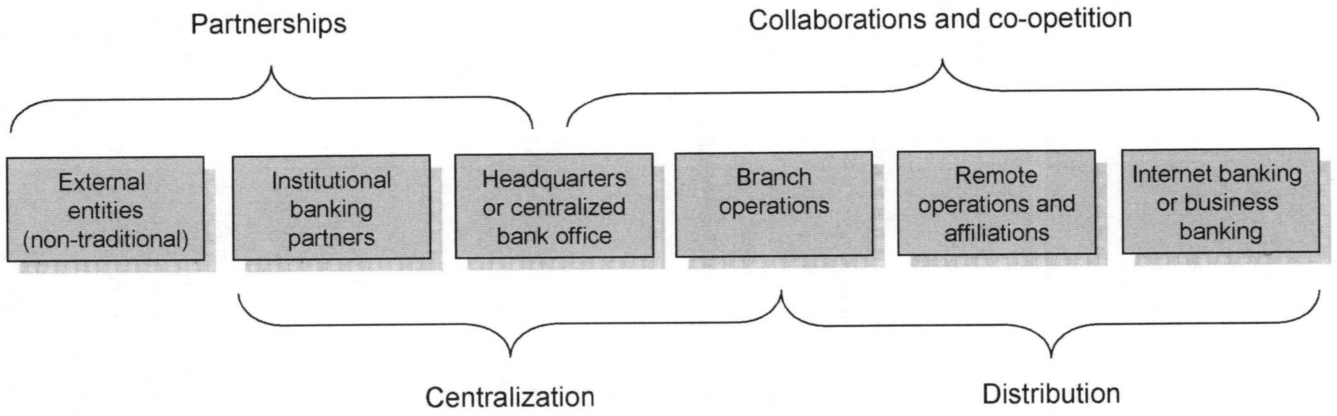

Figure 1.1 The topology of retail banking

partnerships supply access to financial products that are complementary to the firms' services, such as access to new markets and technological capabilities or competencies which are not found within the organization. Partnerships can also be based on an exchange of capabilities or banking competencies, and they can sometimes perform centralizing functions or activities designed to aggregate products and/or services. Centralizing functions, on the other hand, are combinations of technological services designed primarily for cost reduction or cost containment, such as consolidating call centres or establishing a large branch to be used as a financial services centre with access to highly specialized banking expertise. The component of distribution has the primary function of providing customers with access to financial products, markets and, more recently, to non-financial products such as home furnishing, auto supplies and other lifestyle products. Banks are realizing that for branches to remain a viable and effective channel to customers, three strategic investments must occur: skill sets within the branch must be upgraded, so personnel can be fluent in the widest range of products; the physical structure of the branch must be altered to accommodate new approaches to various customer market segments; and investment in brand identity, co-mingled product identities and shared property with another bank or retail partner.

The return of the branch

Traditionally, the cornerstone of a bank's relationship with its customers was the face-to-face interaction at a branch. Customers' use of a branch fell along two distinct channels: use of a teller to perform simple transactions; and the use of a bank officer for more complex actions, such as securing a loan. Technologies like the ATM, multimedia kiosks and the Internet have been employed to automate many of the typical transactions that were conducted through the teller channel and several of the functions of the bank officer. The technological mêlée of the dot-com years offered many retail banking institutions a vision of the future in which the number of physical branches would be substantially reduced and customers would flock in record numbers to conduct all their banking in cyberspace, with customer support centralized into large, regional call centres. What many institutions overlooked was that not all customers in all market segments would opt for technological alternatives to traditional channels at the same rate.

Branch banking versus Internet banking is one obvious example of the misconceptions that banks have about technology and the products and services they offer. For example, in the northeast of the US, a large percentage of the population is composed of young, urban professional individuals and middle-aged individuals who are technologically savvy. Although many customers opt to use the Internet or telephone banking, in a city such as Boston banks tend to keep their branches open on one or more weekdays until 8 pm, allowing customers returning home from work to stop and consult with advisors at the branch. In Cambridge, England, on the other hand, where the segments of population are similar to suburban Boston, composed of retired people, university students, most of whom do not have Internet facilities available or the privacy required to do Internet banking, and young professionals in the technology innovation centres and biotech sectors, banks are closing down branches and restricting their hours of operation (a large bank which claims to be multicultural, for example, no longer provides Saturday branch operations as of 2002, which is inconvenient for its Islamic customers whose week begins on Saturday.) A look at the branch on a Tuesday at noon shows how little the management of that branch understands its customers' needs: queues are quite long and tellers are busy with customers who still withdraw cash from the teller rather than the ATM because they feel more secure having the bank's stamp in their savings book.

In the late 1990s, with the industry frenzy created by the Internet, retail banks realized that they could lower costs by closing branches and increasing the use of computers with a rapid migration towards self-service technologies. However, by the year 2000, customer feedback indicated that several major customer segments liked to bank at a branch. It could be argued that as dot-com companies began to falter and collapse, the branch became a competitive advantage. Operating an Internet bank coupled with a branch network gave customers a greater sense of permanence, trustworthiness and stability in the bank. The perception of the customer was that physical brick and mortar banks were more likely to exist next week because they were harder for a company to dismantle, whereas an Internet company could be closed down within a moment's notice.

In the post-dot-com era, retail banks are now opting for branch operations that are more streamlined in process design, offering advice and presenting customers with a variety of options that integrate the physical and cyber worlds of banking. The intent of many retail banking operations across the globe is to create a low-cost branch network that will facilitate transactions while educating customers about electronically delivered services. This has resulted in a large number of banks experimenting with the concept of 'the branch of the future'. As straightforward as this may sound, retail banking branch design, operations and performance measurements are complex and highly influenced by the communities they serve. Therefore, the first characteristic in implementing a branch of the future is that it must be adaptable. There is no single branch solution that appeals to every customer segment or satisfies the needs in all communities. The issues surrounding the renewed interest in branch banking span a number of disciplines within the retail banking institution and, as we will see, are scattered throughout the remainder of this book instead of being concentrated in one chapter. The reason for this approach is so that the future of the branch can be taken in a context that separates strategic issues from tactical actions. That said, to understand the essential value proposition of banking in the future, it is vital to have a broad historical view of how banks as intermediaries generate value. It is to this topic that we now turn.

Bankers: the historical intermediaries

What we know today as 'retail banking' is the product of a long history of organizations that have in one way or another acted as a financial intermediaries in the facilitation of commerce and exchange between people and business. Lopez reminds us that banks in one form or another were present in ancient Mesopotamia, Greece and Rome, reaching a more formal definition within the social structure during the medieval period.[5] In earlier times, financial intermediaries were often non-banking entities formed to satisfy a need in the exchange of goods, services and value, such as the Florentine merchant banks of the early fourteenth century and Belgian inns operating in the later part of the same century. The resulting formal and sometimes informal organizations acted in direct response to a specific market opportunity, and their actions provide lessons that are applicable to today's global banking environment. As in medieval times, the interactions of retail customers, such as paying bills or saving money, and the transactions of business, commonly labelled 'accounts receivable and payable', are at the heart of international, regional and local commerce.

Retail intermediaries

Taking a historical view of banks identifies important socioeconomic behaviours which are timeless lessons that can help to shape the future of retail banking services because they identify recurring patterns. The key lesson is that providing an underlying fundamental value proposition to customers remains the same, while the banking products, services and

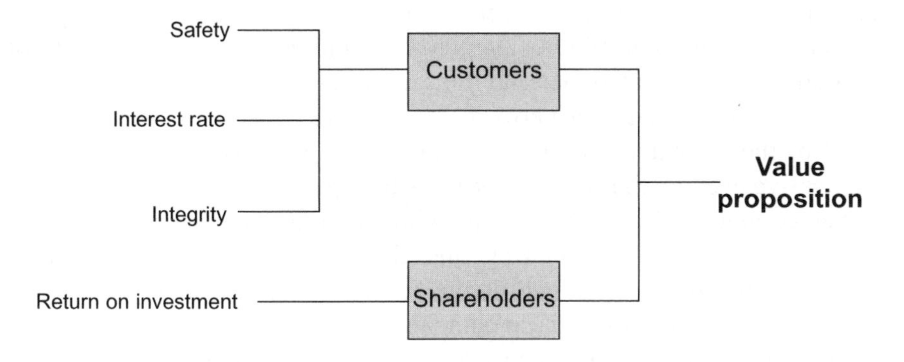

Figure 1.2 Historical banking value equation

technology continue to change. This is evident in the overall value equation for historical banking, illustrated in Figure 1.2.

A quick review of the organizations that have provided banking-like services over the last eight centuries reveals that they share a common purpose, performing intermediary financial services needed for economic activities while providing a return on invested capital to shareholders who had placed their money at risk. For the most part, like their modern counterparts, banks throughout history have experienced a path of maturity in organizational development, in which corporate behaviours change as they are presented with each new market opportunity.

Individuals at all levels of management in retail banks of the twenty-first century should spend a few moments reacquainting themselves with the banking operations of the medieval Florentine super-companies. Early in the fourteenth century, the need for banking services to facilitate trade between merchants in Italy and all corners of the known world gave rise to the three super-companies, Bardi, Peruzzi and Acciaiuoli, with headquarters in Florence. These organizations have been dubbed 'super-companies' by modern historians because they were large organizations engaged in banking, commodity trading, general trade and manufacturing over an enormous geography. In the words of Braudel: 'The Bardi, who had established themselves in the Levant and England, for a while held the whole of Christendom in fee'.[6] The original intent of these companies was not banking, but wool production. However, the need to finance their rapidly expanding operations and, more importantly, to optimize their supply, transportation and distribution chains made them change their focus.[7] Quickly developing a complex partnership of organizational structures that would easily be recognized by anyone in business today, these firms evolved from merchants into merchant bankers and, finally, complex corporate entities rivalling modern corporate enterprises. Employing the advanced technology of double-entry accounting and other methods of accounting for their activities and transactions, they established, during the course of two decades, a network branch and subsidiary companies in most of the known world. The types of banking services they offered is impressive even by today's standards, as they provided an array of international commerce services from banking, currency exchange, letters of credit, insurance, manufacturing and distribution services, as well as providing the financial infrastructure for the papacy.[8] There are several lessons we can learn from these companies as we examine their behaviour in the context of the socioeconomic conditions of both the fourteenth century and the twenty-first century. Firstly, similar to banks today, the Florentines went through a period of almost unbridled expansion, paralleling the rise in trade as the medieval economy expanded. Secondly, they realized that opportunities for securing better returns on investment existed beyond their ability simply to provide banking services, as they also engaged in providing ancillary trading services such as trading jewels, plates, English lead, Gascon wines and a vast array of other precious commodities, even supplying the great wardrobe of England's King Edward I.[9]

Today's need to expand retail banking services by linking or affiliating with non-banking products and services is strikingly similar to that of our medieval ancestors.[10] Loyalty merchant schemes in the UK such as Sainsbury's Nectar programme, which integrates retail sales with retail banking, product cross-selling activities like China's Dah Sing Bank, which uses data-mining technology for customer/product matching,[11] and other business objectives replicate the medieval bankers' expansion plans by incorporating an ever-growing network of connected relationships. Like banks today, medieval bankers were armed with superior technologies such as double-entry bookkeeping and their services were complete with identifying markings or icons which we would interpret today as corporate logos and a branding strategy. The medieval super-companies rapidly grew into vast organizations, only to collapse and fail in 30 short months just after 1343. As we shall see, the medieval bankers made several fundamental mistakes which today's retail banking professionals should factor into their strategic plans.

Medieval bankers were opportunist; their acquisition strategy was calculated to provide a wider selection of goods and services to existing and emerging markets, parallelling modern banks in the post-dot-com era. However, banks in the Middle Ages were both moneylenders and merchants, as lending money and financing trade was a critical way to employ surplus capital.[12] Echoing a strange similarity to the twenty-first-century banking institutions, the factors that contributed to the medieval bankruptcies followed an economic boom period resembling the dot-com investment years.[13] Medieval banks failed due to three key factors: excessive loans to governments to finance wars (which today can be equated to high-risk ventures); a reverse in the gold to silver ratio which destabilized the two-currency monetary system (which today is analogous to the uncertainty of the euro's interaction with other European currencies); and a sudden change in international trade resulting in a loss of fee income which rapidly reduced margins.

In hindsight, one can review the actions of medieval bankers and develop an understanding in which their mistakes become obvious to the modern bank manager. As medieval banks expanded and extended themselves beyond their core competencies, they built organizations that were laden with bureaucracy. When the combination of adverse conditions occurred, it caused the infrastructure of organizations to implode, crippling their ability to function profitably. An oversimplification of the state of medieval banks during the 1340s is that they lost sight of their core competency, banking, which is the fundamental management of the gap between deposits from their merchant activities and partners and loans extended to external entities, making them rely heavily on fee income. The lesson for modern retail banks is that the medieval super-companies, with their vast reserves and a workforce greater than most medieval governments, fell victim to their own greed. The underlying bureaucratic infrastructure could not sustain operations in the face of a rapidly changing business environment.

Core competencies

Unfortunately, today we take comfort in the concept that computer technology enables firms to avoid the circumstances that led to the downfall of the Florentine banks. The modern assumption is that the advanced capabilities of technology will insulate most retail banks from these problems. Yet, technology, and its resulting legacy systems, has begun to hinder most organizations' ability to implement new systems. This is evident in the rise of new market entrants that used the Internet and other technologies to bring Internet banking rapidly to the market, while most traditional banks came to the market late, as noted in the testimony of Edward Furash to the US Senate's Banking, Housing and Urban Affairs Committee in 1998:

> New financial technology has enabled capital markets players to substitute for banks by drawing deposits off into mutual funds and making loans possible through securitization or creative debt issuance.[14]

Therefore, the question remains: will today's financial services organizations make the same mistakes as their medieval counterparts and allow infrastructure to become their competitive Achilles heel? Are the greatly reduced spending levels on technology infrastructure, back-office systems and other capability-building technologies any indication that the first steps in that direction have already been taken? Before the dot-com meltdown, many banking professionals and senior managers were quick to say that the sophisticated markets of today had little resemblance to the socioeconomic structures found in medieval Europe, and that these types of catastrophic events could not happen within modern financial institutions.

Retail banks today have three competitors: other traditional banks, new market entrants and their own organization. Traditional banks offer competitive pressures based on better service, greater brand identity and competitive rates. New market entrants compete by introducing new products, employing technology in a new way or offering lower rates to persuade customers to become clients. The most damaging competitor will be the bank's own internal organization, which acts unconsciously to hinder its ability to compete by not responding quickly to traditional competitive threats and operating with an incumbent cost structure that is not as streamlined as new market entrants. In the past, retail banking organizations introduced new products before they had perfected core services to support the products as part of a comprehensive offering to customers. Historically, banks have enjoyed the luxury of this approach because of the intense capital investment needed to compete in the market. Technologies such as the Internet, biometric devices, cell phones and other retail delivery devices, coupled with changes in legislation and regulation, have changed the competitive landscape drastically during the past few years.

Belgian innkeepers: the new market entrants of the fourteenth century

Unless you have been working at a retail branch located on Mars, you will have noticed that the Internet is rapidly changing not just who can provide retail banking and investment services, but also how consumers and businesses gain access to financial services. Technologies such as the Internet, WAP phones, telephones, ATMs, Internet service providers, eMarkets and other linked non-banking services are all considered access pathways or portals, each potentially a viable channel to customers. Retail banks have developed mechanisms of their own to leverage these avenues to customers, or they are now collaborating with existing customer intermediaries or have joined forces with new market entrants themselves to retard customer attrition. The behaviour of today's new market entrants in banking brings to mind Hunt and Murray's observations of inns operating along the trade routes in the post-Black Death period of the later half of the fourteenth century in Belgium, which developed support services to facilitate commerce:

> Inns played a key role in the movement of goods along the overland trade routes of medieval Europe, and innkeepers provided not only lodging, but also warehousing, expert help with local governments, and even emergency financing. The last medieval inns of Bruges were unique in providing all these services plus brokerage, banking, and finance on an ongoing basis – in short all the services necessary for doing business.[15]

The value proposition of the Belgian inns reflected the changing needs of the maturing trading routes. Like many new market entrants into retail banking during the post-dot-com period, in the fourteenth century, Belgian innkeepers did not hold a collective meeting and decide to get into the banking business; they simply capitalized on the needs of their customers. Today's competitors exhibit the same behaviour, as can be seen in the supermarket Tesco in the UK: Tesco has identified a market niche and supplies a series of services that customers want, that is, convenient banking that can be done while doing something else.

'Hotter than a vindaloo'

Taking a macro-level view of banking services over the past 600 years, we see that banks perform six fundamental functions:

1. facilitating exchange with services such as clearing and settlement
2. providing risk management, with insurance and other mechanisms to hedge and diversify
3. business funding and sourcing
4. transferring purchasing power across time and distance

5. scrutinizing the performance of borrowers by eliminating disincentives
6. disseminating information on the relative supply and demand for credit.

These functions were traditionally constructed into specific banking products which, in turn, were designed to optimize the resources of the institution, in order to maximize returns to the shareholders. This method, which has served banks well in the past, is potentially an institution's vulnerable spot now because the competition has changed and customers have greater choices for their funds beyond banks.

From a customer's view, retail banks have a confusing array of products, requiring continual diligence in understanding fee structures in order to keep abreast of how much of your wealth is eroded by the bank's need to make money. This problem was created largely by technology, as 30 years of technological implementations have fragmented banking systems. Having had separate computer systems for deposits, loans, credit cards and a plethora of other services, retail banks are moving towards internal account aggregation or account linking. It could be argued that technology has given bankers the ability to service increasingly larger volumes of customers and transactions while, at the same time, detaching them from the reality of their customers.

The key to the future of retail banking is to anticipate customers' interests, needs and desires and make appropriate offers, linkages and other mechanisms to facilitate the transactions that follow customer behaviour. Anticipatory financial and commerce services increase the customers' relationship with the bank and reduce a competitor's ability to lure them away by offering a product with a low introductory rate. One example is the Halifax building society's 2003 marketing strategy of television commercials using Indian music and images of Indian geography and culture to captivate the large Indian market, which resides in the UK, and those newly arrived carrying large amounts of savings to establish a business in the UK. Anticipatory banking rests on the organization's ability to detect patterns in customer subsegment behaviour, and equate the resulting trends to lifestyles and events. It is to this topic that we now turn.

The new lifestyle approach to global banking

On the surface, everyone has a different attitude towards spending and saving money. To some people money is a tool, to others it is a means and to others it represents mere survival. People typically go to a financial institution when they have too little money or an oversupply of funds. In all cases, people look to a retail bank for a solution to some monetary dilemma. Therefore, the principal product of retail banks is a solution that fulfils an individual's financial need or, more precisely, a set of integrated solutions that support the individual's lifestyle and financial responsibilities. Rossier rightly points out that money transcends its definition as a medium of exchange backed by the full faith and credit of a sovereign state:

> Money is an emotional commodity as, in turn, it represents a person's security, health, happiness, prestige and power. Many things are dependant on money, even if it is said that 'money can't buy happiness'.[16]

How people use money and subsequently organize their finances to facilitate their life is driven by their attitude towards saving and spending. These two fundamental factors are in turn shaped by a plethora of factors such as culture, inherited family attitude, social standing, dreams, ambitions, goals or lack thereof, careers, blunders and many other factors that are a result of the lifestyle they wish to lead and the level of maturity they have achieved in their life cycle. One key element that many people forget or choose to ignore is that financial success stems from the rigour of a comprehensive financial discipline. Financial discipline is not about establishing direct debits or automatic bill payments; it is a philosophy of running the financial aspects of your lifestyle in a manner similar to managing a small company (managing cash flow, justifying acquisitions such as a house, car, furniture and other durable goods, determining levels of investment in staff such as one's own education and your children's education), and establishing operating levels of spending for day-to-day life events. Retail banks that use traditional market segments are discovering that when other competitors use the same method they become locked in a head-to-head competition with each other, while non-traditional new market entrants are targeting un-served niche markets that are rejected by traditional segmentation. New market entrants such as retail stores are drawing on attributes such as lifestyle buying habits that drive customer behaviour. Traditionally, retail banking demographic segments have been delineated primarily by income or asset size, and assume that people within a market segment adopt a relatively similar behaviour when they approach banking products.

Since the advent of computer technology, retail banks have segmented their markets by employing one or more of the following methods:

- *Geographical segmentation* divides customers by various geographical units (address, post codes, towns, cities, states, regions such as north/south or lowlands/highlands, and countries or groups of countries such as Benelux. Certain customer behaviours can be identified by this method such as Americans hold a higher percentage of risk in their portfolios than Europeans.

- *Demographic segmentation* segregates customers into groupings based on characteristics such as age, family size, occupation and gender. Purchase behaviours and product use within each grouping can be monitored, measured and associated with a specific product offering. Demographic data can be refined into smaller subsegments and regrouped and correlated or sorted by geographic data.
- *Psychographic segmentation* compartmentalizes customer groups based on personality characteristics, socioeconomic status, means and lifestyle. This can be seen when retail banks market to groups with a special interest such as sports or leisure activities, and people associated with charity giving and other loyalty schemes. In most cases, each segment is offered a banking product that caters to, amplifies or reflects the individuals' interest such as a credit card supporting a sports team or dinosaurs printed on cheques.
- *Behaviour segmentation* separates customers based on how they use a specific banking product or group of products, their attitudes towards the product's performance and the benefits that they perceive as valuable, such as breaking down credit card products to cater to special needs such as self-employment, bad credit histories, or creating products for a subsegment such as fee-sensitive customers.

How people match their lifestyle choices with banking products has been an increasing area of study since computers began analysing customer behaviour in the 1960s. Essentially, individuals use retail banks for three primary functions: to make payments, save for the future and insure themselves against life's vicissitudes. Bank accounts (including investment accounts and other ancillary financial instruments) represent temporary places to store one's money until it is needed at some future time. Retail banking products have been developed over time to represent the various activities and transactions that were required by previous generations of banking customers. Over time, these products become commoditized, reducing the fee that can be charged for the service. More importantly, social trends reshape customers' attitudes towards how they use money, leading to a redefinition of basic retail banking products. Therefore, retail banking products are cyclical in nature, changing as the social attitudes and lifestyle which they support evolve to represent the economic conditions of the people within a banking area. Catherine Smith describes two key concepts in positioning retail banking products: a targeting approach called *life-stage analysis*; and *lifestyle marketing*, which examines the kinds of activities in which people engage.[17]

The life-stage approach

The life-stage approach organizes events which occur during a person's life into a planning horizon and can be employed to identify the banking products to be used as a customer matures. This approach to marketing banking products is not new; however, over the past decade, advances in the technologies used to capture, process and correlate data on the specific products used by customers made this approach more viable. Life-stage marketing, used by organizations such as the Henley Centre[18] in London, realizes that the various stages in a person's life, such as going to university or an event such as marriage, trigger particular needs, wants or desires. This approach recognizes these changing priorities, and targets existing and/or likely customers with appropriate banking products. The Henley Centre notes that life stages, and their associated planned and unplanned events, followed a predicable pattern until recently, when the increasing rate of divorce and number of childless couples signalled a shift in Western society towards greater individualism.

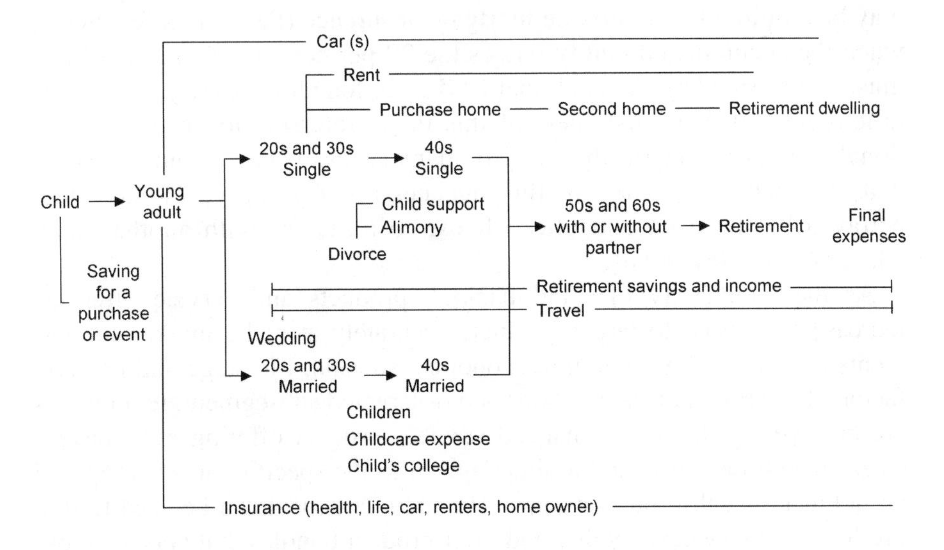

Figure 1.3 Life-stage approach

Source: Adapted from Smith 1990.

Life-stage marketing is but one step towards achieving customer intimacy because it enhances the relationship with the customer by relating specifically to what the customer is experiencing in his or her life. In the UK, Affinity Solutions developed a methodology to acquire and retain customers based on the life-stage marketing approach, which financial institutions such as the Alliance & Leicester used in the partnership strategy for their 'money back' credit card, Marks & Spencer in launching a new household insurance product in partnership with Norwich Union, and MoneyeXtra, to target, facilitate and negotiate commission-based partnerships.[19]

The lifestyle approach

Alternatively, the lifestyle approach assesses the consumption and saving behaviour of individuals to identify banking products, which facilitate their current lifestyle. This approach is effective in organizing a customer's financial needs with products. However, its shortcomings are that often customers do not reassess their needs as their lifestyles change. Sometimes, paying excessive fees for a product which is no longer adequate to a customer's lifestyle erodes the relationship between customer and bank. For example, when a young North American adult acquires a mortgage with less than a 20 per cent down payment, he or she may be required to pay private mortgage insurance (PMI). In a few years, when the accumulated equity passes the 20 per cent threshold, he or she must be informed by the bank that PMI is no longer necessary. Few institutions remind their customers of this fact, preferring to keep the additional fees for as long as they can. In many cases, when customers realize that they have been paying this unnecessary fee for years, they feel betrayed by the bank and often choose to refinance with another bank when rates are favourable.

As the complexity of retail banking products and service offerings increases, the need to target products accurately at niche market subsegments is driven by behavioural, economic, societal, life-stage and lifestyle factors. Regardless of the method used or targeted subsegment, retail banks are discovering that each financial services product offering must have a clear value proposition and a direct appeal to the specific target group and an indirect appeal to other groups. The indirect appeal can be used to link products and services together and offer product bundles that appeal across market subsegments, such as the Sainsbury's Nectar card loyalty scheme. The key is that value propositions are relative to the customer's perception

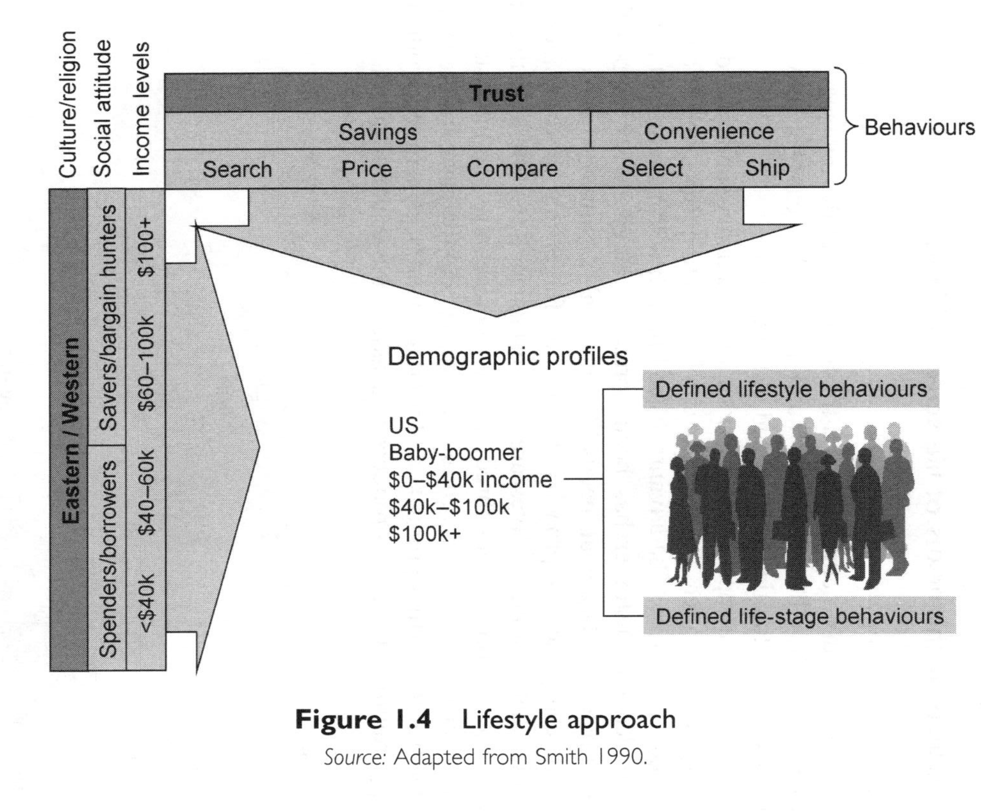

Figure 1.4 Lifestyle approach

Source: Adapted from Smith 1990.

of value and must be deliberately matched to products. Moreover, the value proposition may wax and wane due to changes in a customer's attitude, life stage and lifestyle. When a value proposition begins to wane, it presents, for a limited time, an opportunity for the retail bank to offer another product with greater appeal, based on past customer behaviours.

Products at the nexus of life stage and lifestyle

It is essential that retail banks thoroughly understand these two concepts and the clear distinction between them because at the intersection of these two approaches lie customer touch points that can be converted into targeted opportunities, as depicted in Figure 1.5.

Each of these approaches provides a mechanism to understand customer behaviour and offers insights that can be used to develop specific products. In Smith's words: 'The advantages of lifecycle selling is that, at any stage, provided the customer has been correctly categorized, it is possible to anticipate his financial needs.'[20] Financial institutions make mistakes when using these approaches when they forget that the customer is not static, that customers' lives are in constant motion. The effective use of these tools comes from three separate but equally applied uses of both mechanisms: *matching*, *motion* and *matrix*. Firstly, customer behaviour is matched to existing products and used to identify gaps in the product mix, opportunities for new products and assess the existing product offering

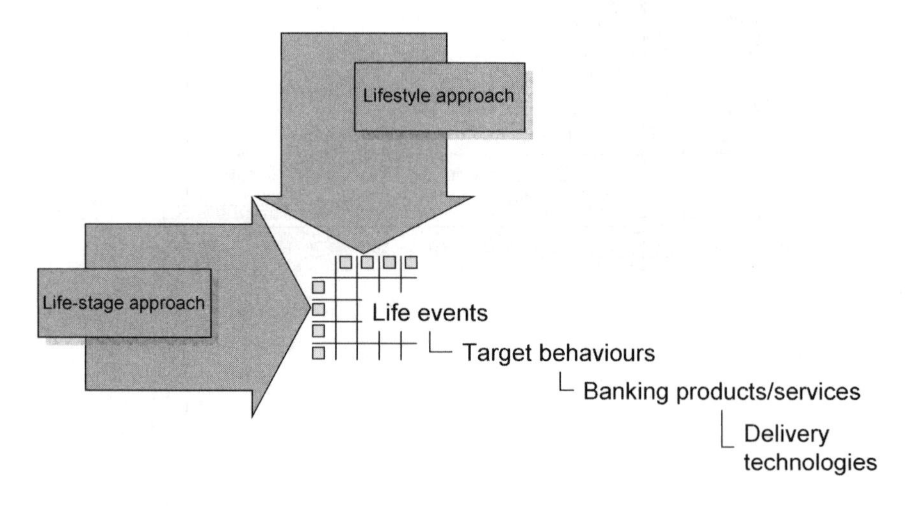

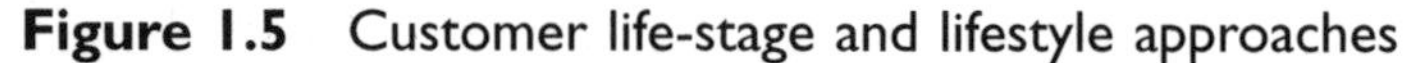
Figure 1.5 Customer life-stage and lifestyle approaches

against the competition. Secondly, relative customer motion can be measured and assessed. This is an area where many institutions make the biggest mistake, failing to realize that a customer is in one life stage only temporarily and invariably changes lifestyles. However, combining these two approaches creates a useful matrix that enables the matching of life events and lifestyles with products, channels and technologies, as illustrated in Figure 1.6.

At the intersection of a customer's life stages and lifestyles are products, transactions and delivery technologies. Each type of transaction presents an opportunity to be packaged into a form whose cost of execution is perceived as valuable to the customer.

Life-stage-focused retail banking products are designed to facilitate behaviour. For example, the Citizens Banking Company has a Kid¢ents programme which offers a savings club, savings accounts, a kids' certificate of deposit and a newsletter.[21] The Washington Mutual Bank of Seattle recognized the potential for educating children to the fundamentals of money when it instituted its school savings programme in 1923, giving students hands-on lessons on how to handle money responsibly.[22] Eighty years later the tradition continues at Washington Mutual's financial centres, where elementary schools and parent volunteers organize bank days at school to teach students positive saving habits.

Conversely, lifestyle-focused products are designed to enable the individual to select and tailor the product to meet his or her need. One

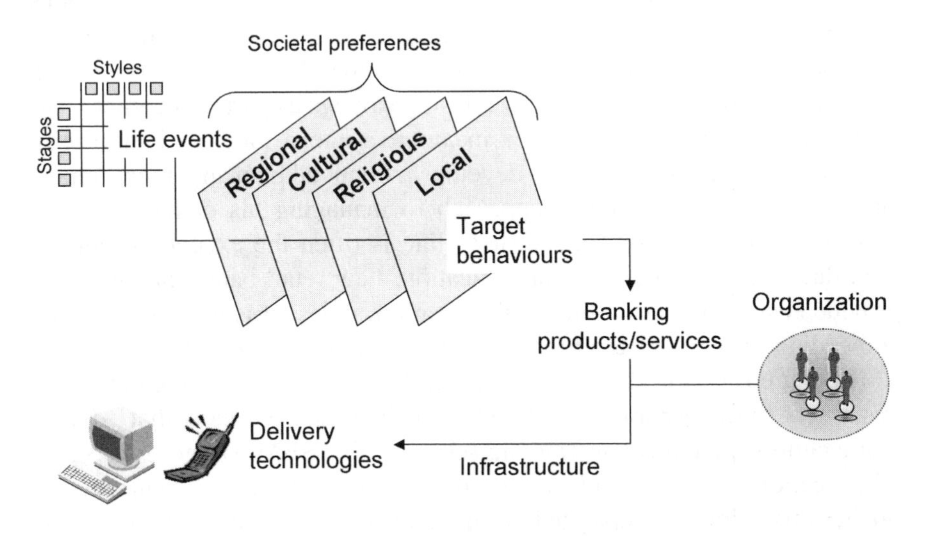

Figure 1.6 Customer product matrix

example is the Halifax credit card creator, which takes a person through four simple stages to customize the card to match financial and lifestyle needs.[23] As banking products become more customizable, they become more complex, especially when products are taken in combination with each other. This added complexity is a double-edged sword, with the additional cost of operations offset by the efficiencies of transaction-processing technology, and a hidden cost in the higher financial literacy rate needed by the customer. Few institutions are prepared to educate a customer on the idiosyncrasies of financial planning, cash management and other financial disciplines because, once educated, the highly commoditized nature of retail banking products could lead a customer to choose another institution for services.

Educating the customer

Consider for a moment the savings account. People regard it as a place to store money for the future, a simple mechanism that transfers an individual's purchasing power from the present to the future. However, is a savings account the best mechanism to accomplish this for all customers? Is it free of risk or void of real growth? Bankers realize that the saving function can be accomplished in other ways, such as investing in common stock and other long-term financial instruments. Each alternative offers a varying degree of risk and return. For example, a savings account comes with an implied guarantee and is associated with low risk, whereas stocks and shares are considered higher risk because the underlying value of stock (its share price) fluctuates with market demand and is dependent on economic factors beyond its control. Using savings as part of a comprehensive strategy to balance risk, as a means to achieve long- and short-term goals, requires that the customer develops a financial plan and, more importantly, practises a disciplined approach to managing his or her finances. However, this prudent financial discipline is often the exception, not the rule, due to inadequate financial education. Few retail banks can afford to provide customers with a financial education, unless it is accomplished by embedding the education into the use of the products themselves.

The State Bank of Mauritius has embarked on an approach of educating customers by incorporating ancillary functions and products that educate while children actively use banking services. The SBM Amigos offers free IT education for kids aged 6–17, as shown in Figure 1.7. The bank accomplishes this using two separate but linked means: by establishing minimum requirements for customers, such as maintaining an account balance of

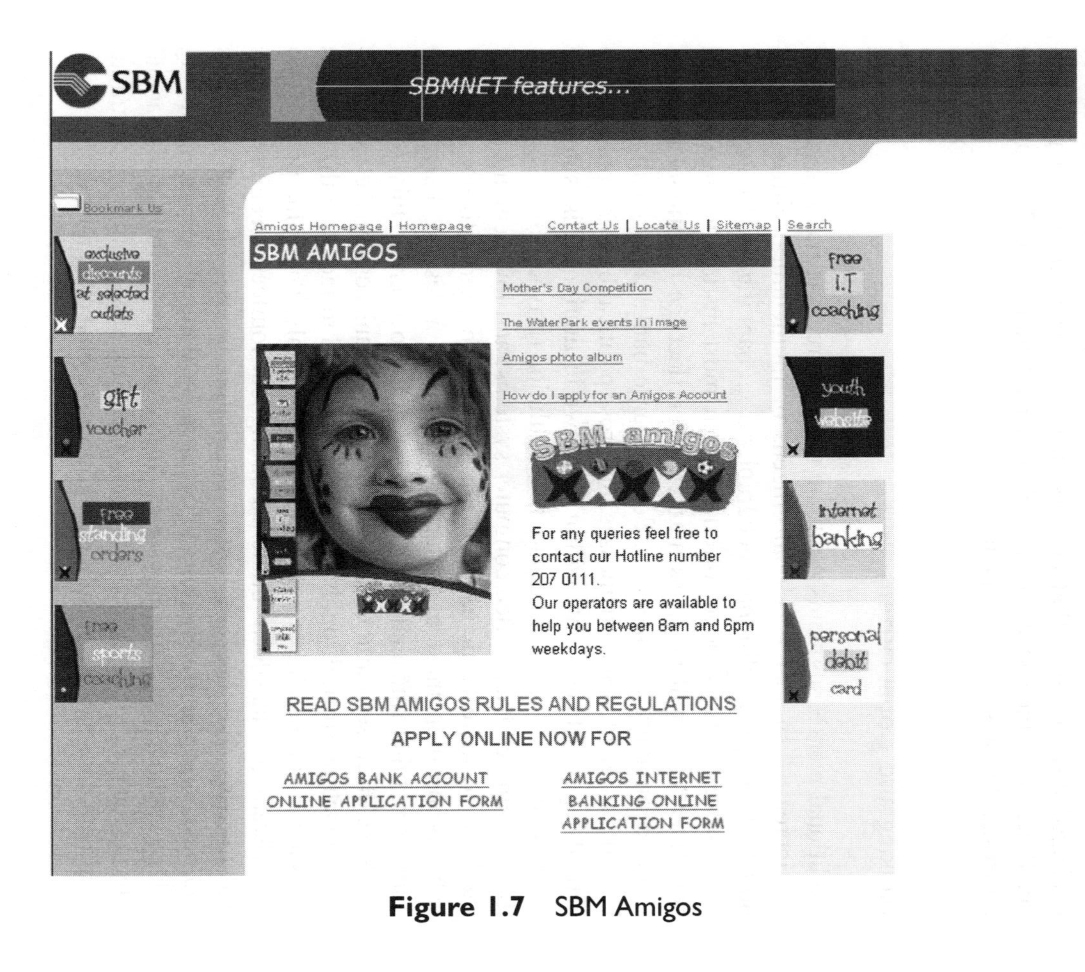

Figure 1.7 SBM Amigos

MRs 10,000 or more, and, on the delivery side, partnering with NIIT, a global IT solutions corporation that provides qualified customers with access to a free IT coach.[24] In addition to an IT education, the bank also brokers access to a sports coach for child depositors aged 8–17.

Educating the customer does not have to start with children; it can be packaged into products that are designed for a special interest group of small demographic subsegment, such as tribal banking for Canada's native American Indians, discussed later.

Banking and global citizens

Additional market segments not to be ignored are expatriates (expats) and the increased number of global citizens or multicultural citizens. Technology continues to eliminate geography from banking and financial services. However, the product offerings from most institutions to the retail consumer and small business market still reflect the traditional limits of single community membership. Several large banks offer localized services for individuals and businesses that cross political borders, but few can actually aggregate accounts within their own institution. This is due to one or more of three factors: international regulation (privacy laws); incompatible or unlinked back-office computer systems; and low demand for these services. To increase demand by non-globally focused citizens, a strong value proposition must exist such as providing access to distant equity markets or other financial opportunities. Let us now turn to this.

As we discussed earlier, medieval Florentine banks established an extensive branch network throughout the known world to facilitate the business transactions of merchants with headquarters in Italy. The value proposition for operating distant local branches throughout fourteenth-century Europe was to reduce the time and cost of negotiating terms with local suppliers and buyers, enable transactions to occur in local currencies and removing risk by trading with known partners. Today this classic role of a financial intermediary is changing, as migrating populations require two similar retail banking services: diaspora banking and global citizen banking.

Diaspora banking

I discussed elsewhere a rising opportunity for financial institutions to facilitate growing cultural diasporas, such as the approximately 50,000 people of Brazilian heritage living in Boston, Massachusetts, with strong family ties and social links to their native country. Similar to the value proposition presented by medieval bankers, retail banks have an opportunity to make possible transnational, multicultural banking in communities where individuals are the umbilical cord for financial support to relations in multiple countries.[25] It could be said that the development of extended family units spanning multiple countries is the first half of the definition of a global citizen. Unfortunately, the current operating state of many multinational or transnational retail banks creates for the individual the same or greater barriers as small businesses experience when they attempt international commerce. Diaspora customers who use retail banks offering international services often discover that the fees associated with transactions make banking extraordinarily expensive. However, Pakistan's United Bank Limited *TezRaftaar*[26] remittance service offers overseas Pakistanis a convenient delivery of money to beneficiaries in Pakistan. If we believe that technology can and is reducing the cost of operations and transactions in general, then over the next few years these services should become commoditized, probably by a non-traditional banking company. The opportunity for retail banking institutions is to define a highly specialized new class of financial services products, allowing individuals to participate in financial services which operate in distant regional economies spanning geopolitical boundaries.

One example of multinational intermediation for immigrant populations is the General Bank in east Los Angeles. Realizing that today's immigrant arrives with money and a need to execute transactions between countries, the bank provides services to immigrants from Korea and Taiwan by conducting business in their native language and assists in financing export–import business ventures. Acting in the tradition of the medieval Italian merchant banks, General Bank's strong ties back to Korea and Taiwan enable a unique value proposition to customers running import–export businesses in both countries, because the bank can track the credit history of an immigrant to pre-approve loans. General Bank's value proposition is further enhanced by the foreign currency services that it offers as a result of having detailed knowledge of the economic conditions in multiple locations. The combination of these primary services presents a clear message to its customers: General Bank is acting in their best interest. This value proposition promotes a high degree of customer loyalty which, as General Bank realizes, is the fundamental aspect of its relationship with its customers.

The second type of global citizen is the expatriate or local citizen desiring access to international equity markets and a greater variety of distant investment opportunities. Many financial institutions offer expatriate services. One example is the Bank of Ireland's fSharp expatriate banking, which offers multiple currency accounts enabled with Internet inter-account transfers, multi-country bill payment, consolidated online statements, simple transparent charges, and access to tax advice linked with KPMG in 155 countries.[27]

Diaspora banking provides a gateway to truly global liquidity where a financial institution can assist customers in maximizing the use and value of their global assets. Utilizing technology which is capable of interchanging operations in real time, accounts and asset balances in one time zone can be deployed and used elsewhere as intraday collateral, rather than remaining idle overnight. Although the US still represents the bulk of the world's capital markets, investors seek new investment opportunities so the trading and banking environment will ultimately run twenty-four hours a day, seven days a week. As world citizens become more technologically astute and increasing numbers of households become connected, the need for banking and investment services that span geopolitical boundaries will increase market segment by market segment. Account and bill aggregation and consolidation services will enable families to engage in new types of wealth management and transfer services, while also providing businesses of all sizes with comprehensive cash management and global trade financing.

The simple transfer of funds to and from corresponding transnational accounts located in multiple countries reduces, and will ultimately negate, the reciprocal value in local currencies. Multi-currency deposits in corresponding dynamically self-allocating accounts are moved by an established daily rate at the time of transfer. This mechanism provides a second opportunity to investors looking for currency diversification in their portfolio. Excess or transferred funds can be invested, even if only temporarily, in services offered in distant economies, which might offer a higher rate of interest or greater safety or both. Small investors or traders seeking portfolio diversity in a local market, which requires brokerage and cash accounts, can manage remotely the number of times currencies are exchanged. This is yet another value proposition that provides optimized cash management services to maximize the return on funds in multiple economies. HSBC's CombiNations savings account reflects this trend, allowing its customers to take advantage of favourable interest rates and exchange rate movements for a combination of currencies.[28] Managing ten currencies, such as the Australian dollar, Canadian dollar, euro, Japanese yen, New Zealand dollar, pound sterling, Singapore dollar, Swiss franc, Thai baht and US dollar, with a single account enables multi-currency deposits and cross-currency trends with a single account structure. This in turn reduces the cost of each transaction and lowers total fees charged to the customer.

Moving from products to financial lifestyle solutions measured on wealth growth and cash optimization ultimately leads to the realization that banking fees could be based on the performance of monies invested within the institution. This is especially true when the customer elects to use the one-stop-shop approach and establishes an exclusive relationship with the bank. In this sense, another approach to educating the customer while creating greater loyalty is to provide a mechanism in which services are presented in a clear, concise and easy to understand manner, such as a financial dashboard. The financial dashboard presents a simple mechanism which indicates progress towards financial objectives. Using the centre line as an indicator of a wealth-neutral position, a customer's behaviour either adds or subtracts from the relative lifestyle- or life-stage-based indicator, as illustrated in Figure 1.8.

Customers can gauge their actions according to long- and short-term goals and financial objectives. They see the consequence of their actions relative to their current lifestyle and life stage. The financial dashboard must be applied to each individual lifestyle/life-stage combination because it is safe to assume that one financial solution cannot possible fit all people in all circumstances. The left side of Figure 1.9 depicts a young adult who has recently purchased a mortgage and a car. He or she has some savings and a small retirement account. The dark indicator line shows his or her relative position towards a healthy financial lifestyle, that is, financial security. The indicators show how their debts relate to their actions, so if they add credits cards, for example, they move towards the right of the new line; if they elect to save money, they move to the left, closer to the wealth-neutral position.

The right side of Figure 1.9 illustrates a customer later in his or her career, having accumulated home equity and a degree of savings and investments. Here the customer can determine which financial products provide the best return under various levels of risk in order to optimize his or her wealth.

Customers intuitively know that their savings and spending habits (and associated actions) determine the rate at which their wealth grows and falls. However, they often forget this factor as they are confronted with life's events. The dashboard method of customer relationship management requires a comprehensive suite of technologies to generate a detailed level of data for the customer. This data can also be used to train branch personnel to be financial advisors, not merely salespeople. The downside to this approach is the 'all the eggs in one basket' syndrome, in which

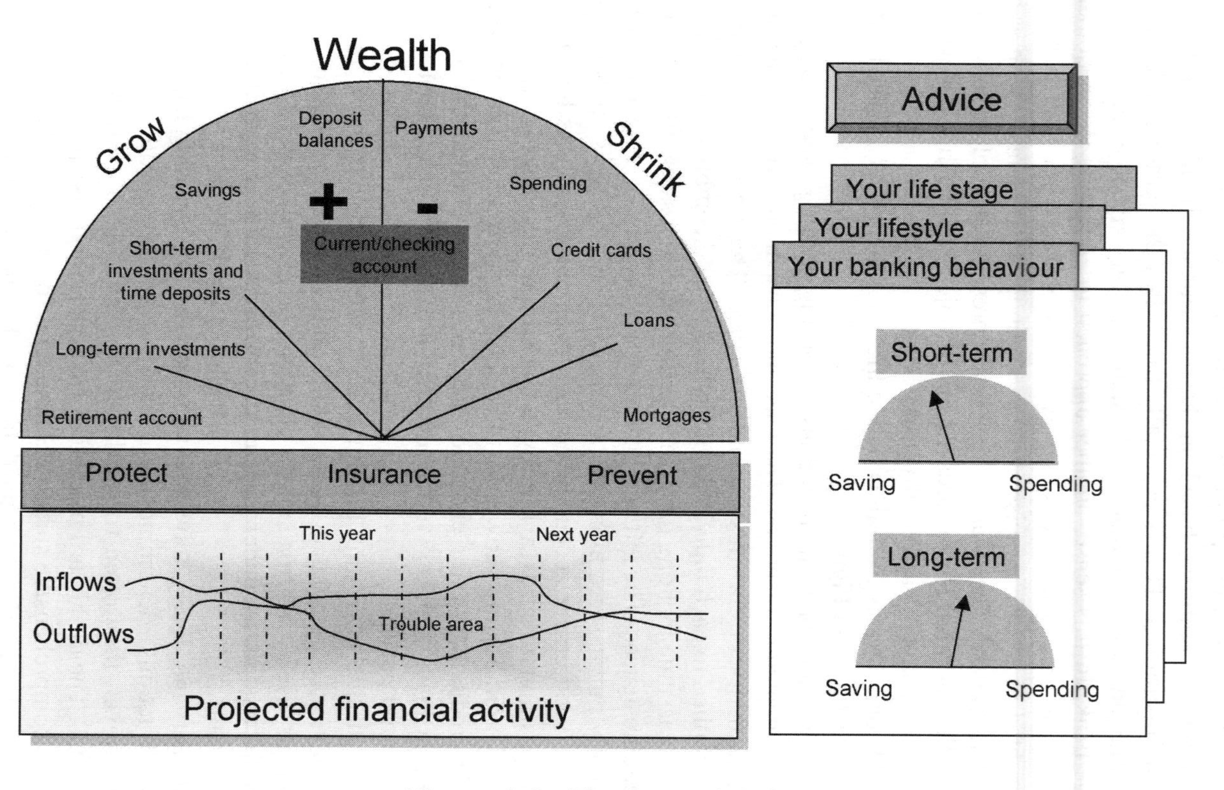

Figure 1.8 The financial dashboard

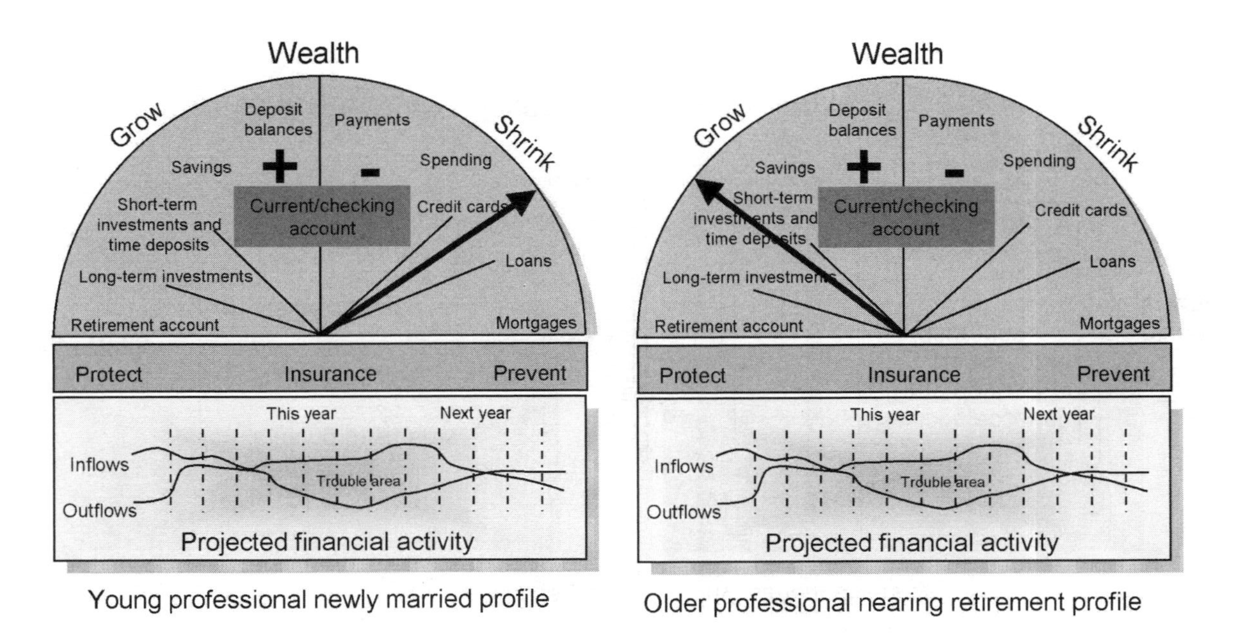

Figure 1.9 Applying the financial dashboard to customers

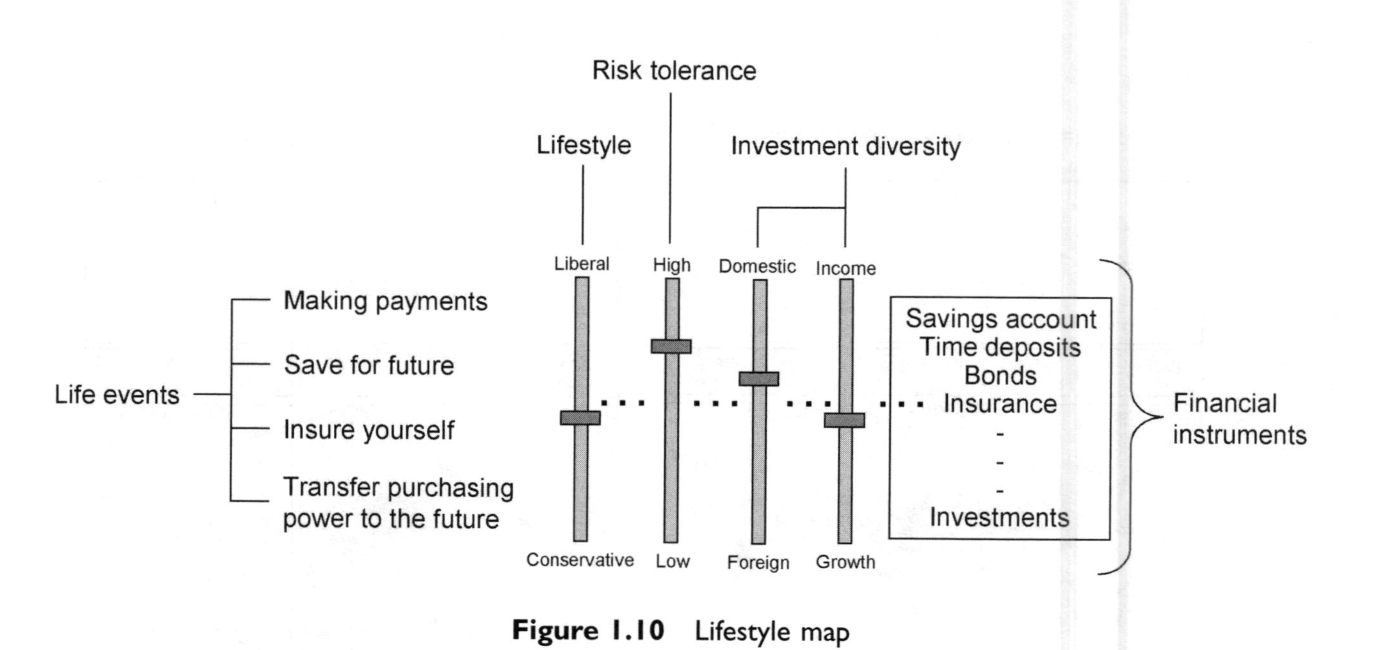

Figure 1.10 Lifestyle map

customers fear that they have committed too many of their financial resources to one provider only. The retail bank can now overcome this fear by educating the customer on the diversity of product portfolios.

An example of this approach is Insurance.com from Fidelity Investment, which has set up a learning centre on its website that enables customers to select the profile that best resembles their lifestyle and then investigate scenarios of life events: 'Different situations require different approaches to insurance. The need for life insurance, health insurance, auto insurance, and homeowners insurance changes according to a mixture of life variables.[29]

Fidelity established nine customer profiles representing a variety of people in various stages of life. Selecting a profile allows a customer to view the corresponding insurance needs and related products. Although Fidelity's profiles are Western-centric and represent American-style demographics, they provide a value framework, which can be adapted for multicultural banking environments.

Lifestyle is inexorably linked with culture which offers an additional variable to the matrix of matching lifestyles and life stages. Retail banking products that cater to variations of cultural or lifestyle banking are rapidly moving from dominant large Western banks to smaller institutions found in all parts of the world. For example, in the United Arab Emirates, Dubai's Royal Bank offers a product entitled Royal Banking, which is designed not for the mass market, but to meet the needs of customers at the higher end of the economic spectrum. This exclusive banking relationship offers an extensive range of financial products and banking privileges tailored to facilitate special banking and lifestyle needs at preferential prices. This level of 'relationship banking' includes access to non-banking services branded as 'lifestyle privileges' that extend to the customer and family invitations to cultural events and theatres, shopping value cards and holiday specials on a regular basis.[30] The services, products, brand image and every aspect of the relationship is designed to cater to an elite customer market segment as shown in Figure 1.12.

Royal Banking demonstrates that regardless of how a product is packaged, the value proposition to the customer must be compelling, clear and simple, and independent from the mechanism of delivery. Technologies such as the Internet provide an important means to enhance a component of a value proposition. They do not, however, represent a market differentiation by and of themselves, except during their initial introduction which appeals to customers who are early technology adaptors. That said, technology applied to banking products plays an integral role in the social adoption of retail services by each market subsegment.

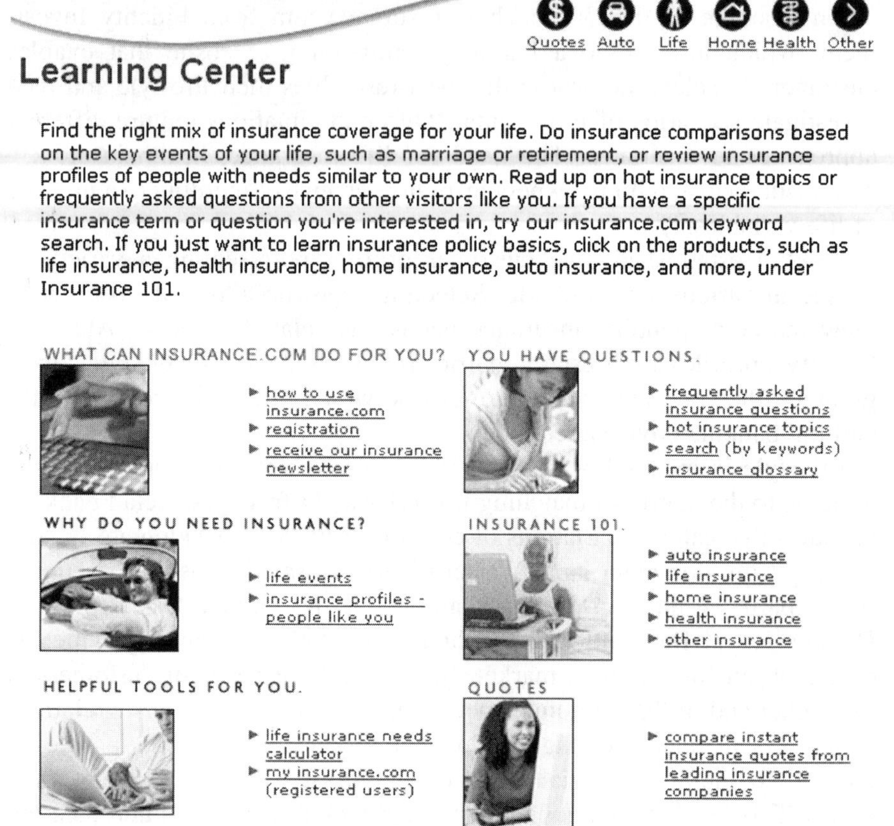

Figure 1.11 Fidelity's Insurance.com

What retail banks learned during the hype of the dot-com era is that applying technology to micro-market subsegmentation can be taken too far, thus alienating customers with choices for the sake of choices. As Wiersema observes: 'Mere variety and multiple choices make choosing the right solution the customer's job. And that's a job they may not be prepared to handle.'[31] Traditionally, profit margins and transaction volumes have driven which products and services are viable channels for fulfilling customer needs. With customers demanding services that are

DUBAI BANK
Products & Services
News Release
Register
Contact Us
Site Map
Home
Royal Banking
Add the majestic touch to your lifestyle
Royal Banking is reserved for the highest echelons of society, including customers such as yourself, who deserve an exclusive range of financial products and privileges tailored to meet exceptional banking and lifestyle needs at preferential prices.
Banking Privileges
Investment Privileges
Lifestyle Privileges
For more information, please visit us today; email us or call toll free on 800-5555

Figure 1.12 Dubai Bank: Royal Banking

customized to fit individual lifestyles, the challenge for retail banks will be to sense changes rapidly in customer attitudes and competitive offerings and use technology to introduce new products. Technology organizations within banks now realize that the rate of social adoption often lags behind the market hype, giving them opportunities to develop products in anticipation of market trends. It is to this topic that we now turn.

The banking chameleon

The traditional view of a retail bank's internal organization is that it reflects a legacy of process compartmentalization, a byproduct of post-industrial assembly-line thinking. The Industrial Revolution led to the establishment of the assembly line which offered efficiency by breaking down a process into its component parts, optimizing the actions of works performed within a specific work activity. This organization of work creates a command and control structure that is hierarchical, resulting in distancing the worker from a holistic view of the process which the company uses to deliver value to the customer. In today's workforce, especially in financial services, few people who have direct contact with customers understand the complexity of the various business processes used by the institution to provide products and services to the customer. The compartmentalization of work activities unfortunately has resulted in a compound bureaucracy, which in many cases distances front-line retail banking personnel from providing a holistic understanding of the bank's total product portfolio. This compartmentalization of activities and products impedes the ability of front-line customer services people to provide customers with services to meet their needs without handing them over to another division of labour within the bank. Organizations have identified this condition as a competitive disadvantage, and, for example, the First National Bank of Botswana has taken proactive steps to correct this by defining its branch of the future as:

> This is a one stop Banking facility whereby there is a movement away from old banking procedures of a front line person handling specific queries. The aim of the Branch of the Future is for any front line person to be able to handle ANY query you may have, this avoids moving from queue to queue to get all your banking done.[32]

To complicate matters further, over the last three decades computer technology has also been applied to this compartmentalization of work, reinforcing the segmentation of tasks, information and process. Thus, data and information about a customer resides in many places throughout the firm in systems that are not integrated. The new generation of technologies including the Internet, collaborative systems such as IBM's Lotus Notes and Parametric Technology's Windchill product and distance-bridging technologies such as Microsoft's NetMeeting are compressing the distance between people and their interaction with a business process. The next evolution for retail banking is to use computer software to re-establish business process understanding and reduce compartmentalization, reconnecting the actions taken by individuals who perform the work with the total customer experience.

The advance of technology has a greater implication for retail banks and any financial intermediary because technology such as digital certificates and eCurrencies will fundamentally alter the social contract of trust in an exchange of value between customers, business and governments. The impact of these advanced technologies that were introduced as byproducts of the Internet has yet to be understood by customers and business. The potential of these technologies will alter the course of global society by ultimately changing our relationship with money, value and exchange. For centuries, the primary ingredient in the value proposition between a bank and a customer is an expressed trust. Over time, the expressed trust became an implied trust, represented by the physical presence of the building, a big steel vault, bars on windows, elaborate alarm systems, bank guards and other devices demonstrating a safe and secure place to put one's money. As money becomes less physical and more electronic in nature, the valued physical attributes of the now implied trust will be discounted or eroded by the customer's perception of the new explicit trust offered by electronic money. Digital currency, with its expressed level of trust in its certification of value, raises the question: how will traditional banks differentiate their perceived value of trust to customers? The management of the customer's perception of trust is critical because the ultimate use of digital technology will, over time, result in the expressed trust of technology circumventing the implied trust of the physical bank. The shift from an implicit to an explicit trust signals an opportunity for traditional retail banks because it demonstrates that the value of the intermediary rests in the establishment, development and facilitation of customer demands, and not in the simple processing of transactions. If the historical use of technology is any indicator of how customers will behave in the future, the expressed trust offered by technology will replace the implied trust that financial institutions have enjoyed as incumbents in a mature retail banking marketplace. Couch and Parker point out an important observation that most banks have not realized when linking trust to privacy:

> Expectations for privacy are far greater on financial websites than on general e-commerce sites. Banks may be in a unique position to overcome negative customer perceptions and gain a competitive advantage over nonbank competitors by leveraging their public trust and strong reputations through effective branding strategies.[33]

The advance of technology, coupled with the ever-increasing numbers of new market entrants willing to offer newer or less expensive retail banking services, mandates that traditional retail banks establish and then, more importantly, communicate to customers a clear value proposition. In the past, the value proposition for retail banks comprised five fundamental principles:

1. *trust* (operating within a set of perceived ethical rules)
2. *security* (strong stone building with classical architecture columns and steel vault door)
3. *fidelity* (dependability operating with integrity)
4. *fiduciary* (an agent of trust and responsibility)
5. *merchantability* (a third-party intermediary that was trusted by both parties engaged in a trade).

Within these five principles, previous generations of banking relationships were established under the proviso that banks provide more than a service to the public because banks act as a public trust. This relationship was an unwritten social contract which was perceived by customers to be valuable because it provided them with a means to interact with commercial providers of goods and services without the risk of storing large amounts of physical currency, thereby supporting a primary concern of their lifestyle. This can be seen in the accounts of the Bank of Amsterdam in 1609, which provided functions of safekeeping and security. The bank also assessed and certified the quality of merchandise and enabled the transfer of payments between parties; although both parties physically came to the bank to conclude transactions, the perceived risks were less than physically handling quantities of gold. This value proposition has been sustained until the advent of electronic money. Rising ATM fraud and cybercrimes due to increasingly clever criminals is slowly eroding the trust element of technology that financial institutions are counting on as part of the industry's identity. Although the bulk of these crimes are still minor isolated incidences, as they become more prevalent in the media, banks will need reassure customers with an explicit expression of trust.

Trust, security and a bank's identity crisis

Sir John Bond of HSBC succinctly expressed the issue of a retail bank's value proposition to customers:

> They want integrity – this is their money, these are their hard-earned savings, they want somebody that looks after it with total integrity. They want fair dealing, they don't want charges introduced without any proper warning or explanation. They want fair dealing in all aspects of their financial affairs, and they want service.[34]

Twenty-first century retail banking must be more inclusive, integrated and able to reflect the intertwined relationships between consumers' lifestyles, the companies they work for or interact with, the bills they pay and the services they consume. Therefore, retail banking can be broadly defined as consumer banking, small to medium size enterprise (SME) commercial banking and a variety of services that are utilized by traditional customer relationships such as investments, insurance and private banking.

It is under this broader definition of retail banking that one begins to see not only how banking services provide a framework for a compound customer relationship, but they also demonstrate patterns of customer behaviour, opportunities for cost optimization and methods of cross-selling, when viewed in a context of the life cycle of the customer relationship. If all banking services are viewed from the perspective of the customer as being a self-contained nano-economic unit, that is, from a purely consumer-centric point of view, an organization providing retail banking products must become chameleon-like in its ability to deliver during the customer's lifetime. In fact, if an institution provides a comprehensive suite of products and services that facilitate the customer's lifestyle as it changes during the course of his or her life, customer retention becomes a byproduct of that relationship.

Traditional retail banking services can be delineated into two, hard to distinguish categories: services for the public or consumers and for people of means and wealth, or private clients. If we subscribe to the notion that technology provides the means to achieve cost efficiencies (economies of scale) and a broader market reach (economies of scope), each resulting in a bottom-line benefit to shareholders and customers, then a logical extrapolation of the applied use of technology is to clone services from one group of customers to another at a cost-effective price point. However, few financial organizations have yet to engage in the mass customization of private client-like services to customers of lesser total wealth. The promise of technology has always been speed, efficiency and the ability to reproduce capabilities. The question remains: why have more comprehensive services been reserved for private clients and not applied to the broader market?

Leading the customer with education

In the past three decades, the technology industry has argued that greater economies of scale and scope can be achieved each time new technology is applied to banking. If this is true, technology should allow us to provide the same level of customer service enjoyed by upper-class private clients to every banking customer, regardless of their wealth. Of course, not all customers require such services, but logic still dictates that the more customers develop behaviours that are alike, the lower will be the cost of operations.

Providing a broader suite of services requires the establishment of an education process that enables a customer to utilize the product offerings in an intelligent way to support his or her lifestyle. Banks will need to educate customers on the benefits and use of their banking services, how to achieve a sound financial discipline, the pros and cons of investment and speculation and prudent preparation for the ultimate wealth transition between one generation and the next. A retail bank's opportunity to educate the customer happens at every customer touch point and with every transaction. Education starts with front-line personal possessing a commanding knowledge of the products and services, and, more importantly, how to apply them accurately to facilitate the customers' lifestyles and provide financial wisdom by revealing to customers how their current lifestyle is part of an overall life cycle in which life events trigger the periodic need to realign banking services.

To embrace the vision of the branch of the future, many institutions will have to undergo a total transformation, while others with need to alter their product portfolios and retrain branch personal. Invariably all institutions will have to make the transition to the future bank style of lifestyle-supporting services.

I discussed elsewhere the concept of how banks have the opportunity to become an aggregator of financial products as an eMarketplace.[35] The Spanish bank Bankinter, an early adopter of the concept, created an online product for insurance-based products, named *Asesor de Seguros* (Insurance Analyst) which has two distinct value propositions: market aggregation and customer education.[36] Bankinter's service facilitates customers in investigating the insurance products offered by competing insurance companies, selecting a policy that suits their needs and taking out insurance online, irrespective of whether they are Bankinter customers. The key value for the bank is that each customer establishes a personalized profile of his or her insurance needs (life insurance, home insurance, health and automobile insurance) which is used to recommend products that best meet those needs. The other element in the value proposition is educational, as the service is equipped with a financial simulator that presents possible solutions to future money problems related to retirement or death.

Banks are realizing that educating the customer must occur through as many channels to market as possible, but the two most popular avenues are the Internet and the branch network. Creating a veritable laboratory for retail banking experimentation and visioning, John Ryan International's Merlin Center in Stamford, Connecticut, stands at the apex of new thinking on branch design. Using a combination of technology and artistry, the open bank is more than a showplace, as it operates using video tellers who can dispense cash and complete transactions using translucent pneumatic tubes, booths that combine real people with a high-tech approach to presenting product materials and advice from experts using video technology.[37] The utilization of kiosks to aid customers in the transition to more online services enables the individual to try online banking without fear of initiating an erroneous transaction that would damage his or her account.[38] John Ryan International is redefining how retail banks look, feel and function by rethinking the total banking experience and the preconceived notion of a retail bank branch.

Industries are often eager to apply technology without thinking how it could alter the operations of the branch, as was learned with the use of automated teller machines (ATMs). According to Retail Banking Research Ltd, ATMs began in 1967, did not become popular until the mid-1980s and banks took 16 years to install the first 100,000 and only four years to reach 200,000.[39] The initial implementations placed the ATM inside the branch, in order to reduce teller queues during branch operating hours. The innovation occurred once the customer could access the ATMs outside the branch, regardless of whether the bank was open for business or not. Customers perceived this innovation in two ways: greater convenience, because they no longer had to take time off work to go to the bank, and a perceived lower cost to banks, because they did not have the added expense of employing people to operate the branch for longer hours. This perception of lowering the operating cost for the bank is the primary discourse raised in opposition to ATM service fees, when service charges began to emerge in 1996. Even though most fees are designed to offset the cost incurred by the interchange between banks, the perception remains. Charging a fee for an added service was a traditional banking behaviour that is now changing, due primarily to increased competition, as noted by Jacques de Saussure of Pictet in Switzerland:

> For 20 years when markets went up our revenues went up without us doing anything. Easiness is additive. There was a tendency to be less cost-conscious.[40]

Saussure makes an important observation: when the ability to charge fees is market-driven and independent or divorced from the ability to deliver the service or manage the cost, the impact to the organization is magnified when a downturn in the market occurs. In the newly globalizing retail banking market, delivering higher levels of customer service at lower operating cost will become increasingly more competitive as new market entrants begin offering banking services. One mistake banks make is to view their branches of the future as experiments in delivery capabilities and not as measured variations in the effectiveness of their overall value propositions. The branch of the future, in whatever form, must incorporate customer education, a means to leverage employee knowledge, include a high degree of technological capabilities and, most importantly, demonstrate the bank's competencies to generate long-term financial stability for the customer. How do banks today face the challenges of customization in a world that is striving to preserve culture?

Global cultural values and customization

Before our entry into the third millennium, banks found their market distinction in a combination of technology, rates and levels of customer service. As the world of financial services and, more specifically, retail banking becomes increasingly globalized, institutions and new market entrants have realized the growing importance of culture, local values and other social factors, not just in the development of products and services but in the underlying definition of their value propositions. Comprehensive value generation in the global banking environment consists of customizing banking products to leverage cultural values and other local idiosyncrasies. What is clear is that banks do not cater for cultures; cultures respond to banks. For example, a traditional bank, with headquarters in one country, acquired a smaller competitor located in a neighbouring country as part of a growth strategy. Immediately the bank introduced its brand image, used its logo, replaced signage and all other visual images of the acquired bank. Next, the bank, confident of its superior product offering and brand recognition, started to convert customer accounts to the new operating entity. During the succeeding weeks, the customer attrition rate soared as accounts left the bank in record numbers. Amidst this customer exodus, the bank asked customers why they were moving their accounts to other local banks, only to discover that the population simply did not like the premise of a 'foreign bank', preferring instead a local, close-to-home feeling institution. The new signage was replaced with the old, but this time, the new logo was placed discretely in the corner.

However, banking innovation that drives and shapes a customer's need for services does not always have a high technology component. One example is the 'pigmy deposit' at India's Syndicate Bank in Karnataka, launched in 1928 by one of the bank's founders Dr Pai to encourage the habit of thrift and small savings by bringing the bank to customers, therefore making it a convenient habit.[41] The pigmy deposit product is the cornerstone of the bank's brand identity, which fosters a sense of service to the community, by dispatching agents to the customer's home to collect deposits at regular intervals, eliminating the need for small savers to go to a branch while increasing the personalization of the bank. Syndicate Bank collects deposits as low as one rupee daily for 63 months at the doorsteps of 1,232,000 depositors (12.32 lakh[42]) using the bank's 3700 authorized pigmy agents, with an average daily collection of over Rs 2 crore[43] (€364,789); at the end of December 2002 the bank's total deposits were Rs 1120 crore (€2,042,819,795). The pigmy account allows depositors to borrow up to 75 per cent of the balance in the pigmy account.[44]

If one looks at the behaviours of non-Western banks in all parts of the world, one element becomes clear: the objectives of these institutions are less profit-centric than those of North American institutions, focusing on providing banking services as a variant of social benefit, providing people with services designed to provide access to capital and a mechanism for savings. This becomes apparent when observing the motivation of Islamic banks, which is based on justice and fairness in which the exchange of value between parties is a partnership (*musharakah*) in financing, making the financier a participant in the risk. Saad Al-Harran places the fundamental differences between Islamic and Western-based, profit-oriented banks in the following manner:

> Since Islam is a social system imparted by Allah to mankind, and man has accepted the responsibility to be His viceregent on earth, man will be accountable for his deeds and actions. This argument can also be applied to Islamic financial institutions which should and must play an important role in the world financial system to bring about relevant, positive changes.[45]

In Saad Al-Harran's view, Islamic banks are not free to do as they please; they are responsible to a higher authority (Allah), having to integrate moral values with economic activities, and using money and property as social tools to achieve social good. Unlike their Western counterparts, Islamic banks operate to provide credit to the poor or people who possess talent and expertise but cannot provide the collateral required by conventional banking institutions. Additionally, the expressed purpose of an Islamic bank is to manifest social harmony, derived from the Islamic concept of sharing and caring, in order to achieve economic, financial and political stability. One can see how this differs vastly from the objectives of Western banks to return profits to shareholders. Interestingly, the Islamic view on usury is strikingly similar to the view of the Christian Church during the Middle Ages, in which thirteenth-century theologians and canonists condemned usury (*mutuum*) or profit from a loan.[46] What Westerners tend to overlook is that during the medieval period, the Church had a much greater influence on the behaviour of society than today. The centrally operated church provided rituals, dogma and Church doctrine, which evolved into today's Judaeo-Christian morals and ethics.[47]

Aggregating cultural diversity

The opportunity for retail banks in a global environment is to incorporate the banking needs of all socioeconomic dimensions of society with an understanding of cultural biases towards banking practices, thereby aggregating cultural diversity rather than causing it to conform to a standard generic banking model. Banking product design starts at a macro-level, where the customers' economic stance is measured against the overarching set of cultural values, as depicted in Figure 1.13. Each dimension of the matrix can be further refined to incorporate varying degrees of granularity. Ultimately, patterns emerge, thus revealing a common set of customer

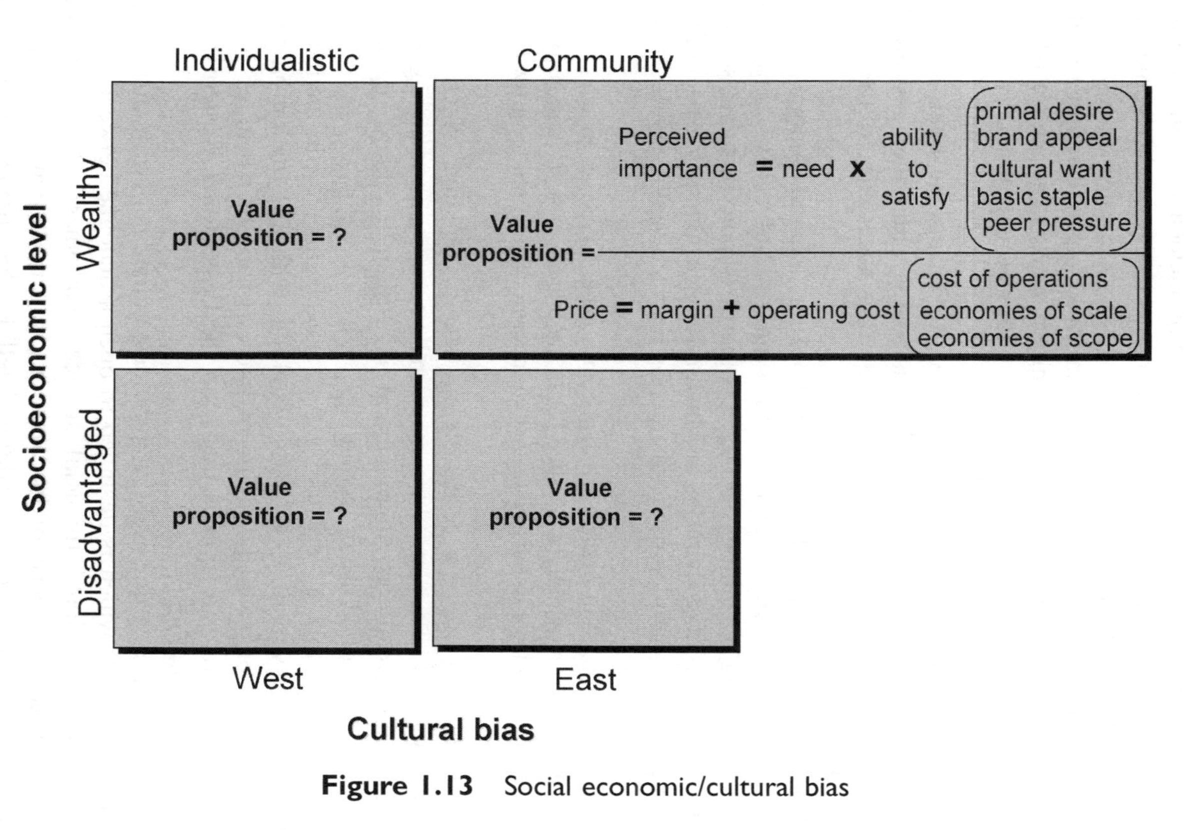

Figure 1.13 Social economic/cultural bias

values across all cultures and a separate set of values common within a cultural context. Hence Islamic banking shows itself as essentially different from Western banking, which is constructed around a core set of beliefs. Islamic banking, although adopting elements of the Western model, preserves variations that are indigenous to the specific geographic region which it serves.

Islamic banking is not simply a mechanism to facilitate commerce; it is a part of the social fabric of the community it serves. The aim of Islamic banking is to create a just society and eliminate exploitation with the application of shariah (Islamic law) on banking operations and financial instruments.[48] The teachings of the Holy Book must be interpreted by Islamic scholars who often sit on religious boards within the bank, and by individuals who are taught to make choices according to their own personal beliefs.

Trisakti International Business School in Jakarta, Indonesia, has launched the Islamic Business and Finance Netversity, employing distance-learning technology to train people in Islamic financial services about the cultural idiosyncrasies of Muslim finance. One key aspect of this learning is the recognition of the distinction between banking philosophies:

> From conventional insurance to Islamic insurance; from risk transfer to risk sharing; a shift in paradigm is called for in the interest of social solidarity. Get trained to participate in this sector that has enormous potential for growth.[49]

The school also offers a certificate in Islamic banking, which covers Islamic financial law, Islamic monetary and macroeconomic management, Islamic commercial, development and investment banking, regulatory issues and the applied use of technology.

The Islamic Banking Network[50] acts as a mechanism to educate individuals in the idiosyncrasies of Islamic banking, with information on products, questions on *riba* (the taking of interest) and other banking issues, and has a host of partnerships that span the Eastern and Western hemisphere, as seen in Figure 1.14.

The Muslim Investor website provides individuals with an 'ask-a-scholar' feature,[51] which is designed to open a dialogue between Islamic scholars and individual financial services' customers. It appears that Islamic banking is ahead of its Western counterparts when it comes to educating customers and embedding itself in the community. Whereas most Western banks have charitable programmes that are often simply conduits to national and local charity organizations, Islamic banks, private or government owned, are a part of the social infrastructure.

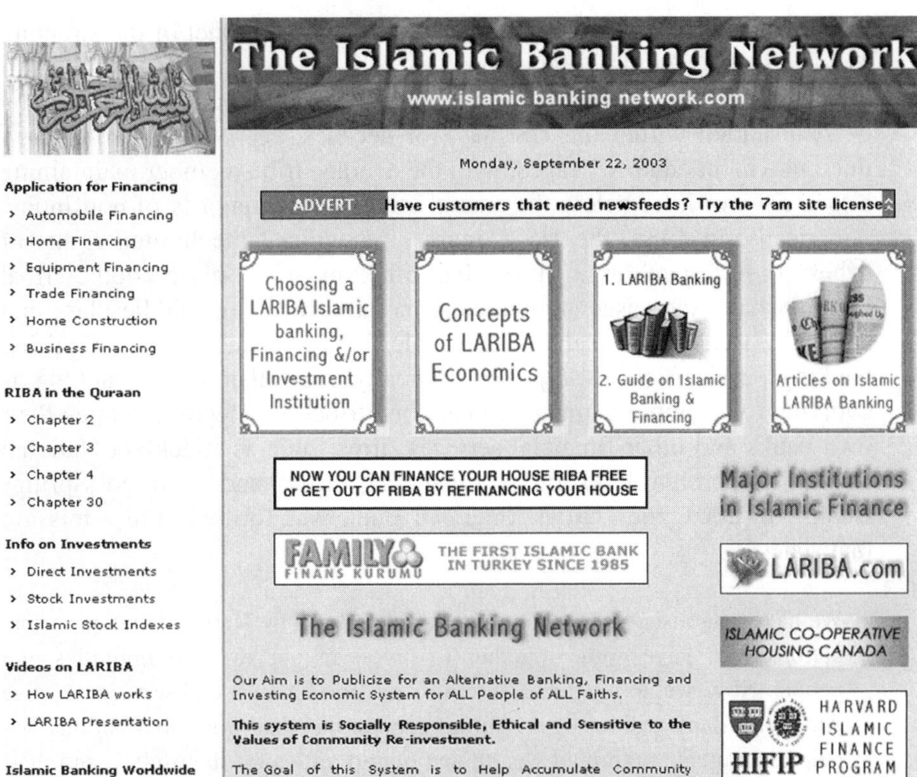

Figure 1.14 Islamic Banking Network

Banking on the edge of society

A euphemistic term in the financial services industry is the great 'unbanked' or 'unbankable' people, referring to people at the bottom of the socioeconomic spectrum who live on the edge of insolvency. Often these individuals teeter from month to month at a level on or below the poverty line that exists within a particular nation state. Providing services to this demographic subsegment has traditionally been fraught with problems, most of which stem from a lack of a profitable relationship with the customer. This market subsegment is found in all parts of the world and is not a product of modernity; the unbanked are a byproduct of the structure of society and should not be ignored.

The indigenous American Indian population, which comprises an independent nation within the US, has, for decades, been the victim of high unemployment and low wages, with the average tribe member maintaining a total net worth far below the annual salary of the majority of non-Indian Americans. In 1988, the US Congress recognized the limited rights of tribes to run gambling. Since that time, in some reservations, tribal incomes have increased dramatically, creating a rising middle class and suddenly transforming the unbankable into a demographic requiring banking services of all types.[52] Ironically, now that tribal banking is evolving to resemble mainstream banking, tribes are electing to open their own banks and other financial services firms, such as Blackfeet National Bank,[53] Sovereign Leasing & Financing Inc.,[54] and Borrego Springs Bank.[55] In 2001, the Native American Bank was formed with a mission that states:

> We have established a bank that is owned and run by Native American tribal nations who have come together to invest in our own communities and people. Now, we no longer have to look outside for financial services. Native American Bank will serve the future generation of all our tribal nations and help them create unlimited wealth and opportunities for themselves and their families.[56]

The eastern Shawnee tribe, which is the majority owner of the People's National Bank of Seneca, Missouri, recently instituted a tribal loan programme targeted specifically to tribe members who may not meet the required criteria of traditional lending institutions.[57]

Aboriginal banking

Created in 1992, one example of culturally driven retail banking is Canada's Bank of Montreal's Aboriginal Banking which caters to native aboriginal communities by providing services designed to contribute to the economic self-sufficiency of aboriginal peoples across Canada.

The Bank of Montreal's value proposition is to establish mutually beneficial, sustainable relationships by designing and delivering, with aboriginal communities, businesses and individuals, a comprehensive range of financial products and services, which has evolved into the Aboriginal Banking Network.[58]

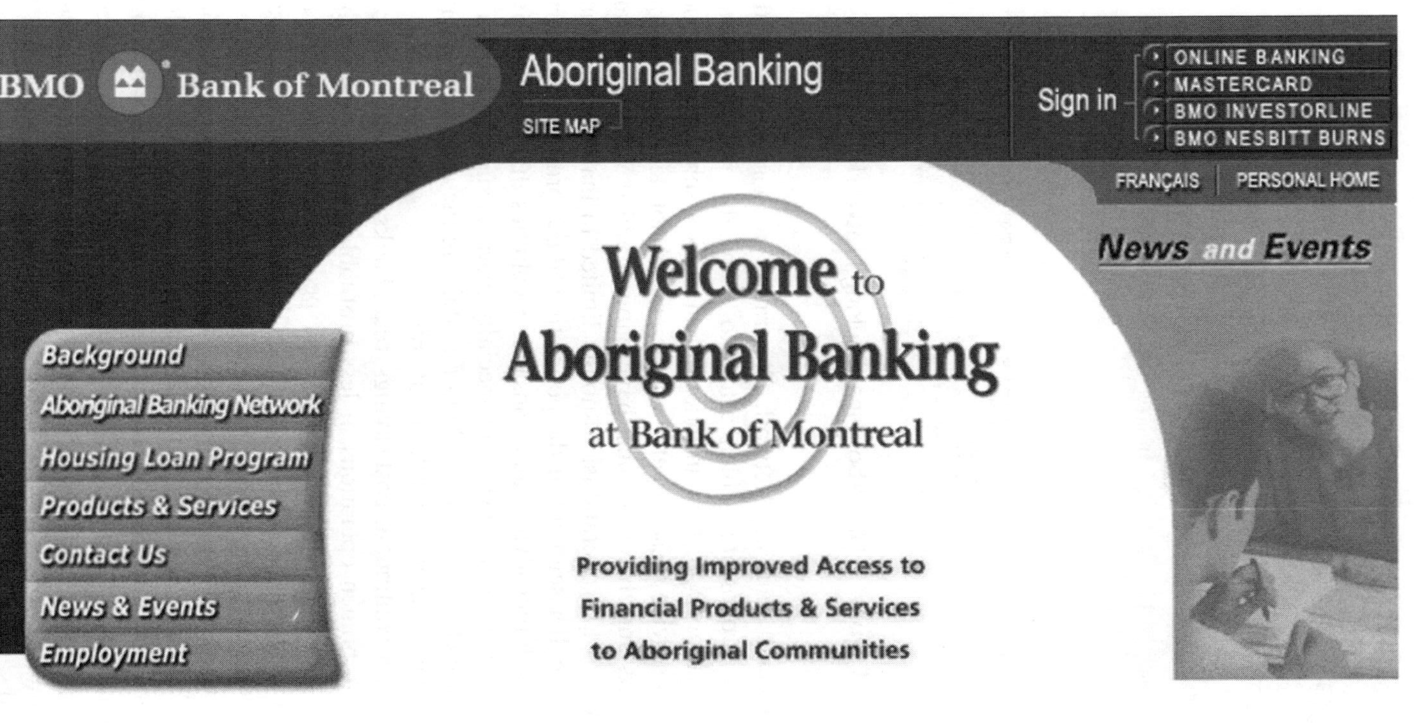

Figure 1.15 Aboriginal Banking

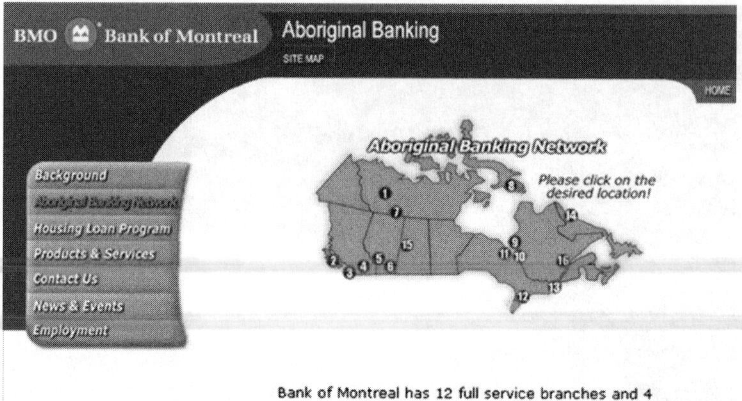
BMO Bank of Montreal
Aboriginal Banking
SITE MAP
HOME
Aboriginal Banking Network
Background
Housing Loan Program
Products & Services
Contact Us
News & Events
Employment
Please click on the desired location!
Bank of Montreal has 12 full service branches and 4 community branches serving Aboriginal communities. Nine of these branches are located on First Nation Territory and most are staffed by Aboriginal employees who are members of the community. In some branches, banking services and basic banking forms are provided in the traditional language of the community Bank of Montreal serves.

Figure 1.16 Aboriginal Banking Network

The Aboriginal Banking Network illustrates another aspect of the customer value proposition which caters to a specific need, generated within what is in every respect an independent market subsegment. Products created to service these targeted customers are not designed to apply to all customers and therefore must have enough added value to sustain any additional cost of operations. Although limited in market appeal and confined to a smaller segment of the population, these products and services generate customer loyalty and transaction volumes that are exclusive to one single banking relationship. In specialty markets such as aboriginal banking, the branch plays a vital role in maintaining the relationship with the customer, particularly in smaller rural areas.

In the quest for continuous cost savings, retail banks have opted to close and consolidate branch operations in less profitable or rural areas. This action makes sense from a profit and loss perspective, especially when an increasing percentage of these populations begin to do their primary banking on the Internet. However, in a rising number of cases, this course of action has alienated some communities and given rise to organizations such as the Campaign for Community Banking Services (CCBS), which campaigns for the continued existence of suitable access to banking services within communities. The CCBS's argument is built on a simple three-part agenda: access to retail banking services sustains local commercial activity; current banking trends are creating areas of financial and social exclusion; and segments of the population such as the disabled and elderly are not being served. These observations have not just been formulated into a series of complaints; the organization has endeavoured to make a case for neutral bank branches.[59] Traditional banking service providers that take an adversarial view of groups such as the CCBS are clearly missing a market opportunity. It is rare that any market segment will provide so much detailed information on the needs of individuals within the segment. We could say that these groups are providing free market intelligence, which retail banking institutions are not taking full advantage of and thereby creating an opportunity for a new market entrance by a non-traditional banking service provider.

Regardless of the political motivations of special interest groups, the concept of a neutral bank branch is one worth contemplating in the context of future bank strategies. Branches resemble retail store outlets in which products and services can be purchased via the infrastructure of the high street. In the last quarter of the twentieth century, shopping centres and later shopping malls consolidated retailers into a shared infrastructure that reduced the cost of operations by spreading many fixed and variable costs across several retailers. A similar case could be made for several retail banks operating effectively out of one physical branch location as an anchor point for brand identity and special services. This neutral bank branch provides key services such as remote teller services, customer education using interactive kiosks, and can be equipped with transient office space for bank representatives to use for face-to-face appointments with customers.

Retail banks are striving to develop a generic global value proposition in order to optimize costs and lower total operating expenses. A generic value proposition can be based on a set of societal values that transcends cultures and geopolitical boundaries, such as the desire to better one's lifestyle, prepare for your children's future and plan your retirement. Generic cross-cultural values are not as rare as one might expect. John Maynard Keynes provides insight that is at the heart of retail banking services' value proposition. In his view, individuals are motivated to save and spend by subjective social incentives such as precaution (against contingencies), foresight (to provide future relations with income), calculation (saving now for spending later), improvement (to increase expenditure gradually), independence, enterprise, pride and avarice. The reasons that trigger these events and resulting transactions include, but are not limited to, enjoyment, short-sightedness, generosity, miscalculation, ostentation and extravagance.[60] Keynes' recognition of consumers' motivations continues to be true even when these motivations are projected against a backdrop of a changing family structure in the West (from a nuclear family to a fragmented network of relationships). It remains to be seen if the change in the social fabric of Western nations will transfer to other parts of the world. Yet, Keynes' observations about people's basic needs, wants, desires and motivations have stood the test of time.[61]

Notes

1 T. E. Gregory, *The Westminster Bank:Through a Century,* London: Westminster Bank Limited, 1936, pp. 1–2.

2 Hong Kong and Shanghai Banking Corporation, available at www.hsbc.com, March 2003.

3 C. P. Smith, *Retail Banking Rethink: Strategic Marketing in Action*, Dunblane: Doica, 1990, p. 178.

4 Cosmocrat, definition: a member of a supposed global ruling elite of cosmopolitan businesspeople and administrators. Derivation: meld of cosmopolitan and bureaucrat. Popularized by J. Micklethwait and A. Wooldridge in *A Future Perfect: The Challenge and Hidden Promise of Globalization.* Citation: 'The cosmocrats are becoming a self-conscious class, helped by the way that the global economy is coalescing around clusters such as Silicon Valley, Wall Street, Hollywood and the City of London.' *Financial Times* 27 May 2000.

5 R. Lopez, 'The Dawn of Medieval Banking', in the Center for Medieval and Renaissance Studies, University of California, *The Dawn of Modern Banking*. New Haven: Yale University Press, 1979, p. 1.

6 F. Braudel, *Civilization and Capitalism 15th–18th Century* volume II: *The Wheels of Commerce*, London: William Collins & Sons, 1982, p. 436.

7 E. Hunt and J. Murray, *A History of Business in Medieval Europe 1200–1550,* Cambridge: Cambridge University Press, 1999, pp. 102–3.

8 J. DiVanna, *Redefining Financial Services: The New Renaissance in Value Propositions*, Basingstoke: Palgrave Macmillan, 2002, p. 173.

9 M. Prestwich, 'Italian Merchants in Late Thirteenth and Early Fourteenth Century England', in the Center for Medieval and Renaissance Studies, University of California, *The Dawn of Modern Banking*. New Haven: Yale University Press, 1979, p. 100.

10 DiVanna, *Redefining Financial Services*, pp. 173–5.

11 'Dah Sing Bank creates infrastructure for cross-selling', *The Asian Banker*, 9 April 2003, available at http://www,theasian banker.com.

12 H. Pirenne, *Economic & Social History of Medieval Europe*, London: Kegan Paul Trench, Trubner, 1937, p. 127.

13 Pirenne, *Economic & Social History of Medieval Europe*, pp. 192–6.

14 Prepared testimony of Edward E. Furash, chairman of Furash & Company, at the hearing on s.1405 of the Financial Regulatory Relief and Economic Efficiency Act 1997, Washington: US Senate Banking, Housing and Urban Affairs Committee, 3 March 1998, available at http://www.senate.gov/~banking/98_03hrg/030398/witness/furash.htm, January 2003.

15 Hunt and Murray, *A History of Business in Medieval Europe*, p. 162.

16 J. Rossier, 'Ethics and Money: What is required of the banking professional', *La Lettre*, Geneva: Geneva Private Bankers Association, No. 23, March 2003, p. 2, available at http://www.genevaprivatebankers.com/en/lalettre/la_lettre_23_en.pdf, March 2003.

17 Smith, *Retail Banking Rethink*, pp. 177–97.

18 Lifestage Marketing, the Henley Centre, available at http://www.henleycentre.com/henley.phtml, May 2003.

19 Affinity Solutions, Case Studies, available at http://www.affinity-uk.com/casestudies.htm, May 2003.

20 Smith, *Retail Banking Rethink*, p. 186.

21 Kid¢ents, the Citizens Banking Company, Sandusky, Ohio, available at http://www.kidcents.net/2nd_level/about.html, April 2003.

22 School Savings Program, Washington Mutual Inc., available at http://www.wamu.com/servlet/wamu/public/eng/pages/about/community/programs/classroom.html, May 2003.

23 Credit Card Creator, Halifax plc, available at http://www.halifaxcards.co.uk/apply/BYO/index.html, April 2003.

24 SBM Amigos Program, State Bank of Mauritius, available at https://secure.sbmonline.com/forms/amigos/coach.asp, March 2003.

25 See DiVanna, *Redefining Financial Services*.

26 *TezRaftaar*, United Bank Limited, Pakistan, available at http://www.ubl.com.pk/products/tezraftaar.shtml.

27 expatBanking, Isle of Man: Bank of Ireland, available at www.fsharpbank.com, April 2003.

28 CombiNations Savings, HSBC Hong Kong, available at http://www.hsbc.com.hk/hk/personal/invest/deposit/combi.htm, April 2003.

29 Learning Centre, Insurance.com Insurance Agency, Fidelity Investments, available at http://www.insurance.com/profiles_insights/index.asp, May 2003.

30 Royal Banking, Dubai Bank, United Arab Emirates, available at http://www.dubaibank.ae/royal.htm, May 2003.

31 F. Wiersema, *Customer Intimacy: Pick Your Partners, Shape Your Culture, Win Together*, London: HarperCollins Business, 1997, p. 29.

32 First National Bank of Botswana, available at http://www.fnbbotswana.co.bw/glossaryOfTerms.asp.

33 Karen Couch and Donna Parker, 'Net Interest Grows as banks rush online', *Southwest Economy*, Dallas: Federal Reserve Bank of Dallas, Issue 2, March/April 2000, p. 5.

34 H. Engler and J. Essinger, 'Sir John Bond Interview', *The Future of Banking*, Harlow: Pearson Education, 2000, p. 78.

35 DiVanna, *Redefining Financial Services*, especially Part V.

36 *Asesor de Seguros* , Bankinter, S.A., available at www.ebankinter.com, May 2003.

37 Open Sesame, *The Economist*, 18 May 2000.

38 W. Waldron, 'Banking on Tomorrow', *Fast Company*, Issue 51, October 2001, p. 50.

39 Development of ATMs and CDs: The World Market from 1967 to 1999, *The Global ATM Market to 2004,* Richmond: Retail Banking Research, available at http://www.rbrldn.demon.co.uk/history.htm, May 2003.

40 C. Pretzlik and W. Hall, 'Alps provide no shelter for Switzerland's private banks', *Financial Times*, 24 April 2003, p. 18.

41 V. Vijayshanker Bhatt, *Financial Systems, Innovation and Development,* London: Sage, 1995, p. 30.

42 Lakh, a unit of measure equal to 100,000 rupees, source: Library of Congress: Federal Research Division, Country Research, available at http://memory.loc.gov/frd/cs/india/in_glos.html, May 2003.

43 Crore, a unit of measure equal to 10 million rupees (or 100 lakh), Library of Congress: Federal Research Division, Country Research, available at http://memory.loc.gov/frd/cs/india/in_glos.html, May 2003.

44 Pigmy deposit, Syndicate Bank, Karnataka, India, available at http://www.syndicatebank.com/default.asp, May 2003.

45 Al-Harran (ed.), *Leading Issues in Islamic Banking and Finance*, Selangor Darul Ehsan: Pelanduk Publications (M) Sdn. Bhd., 1995, p. viii.

46 J. Le Goff, 'The Usurer and Purgatory', in Fredi Chiappelli (ed.), *The Dawn of Modern Banking*, New Haven: Yale University Press, 1979, p. 25.

47 J. DiVanna, *Thinking Beyond Technology: Creating New Value in Business*, Basingstoke: Palgrave Macmillan, 2003, pp. 181–2.

48 Shariah Rulings, The Institute of Islamic Banking and Insurance, London, available at http://www.islamic-banking.com, May 2003.

49 Islamic Business and Finance Netversity, Trisakti International Business School, Trisakti University, Jakarta, available at http://www.netversity.org/, May 2003.

50 The Islamic Banking Network, available at http://www.islamicbankingnetwork.com/, May 2003.

51 Muslim Investor, available at http://www.muslim-investor.com/mi/, May 2003.

52 R. Wirtz, 'Breaching the buckskin curtain', *The Region: Banking and Policy Issues Magazine*, Minneapolis: Federal Reserve Bank of Minneapolis, September 2000, available at http://minneapolisfed.org/pubs/region/00-09/wirtz.cfm, March 2003.

53 Blackfeet National Bank, 'Blackfeet revivial: Tribal bank credited with breathing new life into reservation', *Billings Gazette*, Billings: Lee Enterprises, 20 July 1999, available at http://www.billingsgazette.com/region/990720_reg10.html, April 2003.

54 Sovereign Leasing & Financing Inc. is a wholly owned subsidiary corporation of S & K Holding Company, Inc., which is, in turn, a wholly owned, for-profit corporation of the Confederated Salish and Kootenai Tribes of the Flathead Reservation. Sovereign was chartered on 15 April 1992 and established primarily as the financing arm of the tribal business corporations, http://www.rdfc.org/mnadfi_members.htm, March 2003.

55 Borrego Springs Bank, available at http://www.borregospringsbank.com/, April 2003.

56 Native American Bank, available at http://www.nativeamericanbank.com/, April 2003.

57 People's National Bank, 'Bank tribal loan program outlined', *Shooting Star Newsletter*, the Eastern Shawnee Tribe of Oklahoma, July 1999, available at http://www.showcase.netins.net/web/shawnee/ss/econoupdate.html, April 2003.

58 Aboriginal Banking, Bank of Montreal, available at http://www.bmo.com/aboriginalbanking/, February 2003.

59 Neutral Branch Banking, Campaign for Community Banking Services, available at http://home.btclick.com/ccbs/index.htm, March 2003.

60 J. M. Keynes, *The General Theory of Employment, Interest and Money*. London: Macmillan, 1946, pp. 107–9.

61 J. DiVanna, *Synconomy: Adding Value in a World of Continuously Connected Business*, Basingstoke: Palgrave Macmillan, 2003, pp. 40–1.

CHAPTER 2

Getting There: Thinking Ahead

> In the future, firms may serve customers by bundling certain financial services that are not currently combined, or they may merge banking-like services with non-banking-like services, such as tickets to concerts and sporting events, and vacation planning. These firms may have electronic delivery vehicles and be accessed through the Internet. In the end, prosperous firms will be those that find ways to deliver services the public wants. Some activities that today we regard as inappropriate, difficult, or illegal for banks will most likely change, and sooner than we expect.[1]

In order to compete successfully in an environment of globally competitive banking services, financial institutions must continually adapt their products and services to represent the values and, more importantly, a sense of benefit that is easily recognizable by the consumer and small businesses. Business gurus have touted the necessities of having a clear business vision that is the synthesis of the firm's value proposition. Financial institutions which cater to the retail banking marketplace are finding that their current suite of products that is the basis of their current value proposition is not aligned to the customers' service demands. During the dot-com frenzy, many institutions interpreted this misalignment as not having enough technological product offerings. Many traditional retail banks found that competition could spring from non-traditional banking sources. As the dot-com phenomena faded, retail bankers realized that the next wave of competition would centre on the formation of horizontal and vertical industry alliances to meet the growing complexity caused by customers demanding products to facilitate their changing lifestyles. To meet this wave of industry-wide change, retail banks must develop a value proposition that is clearly understood by customers. The value proposition is a restatement of the institution's vision.

Business visions for retail banks should comprise a clear statement of purpose that summarizes the overall value added by their service to customers. Vision is not meant to mean the next quarter, but two, three and even five years into the future. Creating a vision and a sustainable value proposition demands that an organization must continually think ahead. Developing a vision is not a one-time event, just as the firm's value proposition is not static, but continually changes, reacting to customer and market demands. Although the creation of a vision and subsequent value proposition appears easy, in reality it is difficult. Vision and value proposition development requires a defined approach, with periodic intervals of strategic thinking events to keep it responsive to changes in the competitive landscape. Today's customers are looking for a retail bank that has global breadth (access to geographically diverse opportunities) but local depth (higher levels of personal customer services and assistance) to meet the needs of their changing lifestyles.

In the post-dot-com economic environment, financial institutions have shifted their focus from strategic endeavours to more tactical manoeuvres, concentrating largely on fixing systems that do not work versus implementing leading-edge solutions. To ward off new competitors, a large percentage of institutions are simply meeting the challenges of the economic downturn by cutting technology spending. Most traditional banks breathed a sigh of relief at the reduction in technology spending, indicating that the dot-com competitors appeared to be less of a threat than previously envisioned. It could be argued that many retail banking service providers have been lulled into a false sense of security and will, yet again, be caught off guard by the next wave of competition. This reactive strategy creates an opportunity for new market entrants and other more ambitious service providers to introduce new products and capture highly specialized market segments in both retail and commercial marketplaces. Financial services organizations offering retail products and services must move from a reactive business agenda to a proactive suite of customer-focused initiatives to remain competitive. Financial services firms taking a strategic stance are concentrating on developing their core skills and internal competencies in preparation for linking with cooperating external entities to form multi-organizational networks of co-branded financial products. As the next wave of competition becomes more complex, retail banks will centre their efforts along two distinct lines of business: becoming a retail banking utility that provides services to traditional banking customers and 'white label' generic services to external banking partners to be rebranded; and/or becoming a financial services hub or aggregator of banking products from other providers and intermediary services.

As retail banking evolves into a network of value-added partnerships, associations and affiliations, the organization will become dependent on transforming data into information and information into knowledge about customers. Ultimately, these three elements will lead to increased business wisdom. The banking industry is amidst a revolution sparked by technology and competition that will alter its relationship with customers and other institutions. This raises questions: which aspects of banking are embroiled in the revolution? Is there a previous banking model that is now more attainable because of modern technology?

If we allow ourselves to digress for one moment and examine the banking model of the early twentieth century, one of the fundamental aspects that appears to be driving today's customer behaviour can be seen as returning to a prior value proposition. Anyone who has watched the classic Walt Disney picture *Mary Poppins* will recall the scene in which the young boy Michael gives the banker Mr Dawes senior tuppence, who then breaks into a song explaining that the boy's deposit makes him part of the railways in Africa, dams across the Nile and plantations of ripening tea. In this whimsical portrayal of the bank model of 1910, we see the crux of today's banking dilemma. In 1910, people who went to banks were depositors, and bankers, using their vast knowledge of financial instruments, invested the funds to produce the highest possible returns within a structure of ethics and morals perceived by the customer. Today, customers themselves are investors, having to use their knowledge of financial instruments to select the best set of offered products to improve their total wealth. Do customers actually want this additional responsibility of researching, analysing and selecting stocks from a host of companies and products, simply to gain a slightly better-than-average return? The startling number of mutual funds suggests that although consumers prefer the option to close investment vehicles, they are not prepared to do the work themselves, opting to have a fund manager who is measured by return on investment. Here again, this may be an indication of the next wave of banking behaviour in which fee income is replaced by returns on funds deposited. A banking environment in which fees are eliminated in favour of payment for services based on delivered value may seem far-fetched, but then again so was Internet banking 10 years ago. Negroponte of the MIT Media Lab argued years ago that the one effect of technology was its ability to initiate a switch in cost per use over time.[2] For example: broadcast television was initially free, paid by advertising; now, the majority of homes pay a monthly fee to receive broadcast via cable.

One thing is clear: the revolution in banking services is not over yet. At the vanguard of the switch from products to services, ultimately becoming a trusted advisor, is the branch of the future.

The branch of the future

The Waianae branch of the future is the Bank of Hawaii's entry into applying new technology, with a fundamental rethinking of branch operations including the use of a biometric hand-scanning security system to control entry into the safe deposit box area and virtual tellers, which serve customers via two-way television monitors. The Bank of Hawaii has taken an important first step in rethinking the customer experience with a branch concierge, a banking expert who greets customers and helps them to find the best way to handle their banking business.[3]

The foundation for services that advise customers comprises two key elements: the ability to sense customers' needs and market trends; and a comprehensive approach to information management. If the retail bank develops the mechanisms to sense customers' needs, then activities that add cost such as applying for a loan become a waste of time. The data needed to make a loan decision is often already within the bank, but located in isolated systems that lack a cohesive integration of data and an analytical engine to correlate information on the customer directly into a risk assessment module. To achieve a higher degree of customer intimacy, customers must have a sense of trust and security that the retail bank's use of their data will not be taken lightly, and that confidential information will not be haphazardly divulged to their partners in the network of value. Trust is not a commodity; it is a component within a relationship that must be earned and learned. In the past, trust was earned by the physical attributes of the bank (big steel vault, bars on windows, marble columns and alarms). Now, computer technologies offer an electronic version of these physical attributes.

This raises another set of questions: why do we trust banks? What makes us trust banks? If the Internet is so perilous, why has there been no significant eBank robbery yet? Taking into consideration the chequered past of computer software quality across the industry, coupled with the inordinate amount of software defects and gaps in functionality, it is surprising that cyber bank robbery has not been more prevalent. However, there have been individual cases of fraud, such as programmers accumulating fractions of cents resulting from rounding calculations, misdirected electronic funds, ATM skimming and other direct attacks on bank security systems. Even though computer hackers have been revered in some technological circles, no group or individual has been elevated to the romanticized level of the bank robbers found in North American folklore. What may be looming on the horizon is the new threat of cyberterrorism or eTerror, which to date has been contained in isolated cases of virus proliferation. Direct retail banking cybercrime is destined to become a widespread problem unless multi-country agreements on prosecution are put in place and law enforcement agencies can collaborate transnationally.

Strategic adaptation

The industry that has traditionally been known as retail banking is dead; we just have not had the funeral yet. This does not imply that customer needs no longer exist, nor does it mean that firms providing banking services are gone; it does, however, mean that traditional retail banking services providers are now operating on borrowed time. If we consider the potential of financial institutions to provide services, the value propositions of incumbent retail banks is a low performing asset. This is due to the changing definition of what constitutes a retail bank, what type of firm a bank is, and what products and services make a bank a bank. It is no wonder that with all the changes in the financial services industry in regulations, products, services and the inclusion of ancillary services, customers are confused as to which services are valuable to their lifestyles. However, as Nietzsche once affirmed, 'from chaos comes order', and over time customers will identify which services are of added value and gravitate towards providers that consistently deliver measurable results. To reduce market confusion, retail banks must develop a value proposition that is clearly understood and recognizable to customers.

For a moment, let us consider several key factors which will reshape the financial services industry during the next 20 years. The first factor to consider is that as the baby-boom generation retires, enjoys old age and eventually passes away, the succeeding generation will experience the second largest transition of wealth between two generations since the Black Death in the mid-fourteenth century. The baby-boom generation has generated vast amounts of wealth and in its later years has embraced services for wealth management and wealth preservation. In contrast, the succeeding generation has so far had little interest in wealth management, and has mastered spending even before receiving its inheritance. For retail banks, this presents an opportunity to educate the next generation of customers to the benefits of the prudent use of financial services products to support emerging lifestyles. The second factor is that with any sharp decline in population comes a corresponding reduction in the number of total customers, translating into fewer customers but with a higher net worth. This may significantly affect organizations which have established an aggressive growth agenda to expand their business, as we shall see in the next section.

Sensing the market and identifying the competitive problem

The inability of an organization to sense social changes that occur over long periods and develop a competitive response to the marketplace is not limited to financial services nor is it an inherent problem within retail banking. In the global competitive marketplace for banking services, sensing movements in the marketplace and assessing changes in customer needs often result in organizations making costly mistakes, when consumer trends and customer data are not understood in the context of long-term socioeconomic behaviour. Fundamental shifts in social attitudes typically happen due to three key factors: an attitudinal transformation that takes place over a number of years, such as a society swinging from a savings culture to a debt culture; specific events such as the impending transition of wealth from the baby-boom generation to the next; or social shifts which can be the result of a technological breakthrough, such as the Internet. In a connected global competitive environment, developing a corporate competency to sense the market and adapt to changing customer requirements is an essential skill that retail banks must master, as Howcroft and Lavis noted: 'Organizations can become outdated simply because they lack the ability to adapt and conform to the requirements of society.'[4]

However, financial services organizations must evaluate the impact of changes in society in terms of relative value on their portfolio of banking products. This can be accomplished first by determining if it is a fundamental change in social behaviour or the result of a short-term social phenomenon such as a fad or desire of a specific market segment. Most long-term social change goes unnoticed by society until it has gained sufficient momentum to be noticed suddenly by business. This can be attributed to either the pace of today's banking environment, which focuses the attention on shorter term events and not long-term trends, or, on the other hand, it is because consumers do not inherently decide to adopt a new behaviour; they must be led by mimicking the behaviour of others. Many people can remember life before email, but fewer can recall life before television, and even fewer can reflect on life before the telephone.

Institutions engaged in retail banking activities must develop capabilities to rapidly assess the cultural and socioeconomic behaviours of consumers and weigh any change against the existing value proposition. Organizations that have developed customer-sensing skills are not shocked or surprised when a new market entrant makes an appearance into a niche market or a highly specialized service. For example, we note the American convenience store 7-Eleven and Verison collaborated to offer kiosk-based online bill payment.[5] The 7-Eleven/Verison virtual commerce value proposition is simple and effective, providing a convenient bill payment mechanism for people who are on the go or do not have regular access to the Internet. The same service is found in Shanghai where consumers have started paying their utility bills at the local convenience store, Lawson of Japan,[6] who operates a joint venture with local utility providers. Strategically for the alliance's partners, this can be seen as a precursor to providing a wider array of financial services operating outside the traditional banking networks.

Gauging customer behaviour

When bankers are asked 'what mechanisms does your firm use to "sense" the market and "gauge" customer behaviour?', overwhelmingly the answer is 'technology, of course'. Technology has a prominent place in the value equation due to its ability to effectively gauge customer behaviour and identify market trends. When used effectively, technology can give a retail bank a competitive edge by analysing behavioural trends in customers and establishing new services to capitalize on not just the change but also the transition. The versatility of technology can be leveraged in numerous ways by facilitating interactions with customers, such as enabling face-to-face video customer services via an ATM machine, providing organizations with sensing mechanisms to detect changes in societal banking attitudes, and local cultural community behaviours. However, technology is only one third of the equation, as the people within the firm and the process for the collection of market intelligence play equally important roles. There are three key issues with people: applied use, skills and cultural diversity. People and their inherent skills are a significant but often underutilized asset of a retail bank. This is not to say that branch and back-office personnel are not working to capacity; indeed, in the majority of institutions, they are overworked. As a deployed asset, the people performing the activities within the business processes of the bank rarely participate in the collection and collation of customer information required for the strategic thinking within the company. Yet they can be a low-cost, non-technological sensor for customer behaviour. At a 2001 banking conference in London, the audience of senior banking strategy professionals was asked a simple and direct question: how many members of the audience have physically had a conversation with a customer of the bank during the past 12 months. Surprisingly, out of 65 attendees, not one hand was raised. This identifies a key problem in today's banking environment, while also presenting an opportunity to change how the bank operates in the development of strategic thinking. As technology relentlessly automates more and more functions within the bank, people feel less obligated to interact with customers unless they are in the direct front line of a transaction. The opportunity to leverage the human assets of the bank can be as uncomplicated as employees asking customers several short questions to acquire customer insight, rather than merely extrapolating the raw data stored about an individual customer. Embedding mechanisms to acquire customer feedback into the corporate culture of the institution should not be an event, but rather the normal course of business, essential to establishing a process that actively senses customer need. Each customer entering a branch is an opportunity to obtain direct customer feedback. Most banks have thousands of these undercapitalized feedback opportunities daily.

The second key issue on the people agenda is the current level of skills within institutions and, more importantly, how those skills are being used to advance goals and objectives. As retail banks continue to transition from transaction processors to product sellers and ultimately to trusted advisors, the skills they need to cross-sell, analyse customer lifestyle requirements and recommend products/services must continually be upgraded and enhanced to include a comprehensive understanding of technology, as well as the changes made to product and service offerings to keep pace with the transition. The issue of people and skills extends to include the management of retail banking lines of business. Smith notes that many managers who came through the ranks over the last 20–40 years are now at the last quartile, of their careers having experienced banking during a period of slow change (1960s), slow but positive change (1970s), the painful realities of adverse change (1980s), and the rapid pace of change spurred on by re-engineering, technology and aggressive growth agendas (1990s).[7] Looking across four decades of retail banking, Smith identifies the considerable problem of a gap in the skills of today's managers, which is reinforced by Essinger:

> The old days when bankers had above all to be numerically literate and not necessarily particularly skilled in dealing with customers are over. Today, inter-

> personal skills are extremely important for bankers, given that numeracy will always be an important factor. Staff recruited to work in branches need to be able to deal with people with ease and also able to demonstrate a genuine interest in the customers' needs and problems.[8]

The final issue is cultural diversity, about which a growing body of evidence indicates that achieving cultural diversification at all levels of an organization enables it to be more agile in its capability to sense and interpret variations in customer requirements and competitive pressures. Cultural diversity is then leveraged by establishing a clearly understood business process in which customer feedback and market trends that are observed by employees can be channelled into a corporate intelligence database.

One aspect of sensing the market is the ability to assess the local environment or, more colloquially, the community's attitude towards financial institutions and/or the individual retail banking centres. In the value proposition to customers, retail banks only recognize this aspect of the customer when a large migration of customers occurs across demographic segments to either a competitor offering a product which is perceived as having a distinct advantage, or a new market entrant launching a completely new set of products and/or a new bank altogether. The early successes of New Zealand's Kiwibank, which operates in a synergist relationship with the New Zealand Post, provides good example of how a new market entrant can rapidly woo customers by providing a clear and simple value proposition that appeals to an attitude within a local market. Kiwibank's value proposition is predicated on two decidedly different aspects of the customers' values: a sense of community and nationalism, desiring to keep the profits of the bank within the national borders; and a direct appeal to low-cost/low-fee operations for the broadest socioeconomic group requiring the least complex financial services.[9] Armed with basic accounts, term deposits, home loans, Internet banking and more complex services such as business banking and credit cards planned for the near future,[10] Kiwibank's story illustrates that new market entrants grow rapidly in niche markets when they satisfy a specific need. Later, having demonstrated the ability to satisfy the customers' basic requirements, additional services can be offered with a lower cost of sales rather than trying to acquire customers with more complex product offerings. Clearly, Kiwibank's customer base and total deposits are a minute fraction of its larger rivals and it does not pose a substantial threat to competition. However, when taken in the context of all niche markets, it identifies the need for financial service providers to develop an understanding of what motivates each market segment in order to address the fundamental elements of their motivations and incorporate these factors into the value proposition.

Howcroft and Lavis make an important point that many retail banks overlook when they incorporate social factors into strategic plans: 'Financial institutions have to ensure that their organizational reactions are based mainly on social change not changes in taste.'[11] When traditional product-focused institutions endeavour to tailor products in an attempt to become more customer-focused or in response to niche market opportunities and/or when a technology suddenly offers a new capability, there is a tendency to develop customer or market myopia. This is when an organization or a group within the organization becomes so engrossed with the development and promotion of the product idea that it fails to assess its perceived intrinsic value proposition to the customer. This was the case, for example, with the mobile/WAP phone share trading, which, contrary to the marketing hype and analyst projections, was embraced by only a very small percentage of customers. In many cases, financial institutions that developed and implemented these types of technological offerings may wait many years for any significant return on investment, or, in isolated cases, may have to retire the product before any financial reward can be recouped.

Ironically, a larger than realized number of professionals in the retail banking industry often labour under the misconception that customers enjoy going to a bank and waiting in queues, which Essinger argues is not true when he reminds us of the real nature of customers' attitudes towards banking:

> People only use banks because they need to, not because they really want to: banks are a necessary evil. Unless the customer is a pathological miser, he doesn't want what the bank can provide (i.e. money and access to payment facilities) but rather what the money can bring. Only the fact that we live in advanced societies which have evolved money as a common standard for barter makes banks, or their money, of any interest to us at all.[12]

People, for the most part, do not enjoy banking because it is not a social experience, it is not personally satisfying, nor does it cater to instant gratification in the same way as shopping. However, what Essinger does note is that there are six basic general motivations for people to use banking services. Each motivation must be reflected firstly in the value proposition to the customer and secondly in the design of the product and service offerings:

- safety and security
- interest or ROI

- convenient access to cash
- convenient access to payments
- access to loans
- status and equality with peer groups.[13]

Each customer motivation can be linked to a customer-perceived element of value, a delivery channel or mechanism, a direct line of business and a specific delivery technology, as depicted in Figure 2.1.

Technology plays an important role in fulfilling customer motivations and it must therefore be used to enable the customer to reach that fulfilment via multiple pathways to the institution. However, developing technological pathways for the sake of pure customer choice is not always an economically viable strategy. Technology always has the potential to add value to a retail bank's operations, customer offerings or infrastructure. Technology's value must be assessed relative to the goal and objectives of the organization, based on quantitative and qualitative measures. The potential value can be plotted on the corporate radar screen to show its value and determine when it should be implemented, as depicted in Figure 2.2.

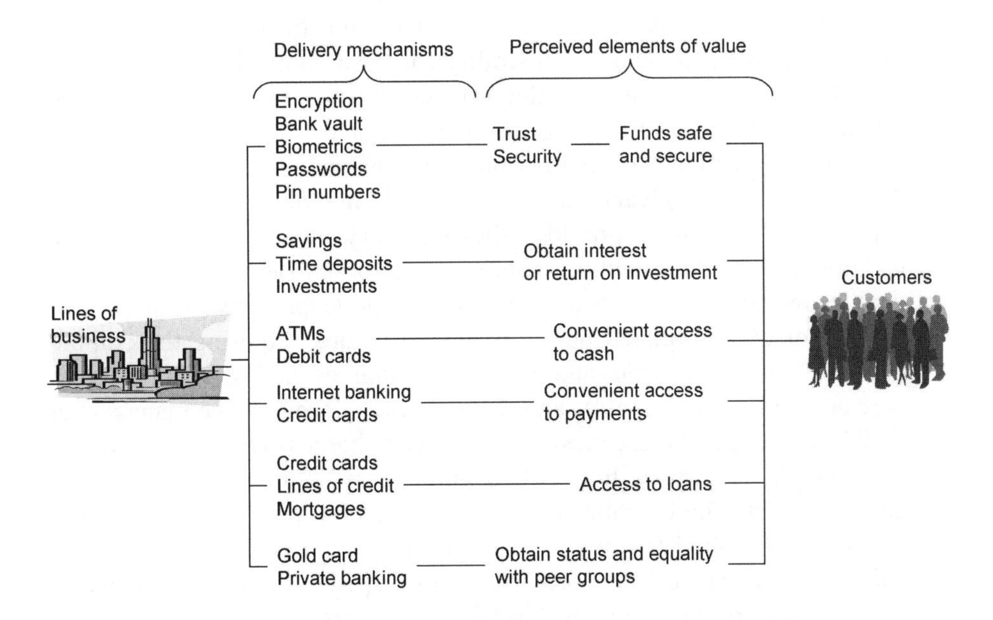

Figure 2.1 Customer motivations and elements of value

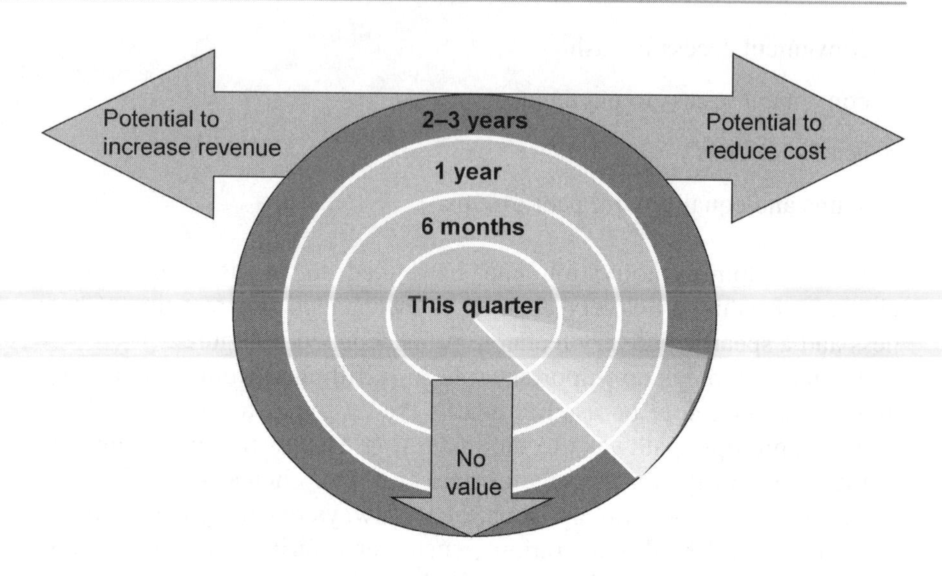

Figure 2.2 The radar screen

Retail banking line managers should be asking the chief information officer (CIO) or chief technology officer (CTO) a fundamental question: will the use of technology enable the organization's banking products and services to lead the competition, follow closely behind or trail badly? Technology must have a strategic intent for the firm to compete in the global environment. The responsibility for technological implementations that alter the business process, the product offerings for consumers, branch operations or back-office processing does not rest solely with the technology organization. Substantive business change and change that hinges on a technological advance must be led and championed by the business. The technology group provides the necessary means to implement the technology, but the adoption rests with the organizational lines of business. However, the leadership may shift to the technology group in cases when projects are related purely to infrastructure, requiring the complex coordination of internal and external resources acting collaboratively between all lines of business and the technology group. Line managers are realizing that it is the organization's ability to harness resources across the firm which determines how, when and where solutions can be rapidly accomplished. The essential issue is that the bulk of technology projects are directly applied to some aspect within a line of business because of some internal desire to reduce cost or in response to an external market force endangering the relationship with customers.

Sensing external market factors and interpreting the trends using a multicultural lens enables firms to correlate the influence of these forces on internal business process change. Put simply, individuals in the various lines of business must learn to interpret external global factors and put them into a context that is meaningful to the firm's value proposition. Technology can be employed to sense and assess customer behaviour and market trends that are linked to a geographic area, such as BNP Paribas's investment in geomarketing decision support systems in France.[14] Using ASTEROP's business geointelligence technology based on new geostatistical analysis and ASTEROP's methodological approach to geomarketing, BNP Paribas optimizes the sales and marketing results of the BNP banking network. The technology enables BNP Paribas to simulate homogeneous trading areas, in effect designing and building territories by linking them to socioeconomic indicators from internal and external sources, which can measure the effectiveness and efficiency of marketing campaigns. Regardless of the software used, it is the combination of technology and methodology that is the fundamental building block to sensing the needs within the retail banking market.

The competitive problem

Competing in the rapidly globalizing financial services industry presents most traditional retail banks with an elementary problem: who is our competition? Previously, identifying the competition was a question of walking down the high street and noting those buildings that were called banks, building societies and so on. Today, the lines of competition have blurred between companies that offer financial services, grocery stores, retail shops, and a host of new market entrants that have realized that facilitating the purchase of their product can be as profitable or more profitable than their direct line of business. The combination of partners that can form collaborative ventures and begin banking and investment services with lighting speed is making the competitive landscape even more complex. However, the establishment of new market entrants presents existing retail banks with a number of lessons to learn and a unique insight into behaviours and shortcomings within a traditional financial services provider. For example, the Emaar Group in the United Arab Emirates, perhaps Dubai's largest property company, acquired a banking licence with the aim of establishing an innovative, world-class financial institution. Dubai Bank's competitive advantage is not to provide services at an immediate lower cost, but a more comprehensive set of offerings or premier services. The bank's competitive edge comes from two separate and distinct sources. Firstly, the new organization is not saddled with long established policies and procedures encased in hierarchical bureaucracy. Secondly, the bank's ability to introduce new products to the market is not hindered by a process of integration with legacy systems.[15] Dubai Bank hedged its success by engaging a set of strategic partnerships that utilizes proprietary tools from Hewlett-Packard and Microsoft, establishing a technological portal called SharePoint to enable collaboration between team members regardless of location.

The simplicity of Dubai Bank's competitive strategy is what gives it a substantial advantage over other banking providers. Its approach reflects the process used by many new market entrants: establish a core processing capability, such as Misys International Banking Systems' BankMaster; and outsource technical leadership, project management, system integration, and implementation responsibilities to Hewlett-Packard Services, and focus on building the retail product's features, brand identity, market awareness and links with an external network of value. The Dubai Bank's value proposition to customers is equally elegant, with services designed to provide 24 hour a day access through numerous channels such as phone, fax, email, Internet and post. The bank uses multiple channel mediums coupled with products that are linked to external value-added services, such as Dubai Bank's VISA card which incorporates a complimentary eGate card to facilitate speedy passage through immigration at Dubai International Airport, and a travel tele-ticketing facility offering a 5 per cent discount on all flight bookings by cardholders.[16]

The linkage to ancillary services and external service partners provides a gateway to the broader issue of how banks will embrace the next evolutionary step in electronic money and payment systems. When banking services integrate with other partners to act as a conduit in the exchange of multiple value systems, such as frequent flyer miles and merchant bonus incentive schemes, they are taking a first step in accepting alternative monetary systems, to which we now turn.

The future of money, payments and value exchanges

To a financial services intermediary, payment services are the engine that facilitates commerce between consumers and business. All customers regardless of lifestyle buy products and pay bills. As a payment intermediary, retail banks sit at the nexus of great change as customers and businesses begin to realize the impact of electronic money and eCommerce. The future of money is a complex subject with tremendous socioeconomic implications and sociotechnological ramifications. For retail banks, changes in the form and function of money are best understood when taken within a historical context. Consulting Unwin Hyman's *Dictionary of Economics*, the definition of money is an asset that is generally acceptable as a medium of exchange, used as a common denominator in the pricing of goods, a unit of account, and a means to store value and purchasing power.[17] Note that the definition does not limit itself to any physical manifestation or substantive form of money. From this and other historical evidence we know that as time passes money will assume a shape and form that serves the needs of society. Therefore, we can surmise that it is not a matter of *if* society will adopt eMoney or eCurrencies, it is a matter of *when*, and under what political and socioeconomic conditions.

The central debate on how the future of money will affect societies and commerce between nation states is beyond the confines of this text. The transition from the physical representations of a nation's value system, which has been manifested by currency in the form of paper money and coins, to the high-tech electronic forms of value-based exchange such as eCurrencies, credit card transactions and other forms of digital money may not be as traumatic or socially altering as one might suspect. If the transition between physical and virtual currency is taken in the context of how society employs money to be a socially acceptable means in the exchange of value, that is, an intermediary in its own right, then the effect on society should be minimal. The history of money reveals that money in whatever form represents a snapshot reflecting the attitude which society places on how value is exchanged. Money is not static; money is dynamic, money is diverse, changing from era to era, country to country, altering its form to be a sign of national identity, personal wealth and economic prosperity.[18] Put simply, the form of money changes as society changes. Our views on cyber-currencies changing the fabric of society are similar to our ancestors' views each time the form of money changed. What is different in today's incantation of electronic money is the fundamental principle behind what currencies in cyberspace represent.

Minting money

What makes modern currencies valuable is the fact that as abstract representations of value they are backed by the full faith and credit of a national government to be redeemed in a tangible form such as products, goods or services. This fact is no longer true with alternative and electronic forms of currency that are backed by the issuer, such as airline miles or electronic fund transfers (EFTs) which are simply promises to pay. Technology is indeed creating a paradox for the financial services industry, global citizens and world governments. The significant difference between cyber-currencies and physical or national currencies is that the issuer of cyber-currencies in effect becomes the minting source. I have argued elsewhere that as eMoney is minted from new sources, the need to certify its value and the legitimacy of the originator will lead to new specialized supervisory guidelines for firms that are certificated authorities and eMoney issuers.[19] In effect, using the digital representation of physical value or currency, any individual or business can become a certificated authority and in theory become a minting source of money in cyberspace. Technically, this is already true when companies issue point schemes, credit notes and other forms of currency representations, although most of them are not negotiable back to cash at face value, such as the DBS BANK and Singapore Airlines KrisFlyer partnership to convert DBS credit card points to KrisFlyer frequent flyer miles.[20] However, as cyber-currencies issued under digital protocols become interchangeable, payment systems may be required to recognize them as legitimate or semi-legitimate, non-sovereign-backed currencies redeemable by the full faith and credit of a network of transnational businesses. One must remember that the minting of any representation of value (digital or otherwise) is backed by the full faith and credit of the issuer whoever that may be. Therefore, it is not beyond the realm of possibilities that digital money or cyber-currencies mark the end of the government monopoly on currency. Conceivably, cyber-currency exchanges could bypass the traditional monetary tax authorities established by governments by simply acting as bartering agents between companies, thereby mitigating taxes and regulation. Solomon reminds us that as the representations of money have changed over the ages, evolving from physical goods money, to paper and accounting money, to EFTs and now to electronic money (eMoney or eCurrencies), the length of time between these transitions has shortened and the rate of acceptance follows recognizable patterns of behaviour.[21] What we can infer from Solomon's view is that over time, new money systems are gradually accepted by society as valid forms of value exchanges. However, the time it takes for the transition to occur is not easily determined, due to many social, political and behavioural factors.

Although technologically achievable, a fundamental rethinking of money and society's relationship with it is no easy task because of its wider implications, as Davies pointed out:

> Despite the antiquity and ubiquity of money its proper management and control have eluded the rulers of most modern states partly because they have ignored

> the wide-ranging lessons of the past or have taken too blinkered and narrow a view of money. Economists, and especially monetarists, tend to overestimate the purely economic, narrow and technical functions of money and have placed insufficient emphasis on its wider social, institutional and psychological aspects.[22]

Taking the discussion of money's future further, Professor Lietaer, research fellow at the Center for Sustainable Resource Development of the College of Natural Resources at the University of California, Berkeley, argues that money is undergoing a fundamental transformation resulting from three mutually reinforcing trends: the international monetary system, geopolitics and information technology. The first two trends identified by Lietaer focus on the direct result of a transformation of the international monetary system attributed to an awareness that 'big money' is now detached from governments, serving multiple masters and becoming increasingly unpredictable. This factor is coupled with new economic globalization driven by corporations and non-government organizations which, acting through deals and lobbies, are important to understand but are outside the discussion of this text. Up until the 1990s, banks had a pseudo-sanctioned monopoly on the relationship between customers and their money. However, what Lietaer identified as the third trend (information technology) has, in the past 15 years, had enormous implications for retail banks, reminding us that the continual evolution of telecommunications threatens a previously established notion that banks were only profit centres as a result of their seemingly monopolistic, regulated entrée to consumers. The vision of the technological future of money has magnified the fact that money is simply an agreement of an exchange of value between two parties. The primary role of a retail bank has been to facilitate the transfer, which now can be negotiated using technology as the intermediary conduit.

Recalling the classical definition of money, the new digital representations, including credit cards, smart cards, eCash, electronic purses, Internet payment systems and even frequent flyer miles and other corporate loyalty programmes, could be considered new forms of currency. Therefore, in support of Lietaer's view, when a company issues a loyalty scheme redeemable in merchandise, another valued commodity, or has value with another merchant, it is technically minting a form currency backed by the full faith and credit of the originating firm. More importantly, as I have argued elsewhere, Lietaer's forecast of an emerging global barter currency must be considered by financial institutions as an opportunity for retail banks to develop consumer and business services to facilitate this new exchange of value in whatever form it takes. The use of a global bartered currency makes possible the formation of transnational alliances, associations and other commercial agreements, which will enable them to work synergistically as a network of value, while these activities rival government-backed currency, primarily due to the fluidity of the bartered currency.[23]

Bartered exchanges and cyber-currencies are not a future technological fantasy; they are a growing global phenomenon, represented by the activities of organizations such as the International Reciprocal Trade Association, which established the Universal Currency, acting as a central accounting centre for corporate barter companies and trade exchanges throughout the world. As a hub to facilitate bartered exchanges, it makes available to members opportunities to sell into an electronically based market and purchase items unavailable within their local system.[24] Bartering intermediaries are emerging in many parts of the world such as Euro Barter Business with exchanges in Belgium, Germany, Great Britain, Romania, Slovenia, Turkey and the US, allowing member firms to swap one commodity for another without the use of hard currency.[25] These barter exchanges facilitate the exchange of goods and/or services for other goods and/or services, circumventing traditional banking products such as the letter of credit and corresponding currency accounts. Australia's Bartercard Trading Program was established in 1991 and has a membership of over 30,000 businesses worldwide, with a value proposition as a third-party record keeper using an accounting/credit unit called the Trade Dollar to record the value of transactions.[26] The value proposition of Ireland's Contranet trades commodities like unused storage capacity and the sale of excess inventory, not limiting itself to simple goods and services. Contranet performs the same basic functions as a commercial bank, providing services to facilitate payments and issuing monthly statements detailing all transactions and balances.[27]

Moving beyond material goods, Barter Talent, part of BarterItOnline, brokers the exchange of professional free agents with the specific project needs of member businesses and entrepreneurs.'[28] Bartering services for equity is a key aspect of BarterItOnline, which provides lessons for retail banks because it is strikingly similar in function to the use of cyber-currencies between trading merchants. BarterItOnline facilitates (acts as a trusted third party) the matching of talent willing to take full or partial payment for services rendered with equity-rich firms desiring highly specialized talent.[29] Retail banks have a unique opportunity to leverage their investments in technology infrastructure to integrate bartered currencies and other value exchange services into their existing corporate and consumer offerings by linking barters with loyalty schemes and other incentive programmes for merchants.[30] Acting as the glue or conduit within a network of value-added partnerships, the retail banking institution can become an aggregator of collaborative services that are linked via multiple mechanisms of value. This in effect makes a retail bank a potential catalyst for co-opetition within consumer markets such as banking, goods and services.

Competing for payments

To compete in a market of co-opetition, retail banks must focus on developing value propositions in two dimensions: the electronic, digital world of 'cyberspace' and the physical, traditional world of 'terraspace'. Payments and other services labelled 'electronic commerce' present traditional financial services firms with both an opportunity to leverage their knowledge of banking products and partner with technology firms, supermarkets and any other organizations, and a problem, which dictates that they provide a clear channel to a targeted market segment in order to be a valuable pathway for businesses. Because banks have not provided this pathway, new market entrants have been rushing into the financial services marketplace. The behaviour of the new market entrants demonstrates that traditional banking products can be duplicated cheaply and rapidly brought to market. As businesses begin to offer traditional banking products, the result will be a continual commoditization of banking products and services, making market differentiation increasingly difficult to establish between banks and their competitors.

Without question, the ability for the world to pay its bills is the foundation of all international economies. Facilitating the exchange of value between trading partners, consumers, governments and markets is made possible by each nation's banking infrastructure. Technology enables the streamlining of the process of payments both foreign and domestic, providing a reduction in both cost and time in the facilitation of global business. What remains to be seen is the role that traditional retail banks will play in these intermediary services. It could be argued that unless retail banking institutions develop a value proposition that clearly demonstrates an added value in facilitating transactions, they will slowly be driven out of most of their traditional services. Developing a comprehensive value proposition for payment technologies that has the potential to alter customers' behaviour, change the fabric of society and influence world commerce must not be taken lightly. More importantly, as banks make the transition to the new wave of technology-laden services, they must be careful not to alienate customers. Rather, the bank must demonstrate to customers that these technologies are a stepping stone into a synergistic economy. Retail banks have an opportunity to play a principal role in educating consumers during the transition to the future state of money in which society values and uses money differently from today.

If history is any indicator of our social behaviour, the next 50 years will see our relationship with money change drastically. Not only will the form or medium of monetary exchange be altered, but the underlying value proposition to people and business will undoubtedly be redefined. Regardless of how the technological aspects of money will evolve, electronic or physical, making payments in whatever form will continue to be an opportunity to add value. Contemporary technologies are capable of reinventing the origination of payments and the settlement of payments between consumers and business on a local and international scale.

Utility companies, cable television providers, telecoms, retail stores and financial services firms are anticipating online bill presentment and account aggregation as new sources of fee income from customers. Paying bills with a single mouse-click and reviewing your accounts from an aggregated statement, while offering greater customer convenience, are part of a value proposition that has a limited lifespan because with multiple providers all offering the same services they will quickly become commoditized. Bill presentment and account aggregation, when taken in the context of a greater product or service offering, act as a mechanism to link products together under a cohesive structure. However, we can argue that consumers' current desire for self-service banking to perform functions such as bill payment is only a passing fad, as more customers realize that they are not saving time, only the cost of postage. Retail banking services must be anticipatory; money should be deposited and bills paid automatically within a range of performance tolerances placing the customer in control. This type of transaction already happens when your mobile phone company texts you, then calls you and finally sends you a letter when your phone bill rises beyond its normal usage pattern. Another example is when a monthly utility bill is typically within a certain range, varying with the seasonal changes in the weather. A customer can set an operating tolerance (a budget) for the expense and elect to pay it automatically unless the amount is greater than, say, 10 per cent of the tolerance limit. The transaction is reflected on the statement and the customers manage their finances by exception not by the individual details. What customers want is advice on how to reduce expenses and optimize cash flow, a competency that banks have and can apply to each individual customer.

The challenge facing retail banks is to create market differentiation by linking banking products and assembling technologies into financial services that engage the consumers in such a way that they adopt the banking channel as the preferred mechanism to supplement their lifestyle. Payment systems and consolidated account reviews are only one aspect of a transformational trend brought about by advanced technologies. New technologies provide the means to rethink the business process and lines of business within the bank. Moreover, the introduction of new payment technologies presents retail banking institutions with the opportunity to redefine the relationship between the bank, customers and money. Retail banks are at risk from disintermediation by losing customers to new market entrants that offer commoditized banking product offerings at a lower price point and with a higher value customer experience.

Looking forward

There is little doubt that physical currencies such as coins and notes will eventually be replaced by various forms of electronic currency; the unknown factor is when and under what conditions the migration will occur. Will this transition between monetary states be limited just to currencies? What role will bartered currencies play in the emerging environment of global commerce? To date, the factors that have prevented the widespread use of electronic currencies have been the lack of public understanding, no clear consumer motivation, a lack of merchant acceptance and a resistance to underwriting the cost of retooling. Perhaps one factor that is often overlooked is trust in the technology. Another factor to consider is the tactile nature of currency, which is a sociotechnological phenomenon best described as that feeling you get when you count a handful of notes or hear the jingle of coins in your pocket. Another factor is the cultural aspect of currency and money's iconography. Although not often acknowledged, people within a nation state feel a cultural attachment to their national currency, such as the US greenback or the British pound. This sentiment was felt throughout Europe as people hesitantly embraced the concept of the euro until the notes were printed and people could relate to the images and iconography of them. The fresh, clean designs of the euro notes symbolize the birth of a new economy, one of the reasons why citizens of the EU accepted the conversion in record time.

From the consumer's point of view, the rate at which society accepts new currencies, payment technologies and other emerging forms of value exchange is a function of three essential elements in consumer behaviour:

1. an implied or expressed trust greater than or equal to that of the existing currencies or payment vehicles

2. an increased convenience in the act of payments, deposits and transfers
3. a perceived advantage or derived tangible benefit over cash.

Taking a merchant's perspective, the value proposition is:

- a minimized risk of fraud
- a reduced risk in robbery associated with carrying cash
- better record keeping
- a shorter receivables' cycle
- lower cost of handling cash.

To financial institutions, the motivation to develop more electronic-based transactions offers the benefit of a lower cost of operations. Electronic currencies, initially not considered as viable alternatives to cash by governments, are now the subject of government research agencies because of their potential lower cost of minting, circulating and tracking through the monetary system. The Gulf Cooperation Council is anticipating a proposed regional monetary union by 2010,[31] which may result in a currency similar to the euro or a variation on the eDinar.

Banks are steering their customers closer toward a cashless society; the motivation is the low cost of operations for the bank and the merchant and greater control of finances for the consumer. However, this appears to be more easily accomplished in smaller populations such as Qatar, where the Qatar National Bank's (QNB) strategy is to link a host of electronic services to enable the population to begin this transition. This can be seen by QNB's linking of its electronic banking initiatives, call center, Al Watani line of home banking services and electronic payment gateway (including utility bill/credit card payment and instant cheque book printing) with its co-branded credit card issued in partnership with MasterCard International and the Ritz-Carlton Doha. QNB realizes that in order for consumers to shift to a cashless society three things need to occur: consumers must be educated in how a cashless system will benefit their lifestyles; a reliable technological infrastructure must exist to facilitate the transactions; and the technology must be prevalent throughout the geography to reach the saturation point of convenience. By linking several initiatives together, it is laying the groundwork for a transition at a pace at which society can adapt to the new, technology-enabled monetary system: 'QNB and its partners have conducted numerous promotions with major shopping centres and international retail chains to encourage the transition of Qatar to a cashless society.'[32]

It is impossible to predict when the world's financial markets, people, nation states and business will shift to a cashless society because the migration will be gradual, not the culmination of a single event or group of sudden events. It is clear that world commerce now has alternative means in which to conduct international and local trade, with a host of payment options that were considered fantasies only a generation ago. As loyalty points, frequent flyer miles, electronic bartering and other non-traditional payments gain favour in certain demographic or cultural market segments, retail banks will need to become even more creative in their approach to facilitating these forms of customer interactions.

Globalization, regulation, mergers and acquisitions

Every time someone makes a purchase, or places an order for a product, he or she is participating either directly or indirectly in global commerce. Goods and services from a local market or a national supplier are wholly or in part a product of corporations from across the globe cooperating in the assembly, construction and selling of materials to be consumed by society. The system by which corporations operate across the boundaries of nation states to exchange goods and services has traditionally been called 'international trade' or commerce. Globalization, on the other hand, is a process that spans this system with multiple transference of social identity during the act of trading.

The media, special interest groups and people in general discuss globalization as if it were a planned event, coordinated by a central malevolent group acting as a modern-day, profit-seeking imperialist. In reality, globalization is a continuous integrating economic process that is neither a product of capitalism nor is it confined to present-day, Western-centric business objectives. It can be argued that the process of globalization is where ideals, customs, values and laws of one group of people, such as a nation state, are transferred to another group of people by a process of domestic and international interchange. In the past, as evident by the actions of ancient peoples such as the Romans and the Greeks, the process of globalization can be defined as a product of conquest, in which the conquerors imposed their ways onto the defeated people. In previous times, up to and including the last vestiges of imperialism in the twentieth century, globalization was an external force, represented by a subjugator, which drastically altered the structure of a local people.

However, towards the end of the twentieth century, with the advent of a series of breakthroughs in communications technology, the process of globalization shifted from an external to an internal social force. Individuals who watch television and use the Internet are becoming, even if by accident, more exposed to the values, beliefs and customs of other cultures, peoples and ways of life. These individuals elect, by their own free will, to adopt elements of other cultures or behaviours from other nations that appeal to their individual sense of value. Because the US has dominated the technological industry and communications media over the past few decades, people have equated this to a larger phenomenon of Americanization or invasion of Western values to all parts of the world. What special interest and other fundamentalist groups fail to understand is that the adoption of cross-cultural values is a result of individual choice. There has yet to be a report on any employee of McDonald's forcing local populations to consume hamburgers and fries at gunpoint. This is an important point, especially for retail banks, because it signals that globalization is shifting from an external force thrust on society – as in previous eras – to an internal struggle between groups in a local society. This shift is at the heart of any new strategies in retail banking because of the implications for brand identities, levels of customer services, product design and competitive strategies. Unfortunately, internal social struggles tend to generate more violent reactions from radical elements within local social groups, often without a clear identification of the alleged common enemy. Because the source of social discomfort is now internal, the enemy is often objectified in the form of the multinational corporation.

Understanding the changing dynamic of globalization is important to organizations providing retail banking services because it is the catalyst for actions within two customer segments: the personal cross-border financial services needs of transnational and/or global citizens; and the rising needs of SMEs to do business in an economy that is less dependent on geographical boundaries.

Transnational/global citizens have two distinct requirements that are directly influenced by a retail bank's knowledge of modern banking: the need to aggregate financial resources and coordinate payments and receipts of wages, dividends, interest and capital gains; and the ability to gain access to distant capital markets to take advantage of a greater diversity of investment opportunities. On the other hand, SMEs have four motivations to become more fully engaged in international commerce:

1. to seek less expensive goods for resale

2. to obtain higher quality materials, components or products than those available in the domestic market
3. to provide a product that is substantially different from the one which can be obtained locally
4. to export local goods to distant markets.

International trade has risen steadily since World War II and increased sharply in the last decade. Traditionally, the SME market is an underserved market, with fees that in many cases hinder small businesses or young start-up companies. In the future, SME banking will require a strong, informed financial partner with resources that can be leveraged across international borders, as seen in SME Banking from the DBS Bank in Singapore, which offers worldwide commercial links, working capital trade services, credit facilities, treasury services, corporate deposits, cash management, business insurance, electronic banking services and resources.[33] Unlike some subsegments of the banking market, SME customers require a higher degree of education to operate in a global environment, thus creating an opportunity for retail banks to partner with external sources, such as DBS Banks' link with Singapore's Standards, Productivity and Innovation Board (SPRING). SPRING offers courses such as 'Understanding the nuts and bolts of business finance', 'Capital investment analysis', 'Is your investment making economic sense?', 'Uncovering hidden treasures' and 'Business opportunity analysis and evaluation'.[34] To aid SMEs in doing business with foreign entities, DBS Bank associated with the Singapore Chinese Chamber of Commerce and Industry to offer SMEs seminars on the fundamentals of doing business with China.[35] These close associations have led to DBS Bank offering a special financing package called 'Grow with DBS', which offers a microloan programme for small businesses.

Mergers and acquisitions

Mergers and acquisitions have been the subject of countless books detailing the actions of institutions from a variety of perspectives. In the context of our discussion on retail banking, it is safe to say that mergers and acquisitions will continue long into the future. The single, most important issue during a merger or acquisition is not to lose sight of fulfilling customers' needs. Customers often feel a sense of disorientation with their financial institution during a merger or acquisition. What can a firm do to prevent this? In basic terms, retail banks can examine their options from the viewpoint of the customer and assess the overall contribution to the firm's value proposition. In some cases, a higher degree of service or a broader selection of products may result in the establishment of a strategic partnership in lieu of a merger or acquisition. The formation of the Liquidity Management Centre, with Dubai Islamic Bank, Bahrain Islamic Bank, Kuwait Finance House and the Islamic Development Bank as shareholders is an example. Its function is to facilitate Islamic inter-bank money market and bond trading, so that Islamic banks can manage their liquidity as effectively as their non-Islamic counterparts.[36]

It could be argued that the competition in smaller country markets is becoming more severe due to two key factors: the complacency of incumbent banks; and the pressing need to increase the efficiency of local banks, which can be seen in the market consolidation occurring in Iceland in 2003.[37] Small country regions have this consolidation pressure in addition to big banks moving into their territory and new market entrants engaging customers through new channels. Therefore, smaller institutions operating in smaller regions will need to develop corporate competencies that enable them to gain an intimate knowledge of their customers, rapidly deploy new products, drastically streamline operations to provide competitive rates and, more importantly, collaborate with external entities to achieve economies of scale and scope. Teplitz and Mills point out that strategic alliances are only effective when the business goals of the financial institution are clearly defined, due to the nature of the dynamic complexities between organizational competencies.[38] Here again, it is essential to have a clear and distinct value proposition when entering a partnership or any cooperative venture, because of the potential to dilute brand and product identities. Cooperative agreements between retail banks, other financial services providers and non-banking entities call into question the mechanisms of taxation, fair trade and other trade barriers that have been erected as part of economic or foreign policy.

Regulation

Led by actions in the US during the Internet boom, governments in all parts of the world began contemplating legislation to tax Internet business activities long before any real value had been generated.[39] In the post-dot-com era, banks, merchants, manufacturers, service providers and people realize that eCommerce is not the quick road to riches, but rather a viable, long-term medium of international commerce and exchange. As world businesses discover the applied value of the Internet and eCommerce technologies to trade, commerce and the lowering of operating costs, governments will reassess banking regulations and Internet commerce taxation. Even though a more cautious approach to business and taxation has set the tone for business today, regulations across world governments have the potential to hinder the physical implementation of technological advancement.[40] Government tax authorities are now realizing the potential lost tax revenues that could result from the widespread use of alternative payment mechanisms. These new payment technologies and cyber-currency schemes offer individuals and business the potential to significantly reduce the cost associated with cash handling, cheque processing and other small-value payments, with the ancillary value proposition of convenience and speed. Rumours of taxing frequent flyer miles and the resale of goods using online eMarketplaces such as eBay have raised concerns about the extent a local tax authority can exercise control over international and local business. Cloaked under an umbrella of regulating laws to reduce risks such as loss, fraud, insolvency, piracy concerns, money laundering, tax evasion, counterfeiting, and consumer protection, Internet taxation will undergo tremendous changes in the future. As retail banking institutions take a larger part in the use of alternative payment schemes and cyber-based exchanges of value, they will need to be more cognizant of local, national and international tax collection regulations.

The advance of technology and innovation

When we think of technology and innovation in the context of retail banking, we immediately think of delivery mechanisms such as ATMs, WAP phones, PC banking and other physical uses of technology. From a strategic point of view, technology and all its innovations must be considered as separate but equal partners enabling the banks' value proposition in two very different ways. Technology that has become highly commoditized can be acquired by anyone, organized into product offerings and used to deliver services in which, in many cases, the key component is reducing operational cost. Innovation, on the other hand, provides market differentiation, stemming from either the creative bundling of technology and corporate competencies or an external source such as a packaging capability. In order to put the applied use of technology into the proper perspective, Smith provides us with an important definition of retail banking products and services:

> Service is a general term, describing an activity or function. Product is a particular manifestation of that activity or function. Services are perennial. Products last only a short time. Any service will be offered through a whole family of products, which are regularly updated to offer the service in the form that is relevant.[41]

Smith's distinction between products and services is critical to the development of an understanding of how to launch, market, deliver and operate banking offerings to customers. Retail banking products that are highly dependent on technology are temporary, limited in time and wax and wane as customer demand changes. In some cases, a banking product will have many years of market appeal, with the technology used to deliver it or the infrastructure to support it changing. However, few technology implementation plans include a retirement clause stating how the technology will be unbundled from the existing system when the next technological advance occurs. In Smith's definition, services are the more appealing prospect for retail banks because they are independent of the underlying technology and their value proposition is not linked to any one means of delivery. Thus it can be said that technology is used as a means to deliver products; innovation occurs and banks can efficiently leverage it when services are redesigned. The retail banks' value proposition is at the nexus of technologically based products and service innovations. Retail banks like their non-banking counterparts have become wary of the 'true' benefits of technology spending in the post-dot-com era. This lack of predictable returns on investments in technology typically has been associated with a fundamental problem with the technology itself. Nothing can be further from the truth. It is true that technology does have inherent problems such as software bugs and other imperfections. However, the factors that hinder an organization's ability to reap the returns from technology investments are the rate in which the firm adapts its business processes, policies and procedures relative to the value proposition presented by the technology and the rate of technological adoption by customers. These two factors – business process adaptation and customer adoption, or the socialization of technology – govern the rate at which businesses can profit from technology, as noted by Howcroft and Lavis:

> Against the apparent advantages offered by the new technologies, there are a number of considerations which should act as a brake on the speed of innovation. At the core of these dilemmas is the whole question of customer preference; there are limits to the speed with which customers will adopt new, technology driven services.[42]

One technology that has undisputedly altered the nature of retail banking, the behaviour of customers and the cost of operations is the automated teller machine (ATM). Initially providing an automated teller service inside branches, it did little more than add capacity and reduce queues. The real impact to banking occurred when retail banks realized that making the ATMs available outside banking hours effectively expanded the branch's ability to service customers. Although the ATM service was limited compared to the full services of a branch, it presented customers with a sudden shift in the bank's value proposition because it increased access to banking services, at times more convenient to customers' lifestyles. In many cases, it eliminated the need to rush to the bank during working hours to make simple deposits and withdrawals. When the ATMs were placed at remote locations, the level of customer convenience improved exponentially. From the customer's perspective of a value proposition, the first generation of ATMs at the branch expanded the hours of operations, while the second generation of remotely located ATMs extended the reach of the bank. However, even with the ATMs' improved value proposition, not all customers gravitated towards using the capabilities to their full extent. This behaviour was often delineated along predictable demographics such as age, in which older customers were less likely to adopt technology as the interaction of choice with banks, as noted by the American Bankers Association.[43]

The next generation of customer-facing technologies, which focuses on automating or facilitating interactions between consumers and retail banks, such as telephone banking, the Internet, mobile banking, and smart cards, follows a similar pattern of implementation, yet each particular one enhances the customer value proposition in different ways, as reflected in Figure 2.3.

As we can see, the firm's value proposition has two key components: a direct value to customers; and an indirect value to shareholders. The customer side of the equation centres on values that appeal to or are directly associated with a basic human banking need, want or desire. These customer requirements vary by either lifestyle or life stage and in many cases are external interpretations of the actions within the customer experience. For example, customers might go to a branch 20 times and experience no queues, perform their banking tasks and convince themselves that the banking experience was quick and convenient. However, one day, they might return to the branch when queues are long and then their attitude towards the bank as a convenient experience is dented, requiring a number of queue-free visits to erase the bad experience. Therefore, retail banks must manage customers' perceptions of the experience

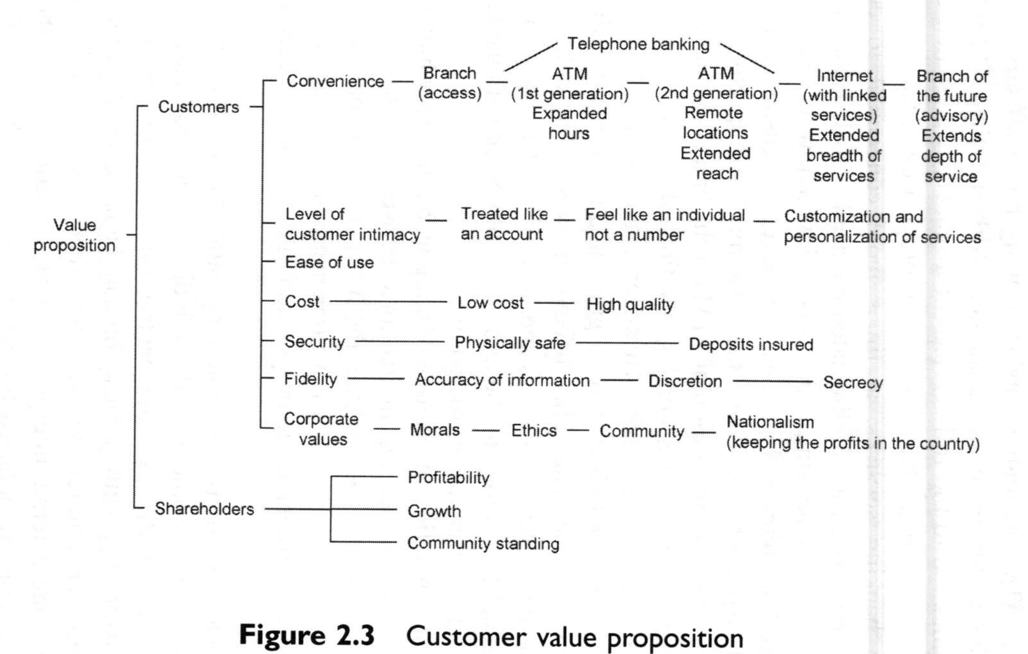

Figure 2.3 Customer value proposition

and expectations of the services used. Expectations, perceptions and experiences are defined, set and managed when the top management of the retail bank originates a vision of the firm's value proposition, sets the example, which is in turn radiated by all levels of the organization. Surprisingly, the branch of the future presents customers with a new level of value but creates a dilemma for retail banking institutions – a higher degree of customer interaction can be maintained via a more intimate relationship with a customer, while, simultaneously, a greater level of aggregated risk is introduced into the shareholder component of the value equation. Put simply, there is an inherent risk with an intimate advisory relationship, when the responsibility of generating wealth and consistent returns shifts from the customer to the bank's ability to optimize its performance. In other words, the customer may have a greater tolerance for paying fees, if the bank provides a solution (technological or otherwise) that facilitates his or her financial needs, but will be more likely to hold the institution responsible for poor performance. That said, advisory services are an innovation only made possible beyond the world of private banking by the use of advanced technologies. Retail banking innovation occurs at three levels: customer-facing technologies such as the branch or Internet banking; infrastructure technologies that alter the cost structure or overall performance of the institution; and the process of innovation that governs the rate of implementation within the bank.

Customer-facing technologies

As I have argued elsewhere, the misunderstood intelligent agent technology is an increasingly important component in a bank's equation of value.[44] According to the consulting company Accenture, personal financial robots – finbots or valagents – will execute transactions on behalf of the customer as agents and fund managers, searching for banking services that meet the requirements of customers' lifestyles. Valagents will move funds automatically, based on predefined risk/return criteria, working as insurance agents that search for products with lower rates and coverage, and personal shoppers that seek out pre-described products.[45]

A *bot* is a software tool designed to interrogate data and search for specific information; supplied with directions, it retrieves answers or values and executes responses on behalf of the originator. Technologies that represent you and perform duties on your behalf are commonly referred to as 'agents', including bio-enhancement, intelligent agents, robots and avatars. Intelligent agents are autonomous and adaptive computer programs, which operate within software environments such as operating systems and database networks. They assist users with routine computer tasks, being tailored to accommodate individual user habits. Finbots for financial services functions can be organized into two distinct categories: active, outward-searching and inward-investigating, data-mining bots. There are a number of finbots under experimentation and other bots that have a direct application to financial services such as commercebot, dataminingbot, governmentbot, knowledgebot, searchbot, shoppingbot and stockbot.[46] The key to developing agent technology for retail banks, according to India's Polaris Software Labs, is to think of customers, not products, and design agents that equate to lifestyles and life events.[47]

Innovation in security

Security is an essential element of the bank's value proposition to customers. Organizations such as RSA Security now offer solutions that include identity management, which provides banking customers with peace of mind and greater self-directed control of their interactions with financial institutions. RSA's technology operates using a combination of electronic tokens and agents to authenticate transactions as they occur, as depicted in the Figure 2.4.

RSA's technology can be applied to a number of retail banking customer touch points, such as Banca Popolare di Sondrio's (Switzerland) implementation of RSA Mobile, which enables customers to enter a user ID and PIN, generating a one-time access code directly to their mobile phone, or FöreningsSparbanken NetTrade's use of RDA SecureID for authentication and secure Internet stock trading.[48]

Infrastructure technologies

Although less glamorous than customer-facing technologies, infrastructure technologies are the key assets to harvest in order to achieve lower operating cost, establish capabilities that can be developed into core competencies and make possible an ever-widening array of customer-facing technologies. This is the case with Electronic Payments & Commerce's vision of a national payment highway, which establishes an infrastructure outside the confines of the retail bank, facilitating services such as electronic commerce and electronic fund transfers for central banks, securities depositories, automated clearing houses and commercial banks.[49] Under a similar line of thinking is the Eleanor initiative for global payments offered by Identrus and a group of founding banks including ABN AMRO, ANZ, Banco Santander, Bank of

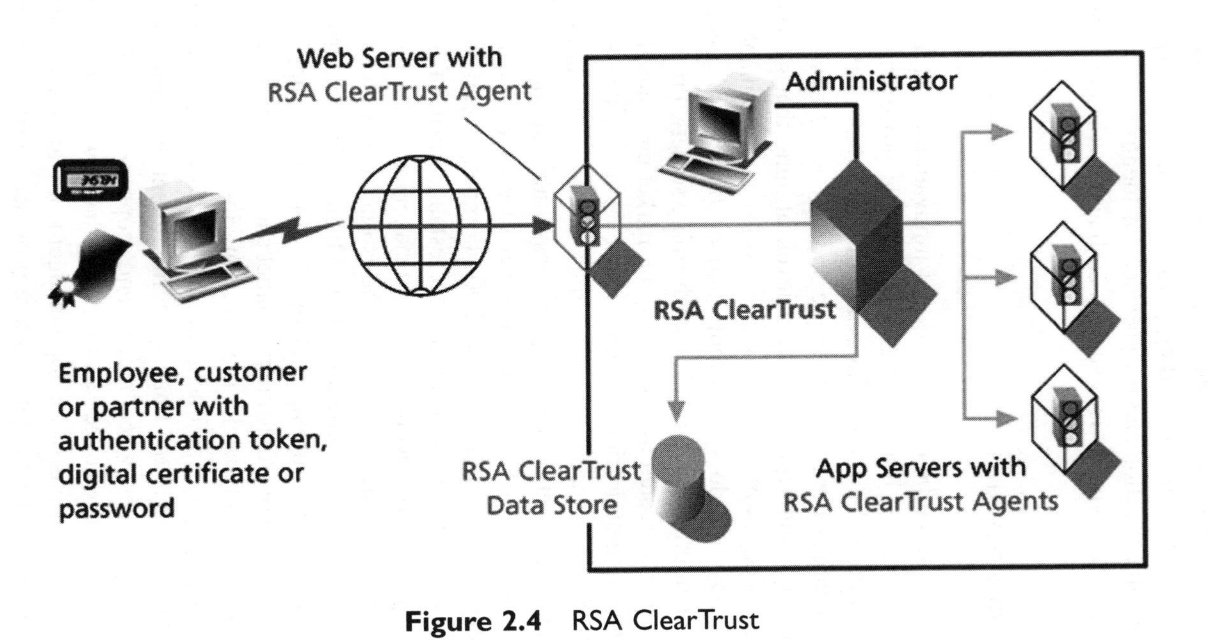

Figure 2.4 RSA ClearTrust

Tokyo-Mitsubishi, Barclays Bank, BNP Paribas, CIBC, HSBC, HypoVereinsbank, Mizuho Corporate Bank, National Australia Bank, Royal Bank of Scotland, UFJ, Société Générale and Wells Fargo.[50] The Eleanor initiative allows corporate customers and trading partners to deal directly with each other using the authentication and trust services of Identrus, while the banks interact with customers via services such as cash and risk management.

The process of innovation

Prether said it best when he commented that innovation is not a product, a technology or a concept: innovation is a sustainable process that must be managed, measured and nurtured; innovation is a product of the organization's culture, which is the result of people and values.[51] Newman elevates the process of innovation to the national level, arguing that governments, industry and universities must band together to form a sustainable cycle of innovation.[52] Innovation does not simply happen because of a company's process or resultant product magically transforming society. Product innovations must be communicated to customers via marketing channels and with the aid of mass communication systems. However, to create new product and service offerings, financial institutions must do three basic things: create an environment for innovation; develop a process within the firm that fosters innovation; and offer incentives for personnel to exercise their ability to innovate and experiment. In the 1980s and 90s, companies learned that innovation requires continual investment and the establishment of a culture in which experimentation is encouraged by management. The paradox that financial services companies must overcome is that within an environment of innovation, experiments sometimes fail. Much is learned from failed experiments, such as market timing, lack of infrastructure to support the new product, gaps in training of front-line personnel and other potential shortfalls in the organization. Unfortunately, most banking institutions do not reward the learning from a failed experiment, due mainly to a lack of expectation management and the size of the financial commitment. Experiments in new product innovations are best when budgets and scope are within the limits of acceptable investment. The key lesson to learn is that new small experiments that manage the expectations of the top management team provide benefits, regardless of their success or failure. Failure provides direct feedback to the organization, identifying areas that require improvement or the rate of new product receptivity by customer market segments. Successful projects can then be commercialized and introduced to the customer base and organization on a larger scale. It is to financial services customers that we now turn.

Social factors and demographics

Social factors and customer attitudes towards retail banking products are as numerous as the products themselves. Organizations providing retail banking services are faced with an opportunity that is a double-edged sword. Higher levels of customer demand predicated on customized services means that products could be targeted at market subsegments, ranked by potential profitability and factored by anticipated revenues. At the same time, marketing campaigns are structured to achieve increased levels of penetration within the market subsegment and coordinated with the management of branches or lines of business offering the product. The effectiveness of the marketing of products directly linked to individual market segments, together with the measured profitability of each product, provides a means for the institution to manage a portfolio of products and services based on a factored aggregated demand.

Culture/gender

Targeting financial services products to market subsegments is not new; what is new is viewing each product as a temporary relationship over the life of the customer and equating the product life cycle to the total realized revenue from the customer. A good example of a highly specialized market subsegment product is the Bank of East Asia's 'dear lady insurance' product, which is tailored for the needs of today's Asian women whose life expectancy is estimated to be longer than that of men. The product allows women to achieve a level of financial independence during retirement years and other life events, such as pregnancy, which comes with an optional 'maternity benefit rider.'[53]

Another underserved (at least by Western banks with Islamic populations) market is Islamic financial services. Islamic banking and investment products are another example of products tailored for a specific market, although Islamic banking has a potential market of one billion people, it can best be defined as investment products that adhere to principles established by shariah law. These principles require that:

- Investments must be free of interest (*riba*) and in ethical sectors in which profits cannot be made from forbidden activities (such as alcohol production, gambling or pornography).
- Wealth creation is a result of a partnership between the investor and the user of capital in which both parties share in the rewards and risks. A

return on invested capital is earned and not linked to profits from the capital and cannot be predetermined from banking products with interest-based returns provided by bank deposits.

The predetermined return on capital invested that is unrelated to the underlying performance of the asset, such as in bank deposit accounts, bonds and other interest-based securities, is not acceptable under shariah law and alters the products and services that can be provided to Islamic investors. However, the Islamic Fiqh Academy and a number of contemporary Islamic scholars do consider equity securities, or the purchase of shares, permissible because the profits returned to an investor from equities are tied to the returns of the underlying company, which places the investment at risk. A key implication of Islamic investment principles is a higher degree of scrutiny on the part of investors when selecting any financial instrument in order to ensure compliance within these religious guidelines. The gap in Western banking services present opportunities for organizations, for example iHilal Financial Services, to offer products specifically tailored to comply with Islamic values and beliefs.[54]

When comparing banking products and services that are tailored for target markets, patterns emerge, revealing a model in which all products, regardless of their target, build their value propositions on fulfilling a single customer need and then build on the initial offering to supply added value.

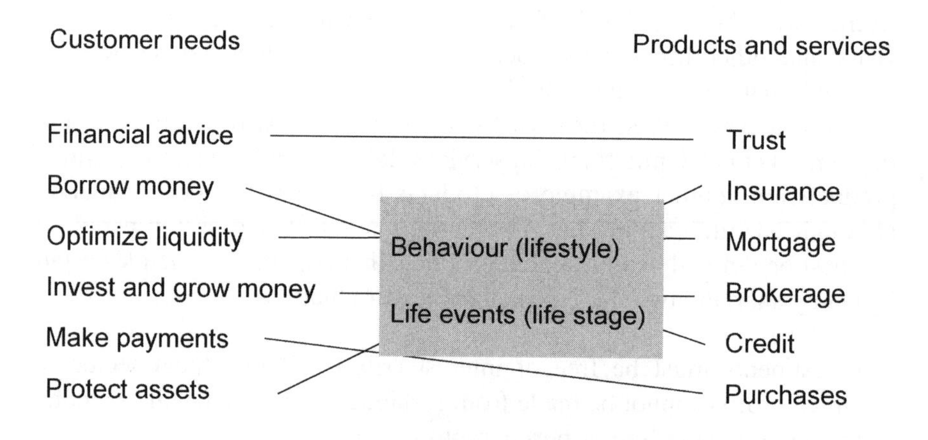

Figure 2.5 Customer needs/product map

Market segmentation

Cultural banking habits are not limited to customer behaviours that are the products of religion, social values and beliefs or local myths; society's banking behaviour is largely derived from the political stability of the monetary system of the nation state. People in North America and Europe, for example, owe their ability to save and invest to the stable supply of money, the security of the banking infrastructure and predictable regulation of the markets. This generates a trust in the banking system that is often taken for granted in the West, and is not always true in developing nations, such as Nigeria:

> Nigerians as a rule are very suspicious of keeping their savings in banks, and with good reason following the spate of bank collapses before the start of the new millennium. Nigeria is a cash economy with an estimated 55% of money held outside the banking system.[55]

A similar feeling of unease in the banking system can be witnessed in South American countries during the recent monetary crisis in Argentina and Brazil. However, market subsegmentation can also address customers based on an economic orientation that can cross geopolitical boundaries, appealing strictly to financial behaviour regardless of lifestyle, such as Standard Chartered's Priority Banking which comes complete with a personal banker. Priority Banking capitalizes on the bank's 140 years of expertise in Asia, Africa and the Middle East, offering financial planning services and customized banking solutions based on the priorities in your life. With 50 Priority Banking Centres in 23 countries, Priority Banking provides priority treatment, banking and investment privileges, personalized service from a relationship manager, a complementary financial planning service, and a portfolio of diverse regional and global investment opportunities.[56] Beyond banking services, Standard Chartered's Priority Banking provides lifestyle privileges, with invitations to lifestyle events such as wine appreciation, talks on jewellery, fashion shows and linked shopping, dining and travel privileges wherever you travel within its international network.

That said, banking behaviour, specifically saving and spending habits, is a compound phenomenon which results from many factors such as local attitudes, cultural influences and a sense of stability from the regulatory authorities within a nation state. When developing a value proposition for retail banking products in a nation state beyond the bank's primary operating country, the role of the government and its ability to shape an individual's banking behaviour must become a major contributing factor.

Government

In the UK, there is growing concern over the complexity of long-term savings products, and the confusion experienced by customers investing in these instruments is leading to pressure on UK banks to simplify products.[57] Although all the product offerings appear to be confusing, however, they do offer customers a wide degree of choice. The underlying problem is twofold: a lack of financial sophistication by the general banking public; and poorly trained banking staff who are unable to advise customers effectively on the products that fit their lifestyles. A third element to this market confusion, which is not limited to the UK, is the growing complexity in national and local tax laws. Together, these factors make it necessary for customers to spend more time in understanding how to apply financial products to support their short- and long-term goals. In response to social and political pressure to simplify savings instruments, Fidelity Investments rightly points out: 'It is people and their financial needs that are complex, not the products themselves.'[58] Unfortunately, people in general spend less time understanding their own personal finance and banking products than they do on their favourite hobby or leisure activity. In Western cultures it appears that customers are more willing to pay for advice, preferring a reduced total return to researching and understanding their financial situation themselves. This social trend, taken in the context of government reports calling for a split between investment advice and the cost/fees charged by institutions, may lead to a new condition, as observed by Tony Osborn-Barker of Deloitte & Touche:

> good advice, like good management, costs money and a ceiling on charges may lead to a two-tier system of savers – the informed and the naïve.[59]

The condition of consumer naivety in savings and investment vehicles is not a future trend; unfortunately, it is a present reality, as consumer unawareness has been developing for a very long time, evident in the rise of managed funds over the past 50 years.

These social responses and government pressures should be welcomed by retail banking organizations because they identify opportunities for financial institutions to engage governments proactively in educating customers on the need for social responsibility in managing their own future financial condition. At some point, individuals must take responsibility for their financial futures and use the government and financial institutions as sources of education in developing and planning their financial plans. For retail bankers, this presents an opportunity to leverage technological resources to educate and inform individuals during the course of their relationship with customers. One of the expressed goals of the UK government, for example, is to encourage long-term savings in order to reduce the total funding needed to sustain social programmes.[60] Retail banking and investment products play a pivotal role in facilitating the long-term financial health of a nation; this is not an elected responsibility of any financial institution but a byproduct of the continuous process of customer education and the quality of the financial advice given. Moreover, as a partner in generating the stability of a nation's monetary system, banks must go through a programme of continually educating the customer to optimize products to support their lifestyle, inadvertently preparing their customers for the future of retail banking, which will be explored in the next chapter.

Notes

1 J. Jordan, *The Functions and Future of Retail Banking*, Cleveland: Federal Reserve Bank of Cleveland, 1996, p. 3.

2 N. Negroponte, *Being Digital*, London: Hodder & Stoughton, 1995.

3 Branch of the Future, Bank of Hawaii, Honolulu, 8 September 2000, available at http://www.boh.com/new/20000908.asp, March 2003.

4 J. B. Howcroft and J. Lavis, *Retail Banking: The New Revolution in Structure and Strategy*, Oxford: Basil Blackwell, 1986, p. 52.

5 C. Haley, 7-Eleven, Verizon offer online bill payment, Boston.Internet.Com, Boston: Jupitermedia Corporation, 9 April 2003, available at http://boston.internet.com/news/article.php/2179111.

6 The Asian Banker Retail Banking E-newsletter, The Asian Banker Interactive, 10 June 2003.

7 C. P. Smith, *Retail Banking Rethink, Strategic Marketing in Action*, Dunblane, Doica, 1990, pp. 12–14.

8 J. Essinger, *The Virtual Banking Revolution: The Customer, the Bank and the Future*, London: International Thompson Business Press, 1999, p. 40.

9 A. Fifield, 'Kiwibank can afford to hold critics to account', *Financial Times*, 24 April 2003, p. 11.

10 Kiwibank, FAQs, available at http://www.kiwibank.co.nz/faq/, March, 2003.

11 J. B. Howcraft and J. Lavis, *Retail Banking: The New Revolution in Structure and Strategy*, Oxford: Basil Blackwell, 1986, p. 53.

12 Essinger, *The Virtual Banking Revolution*, p. 4.

13 Essinger, *The Virtual Banking Revolution*, pp. 5–7.

14 IRIS 2000 and ILOTS, ASTEROP.com, available at http://www.asterop.com/infos-us/CP_241001.html, April 2003.

15 'Dubai Bank setting new standards', *World Finance Magazine* Volume 12, Issue 3, Hewlett-Packard Company, available at http://myfsi.hp.com/magazine/wf12_3/dubai.asp, April 2003.

16 Dubai Bank, Dubai, United Arab Emirates, available at http://www.dubaibank.co.ae, May 2003.

17 C. Pass, B. Lowes and L. Davis, *Unwin Hyman Dictionary of Economics*, Leicester: Unwin Hyman, 1999, p. 350.
18 J. Williams (ed), *Money: a History*, New York: St Martin's Press, 1997, pp. 248–9.
19 J. DiVanna, *Redefining Financial Services, The New Renaissance in Value Propositions*, Basingstoke: Palgrave Macmillan, 2002, pp. 160–1.
20 The Asian Banker Retail Banking E-newsletter, The Asian Banker Interactive, 10 June 2003.
21 E. Solomon, *Virtual Money: Understanding the Power and Risks of Money's High-Speed Journey into Electronic Space*, Oxford: Oxford University Press, 1997, p. 30.
22 G. Davies, *A History of Money from Ancient Times to the Present Day*, Cardiff: University of Wales Press, 1996, p. xvii.
23 DiVanna, *Redefining Financial Services*, p. 11.
24 International Reciprocal Trade Association, available at http://www.irta.com/.
25 Euro Barter Business, available at http://www.ebb-online.com/.
26 BarterCard Ltd, available at http://www.bartercard.com.au/index.htm.
27 Contranet, available at http://www.contranet.ie/contranet/index.html.
28 BarterItOnline: BarterTalent, available at http://www.barteritonline.com/bartertalent.htm.
29 BarterItOnline: Equity Swaps, available at http://www.barteritonline.com/equity_swaps.htm.
30 DiVanna, *Redefining Financial Services*, p. 12.
31 'Gulf Cooperation Council steps closer to single currency', *Gulf Business*, Dubai: Motivate Publishing, November 2002, p. 101.
32 Qatar National Bank, available at http://www.qatarbank.com/, March 2003.
33 SME Banking, DBS Bank, Singapore, available at http://www.dbs.com.sg/sme/, April, 2003.
34 SPRING Singapore (Standards, Productivity and Innovation Board), available at http://www.spring.gov.sg/portal/main.html, April 2003.
35 Singapore Chinese Chamber of Commerce and Industry, available at http://www.sccci.org.sg/index_e.html, April 2003.
36 FI News, Islamic inter-bank trading centre to launch operations, *The Asian Banker*, 14 May 2003, available at http://www.theasianbanker.com.
37 C. Brown-Humes, 'Competition pushes Iceland's bank to form new alliances,' *Financial Times*, 28 May 2003, p. 31.
38 J. Teplitz and C. Mills, 'Filling the value gap in mergers', *The Banker Supplement*, London: Financial Times Business, March 2001, p. 5.
39 The United States 107th Congress has introduced several bills on the issues of Internet taxation: Internet Tax Moratorium Equity Act [S.1542.IS], New Economy Tax Fairness Act or NET FAIR Act [S.664.IS], Internet Tax Fairness Act of 2001[H.R.2526.IH], Internet Tax Moratorium and Equity Act [S.1567.IS].
40 DiVanna, *Redefining Financial Services*, pp. 157–60.
41 Smith, *Retail Banking Rethink*, p. 184.
42 Howcroft and Lavis, *Retail Banking*, pp. 64–5.
43 *Consumer Acceptance of Banking Technology*, ABA Banking Journal Supplement, American Bankers Association, November 1997, p 1, available at http://www.banking.com/aba/issues_sup1197.asp, March 2003.
44 DiVanna, *Redefining Financial Services*, pp. 190–6.

45 Accenture Thought Leadership Research Report, When and how will consumers go virtual, pp. 39–42, available at http://www.fondation-finance.com/ff/FFmailer.nsf/Articles/p33p44/$File/p33p44.pdf, May 2003.

46 Bots by Category, BotSpot, available at http://www.botspot.com, April 2003.

47 N. Narayanasamy, *The Great Technology Paradox*, Polaris Software Lab Ltd, available at http://www.polaris.co.in/media/techquest/GreatTechnologyParadox.pdf, May 2003.

48 RSA Security Inc., available at http://www.rsasecurity.com/products/securid/success/index.html, May 2003.

49 The payment highway concept, Electronic Payments & Commerce Ltd (EPayCom), available at http://www.epaycom.co.uk/, April 2003.

50 Eleanor Program for global payments, Identrus, available at http://www.identrus.com/knowledge_center/library/products.html, May 2003.

51 Donald Pether, speech: The Sustainable Process of Innovation, presented at the Innovation Summit, McMaster University, Hamilton, Ontario, 17 September 2002.

52 Harvey Newman, speech: Creating a Sustainable Process of Innovation, presented at the pan-European regional meeting, World Summit on the Information Society, available at http://www.wsis-romania.ro/conferinta/WSIS-7NOV/SESIUNI-WSIS-7NOV/opening/harvey-newman/HARVEY-NEWMAN-SPEECH.pdf, May 2003.

53 Bank of East Asia, available at http://www.hkbea.com/whp_currnews/news_html/20021008e.html, March 2003.

54 iHilal Financial Services, available at http://www.ihilal.com, January 2003.

55 'Age of Universal Banking', in *African Business*, Number 266, June 2001, p. 24.

56 Priority Banking, Standard Chartered Bank, Singapore, available at: http://www.standardchartered.com.sg/cb/priority/priority_main.html, April 2003.

57 D. Hargreaves, 'Where do you think you're going?', *Financial Times*, 13–14 July 2002, p. 1.

58 Fidelity Investments, Sandler review fundamentally flawed says Fidelity, Fidelity press release, London: Fidelity Investments, 9 July 2002, available at http://www.fidelity.co.uk/adviser/latest/sandler/pressrelease.pdf.

59 Tony Osborn-Baker, *Deloitte response to the Sandler Report*, London: Deloitte & Touche, 2002, p.1. available at http://www.deloitte.co.uk/services/Consulting_Advisory/Human_Capital/Employee_Benefits_Group/Sandler.pdf, April 2003.

60 P. Hollis, 'Sandler Seminar Speech', Department of Work and Pensions, 9 October 2002, p. 2. available at http://www.dwp.gov.uk/mediacentre/pressreleases/2002/oct/sandler-seminar0910.htm, March 2003.

CHAPTER 3

Being There: Preparing for the Future

> Conventional wisdom has perceived that cheap retail deposits were a structural phenomenon rather than something which had to be actively competed for on the basis of price. Structural solutions (i.e. making the branch network more efficient or improving the quality of product designs) are bound to predominate in an environment where the nature of the balance sheet is so complex, not only in the broad categories of funding and lending maturities, but also by the type of sources of funds and borrowers; and where the balance sheet structure is made more complex by processes of irrational pricing, cross-subsidization across generic product types and business sectors.[1]

Retail banks make a mistake when they select one or all of these underlying changes in behaviour and set forth on a technology-driven project that seems to satisfy sudden market changes without considering the broader implications of the implementation. Market trends must be viewed within the greater context of their impact on their ability to drive a customer's future attitudes towards his or her own lifestyle and life stages, as previously discussed. The second context in which these trends must be fully understood is their impact on the financial institution, the products it offers and, more importantly, the processes used by the firm to drive value, to which we now turn.

In Chapter 1, we discussed the establishment of a customer dashboard that aggregates information to indicate progress towards a set of wealth objectives. The dashboard can be a market differentiator by leveraging the Internet with the infrastructure of the institution and/or the collective partners within their network of value. Applying the dashboard concept to the organization delivers data on customer behaviour, the effectiveness of retail banking products and the result of customers' actions relative to the advice given, as illustrated in Figure 3.1.

As financial services companies migrate towards offering advisory services, their advice must be measured against customers' lifestyle choices,

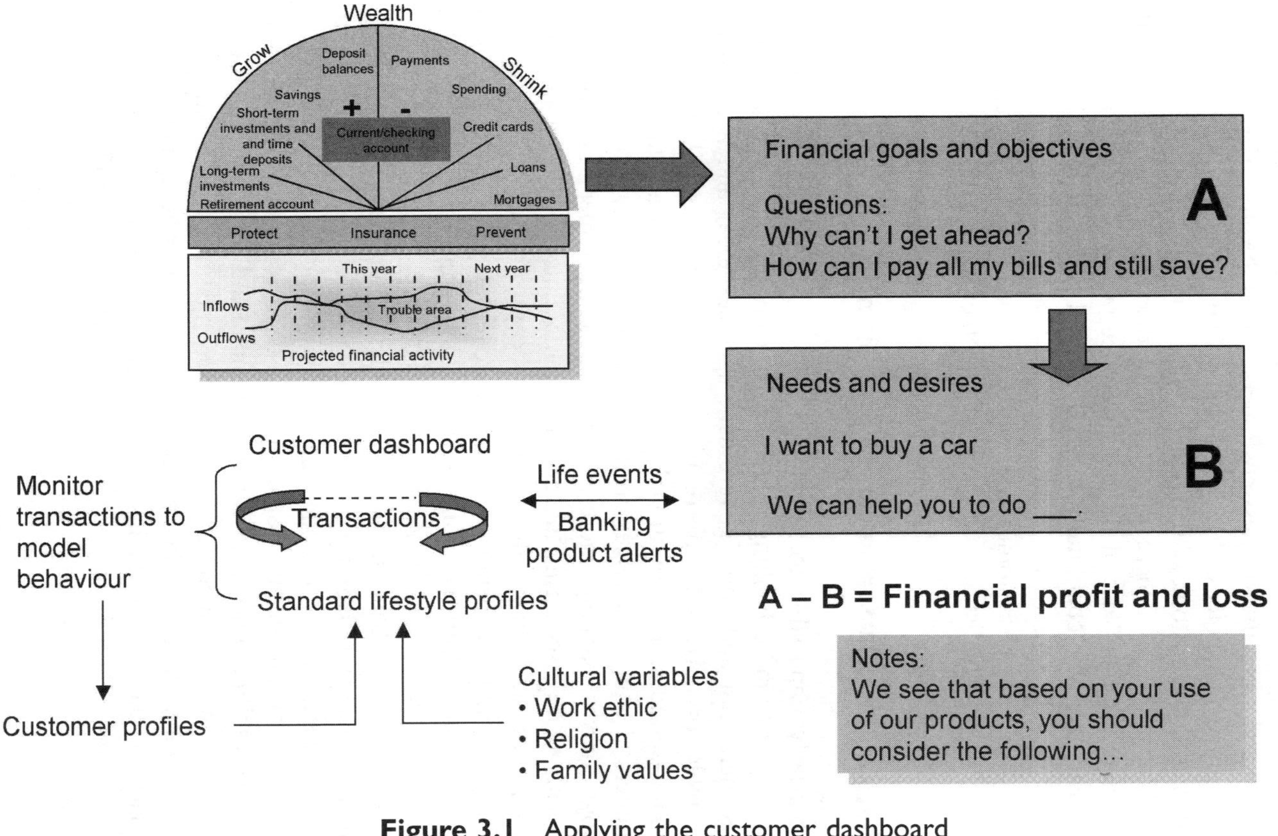

Figure 3.1 Applying the customer dashboard

goals and objectives. The primary reason for measurement is twofold; firstly, to assess the effectiveness of the guidance as a hedge against any unforeseen legal actions by customers in the event that financial goals are not met; and secondly, to assess customers' use of the advice given relative to their life event choices. Utilization of advice by customers must be measured to ascertain customers' behaviours, such as their tolerance towards risk and their ability to adhere to a financial discipline. More importantly, assessing customers' use of the bank's advice provides a lens for filtering out customers who continually seek advice and subsequently take actions that effectively ignore the counsel given. These customers represent a higher total cost-of-customer and might be considered candidates to be handled by a specialist or guided towards another service offering.

What do these factors mean to your firm?

It is nearly impossible to function in today's global economy without having one or more banking relationships. Corporations large and small, consumers rich and poor, government agencies local and national and charitable organizations all require some form of retail/commercial banking services. The traditional boundaries between a retail bank and commercial banking services are becoming increasingly blurred as technology makes banking more transparent to customers and business. Consumers are discovering that adopting a more business-like approach to personal finances gives them power to control more precisely their lifestyles. Traditional banking customers are learning that just as cash flow is the mainstay of business, it is vital for facilitating their lifestyle. Electronic commerce technologies enable society and business to form relationships between banking service providers, merchants and customers that are increasingly based on a network of added value. Financial institutions can capitalize on this phenomenon by placing the relationships they forge with consumers and business into an economic model that becomes a seamless selling process, integrating financial and non-financial products that coexist within the context of a customer relationship. The integration of computer systems and the continuous process of bringing new products to market mandates that the institution's core banking system and delivery infrastructure should be robust and capable of swapping functional components. We can argue that in the case of retail banks, the need to update their core systems more frequently to remain competitive is increasing, with smaller banks maintaining a competitive advantage over larger institutions because they can be more aggressive in their approach.

Smaller retail banks like new market entrants can opt for completely new back-office systems because there is less organizational inertia to overcome in order to complete the change. New market entrants are at an even greater advantage because they come without the pre-existing structural bureaucracies inherent in delivering traditional banking services.

New market entrants

Organizations outside the retail banking industry will continue to enter the market and provide customers with services along three distinct lines: products that are completely new; existing products at a lower cost to the customer; and products linked to non-banking products. In all three instances, the introduction of a new market entrant's product is an indicator of a market opportunity for existing retail banking providers. New products are typically the result of an advance in technology or the establishment of a new capability. In 2000, Engler and Essinger noted that the biggest competitive threat to traditional banks is from non-banking new market entrants such as retailers, because they present customers with the dual value proposition of acting as a primary conduit to both money and goods.[2] This trend is confirmed by the successful entry of Tesco and Sainsbury's into financial services in the UK. In the US, Wal-Mart and GE's moves towards providing retail banking services have been blocked by regulation. However, proposed changes in legislation would allow them and securities firms such as Morgan Stanley and Merrill Lynch to offer services and change the face of competition.[3] Other new market entrants are traditional banks partnering with other financial services providers to establish new Internet-only banks, such as Japan Net Bank which is a consortium of Sakura Bank, Sumitomo Bank, Nippon Life, Fujitsu, Tokyo Electric Power and NTT DoCoMo.[4] The high concentration of ATM technology per citizen in the Japanese banking market is a sociotechnological phenomenon that presents lessons for the West. With only 4 per cent of the land mass of the US and 130,000 ATMs compared with 190,000 in the US, Japanese customers have a greater utilization of technology-based banking services than other cultures, performing a majority of transactions via cellular phones and the Internet.[5]

Market-sensing organizations will evaluate new market entrants' products against their own to identify the gap in capability or technological deficiency. New products from new sources present an opportunity for retail banks to reassess their products in a new way, and not just against existing competitors. When a new market entrant introduces an existing product, at a lower cost, it signals one of two conditions: the new market entrant is offering the product at a loss to attract customers and anticipates recovering the cost over the course of the relationship; or it has a lower operating cost structure. In the latter case, an existing retail bank now has an opportunity to re-examine its cost of service through a new lens and, in many cases, will find that the lower cost can be attributed to a less hierarchical organizational structure and/or a significantly streamlined business process to support the lower cost product. The most difficult competitive scenario is the introduction of a product linked to a product or service that is external to the banking product. Financial products that are linked to an external product indicate that the relationship with the customer already exists. To compete in this environment, the company must woo customers away from both a product and a relationship. Therefore, the retail bank must expend additional energy to attract and retain the customer which ultimately leads to an even higher cost of sales. Industries such as carmakers are realizing that activities which follow the sales of their product now command a higher profit margin and are an essential part of the long-term customer relationship.[6] This is important in the case of cars because of the cyclical nature of the customer transaction. The carmaker wants the customer to choose them again for the purchase of the next car. Therefore, the more the relationship remains in the control of the car manufacturer or its consistently branded subsidiaries, the lower the cost of sale on retaining that customer. The opportunity for retail banks is to partner in this customer relationship by co-branding products that are seamless to the process, such as knowing the customer well enough to eliminate the loan origination process by pre-approving the loan for purchases within the network. A bank collaborating with a car manufacturer as a node in the dealer network acts to facilitate loans. A proactive approach links the dealerships to the bank by assessing customers' behaviours such as when they show an interest in a new car by taking a test drive, or, by monitoring their cars' maintenance records, a potential new car purchase event can be predicted or even encouraged by reminding customers that they have a pre-existing line of credit that requires no loan application.

However, unlike life events that are to some degree predictable, many external events such as natural disasters, geopolitical conflicts, civil unrest and complex family problems can influence customer saving and spending behaviours in both positive and negative ways. Natural unplanned events, such as the outbreak of severe acute respiratory syndrome (SARS) in China and elsewhere do present an opportunity for firms to assist customers in new ways. Since the outbreak of the virus, a significant portion of the population has been staying home, working, shopping and playing online.[7] With the surge of people going online and the subsequent demand for broadband services, the overall market for eBanking services has taken a quantum leap towards presenting financial institutions with a previously non-Internet banking demographic. Even as the spread of the virus subsides and usage levels recede from the peak generated by the initial outbreak, homes that were previously not online are now still online, and they will not be uninstalling the Internet.

Globalization and the synconomy

In *Synconomy*,[8] I argued that the nature of business is fundamentally changing: as business processes begin to interoperate between geographically dispersed corporate business partners, they are directly influenced by culture, collaborative actions, co-opetition and the generation of value, which creates a synergistic relationship between internal business processes and macro-level economic networks. Put simply, for corporations to add value in the new century, they must operate in synergy with the economic values of their business partners. For retail banks and financial services organizations in general, the capabilities or productive output gained by combining the core competencies of the individual organizations and their underlying business processes is greater than the sum of its parts. In a synergistic economy, the combination of financial products and services develop, over time, into a capability that acts separately from the traditional external forces that previously shaped its corporate behaviour. A financial services synconomy exists when firms offer retail banking products, investment services and provide infrastructures that facilitate commerce. Operating synergistically in a network of value, they generate a value proposition to customers greater than that which can be achieved by the sum of the individual organizations. This is critically important to retail banks because it identifies that few (or no) traditional institutions will be able to service all markets at all times with all services unless they are part of a network of value. Therefore, a key lesson is that at some point a bank can become so big, with such a wide array of services, that it is no longer effective, which contrasts with the notion of a one-stop-shop banking experience within a single institution.

When retail banks consider globalization in their strategies, they must take into account the following context; as said above, in previous centuries, globalization can be considered an external process of conquest, in which one faction imposed its cultural rules on a local conquered population, maintaining order and propagating a homogeneous social behaviour. A historical oversimplification of the globalization process is that prior to the end of the twentieth century, globalization was an external force which determined the commerce, culture and societal structure of a nation state. However, with the advent of television and later the Internet, the fundamental process of globalization is no longer based on nation states conquering one another. Globalization has now evolved into a process in which ideals, values and social attitudes are more freely exchanged, resulting in people within a local culture electing to adopt or attain various aspects of an external culture or imitate other people's lifestyles. This process of progressive awareness due to a global interconnected technological infrastructure effectively shifts globalization from an external process of cultural imposition to an inclusive process taking place within a nation state by individuals making personal choices. There have been no reported cases of fast-food restaurants forcing people to eat hamburgers and fries at gun point. Retail banks must be cognizant of this social phenomenon and realize that within any local geography there are groups who will prefer to preserve their national identity, culture and values. Globalization will undoubtedly foster violent reactions in social organizations and special interest groups. As people use technology in all its forms to develop a greater awareness of world affairs, cultures and beliefs, retail banks will need to strike a balance between the desire to direct customers to a standard Western-style approach to banking and the adaptation of banking products to more closely reflect the culture in which the product will operate. Retail banks must customize products and services to deliver maximum product and service appeal to significant market segments. The imperative for retail banks operating in a synconomy is to design strategies that focus on optimizing economic motivations, such as economies of scale and scope, while they also develop tactical initiatives to leverage cultural aspects such as product preferences or savings and spending habits. To make this shift, companies must view their lines of business, the technologies used to support business processes and the composition of the skills employed in order to construct a business that is agile enough to change as business conditions continue to evolve in the global synergistic economy.

Organization, business processes and skills

Retail banks and financial institutions, like their non-banking counterparts, are often founded on a simple premise: to satisfy a consumer need which manifests itself as a market opportunity. Under a hierarchical corporate structure, an organization forms to establish a set of work activities resulting in an optimally constructed process for fulfilling the market opportunity as an intermediary with a retail banking product or a service. The organization forms a value proposition and either by design or accident establishes a normative business model. At some point in their history, all retail banking institutions have evolved from this series of business building events, and through the cycles of customer demand strive to achieve lower cost optimization of the firm's operating state. Typically, retail banks achieve business process optimization by either streamlining process steps by applying technology for higher transaction throughput or an increase in the productivity of personnel, or the bank endeavours to optimize the interactions between its customers, other banks and partnerships.

Today, organizations that are intermediaries in the financial services industry realize that their perceived ability to add value is beginning to be questioned by customers. This market trend is causing many companies, especially those engaged in retail banking, to re-examine their primary definition of the business model and underlying business processes. Like their customers, banking service organizations are asking, 'What is a bank and where is it going?' As retail banking organizations review and analyse the connection between what they do and how they add value, they discover the relationship between the hierarchical structure of the organization and the steps in their business processes. Bushe and Shani remind us that the structure that divides and coordinates labour dictates the behaviour of the people within the organization:

> Structures are environments that affect how people behave. They channel effort and energy in a particular direction. When they are well designed, they support employees in accomplishing their tasks; when they are poorly designed, they can get in the way. Since they channel effort, changes in structure can lead to changes in how people behave at work.[9]

Keeping the relationship between structure, process and behaviour in mind, when retail banks revisit their value propositions, they invariably, although not intentionally, forget a critical factor which governs value creation – their relative position in the cycle of business and market maturity. As a bank grows and develops, its business processes pass through a cycle of business maturity. The early stages of business development are often dominated by a strong leader who establishes the boundaries of the business, its processes and the limits of the resources employed to fulfil the immediate goals and objectives. As the organization forms, grows larger and becomes more complex, the leader is replaced, functionally, by a strong management team that has embraced the leader's philosophy of running the company. Over time, further layers are added to the bank, more products are introduced, lines of business expand, mergers and acquisition fuel the growth agenda, and the leadership of the firm becomes diffused into a lower level in the command and control organizational hierarchy. Suddenly, a series of events result in unexpectedly plunging the organization into a competitive crisis, such as the arrival of a new market entrant, a price war or a rapid decline in demand due to changing customer attitudes. It is at this moment that retail banking organizations which do not have a clearly stated and defined value proposition fall into a downward spiral of loss of value-generating capacity. This is often triggered by rising costs that result in the reactionary manoeuvre of downsizing the organization through redundancies. At this point of crisis, many organizations struggle under the weight of their own infrastructure, not realizing that it is an opportune moment to rethink the fundamentals of the value proposition and reshape the organization. Companies that have successfully transitioned from this crisis point often equate their success to one of two essential elements: the return of a strong leader, such as Deutsche Bank's appointment of Josef Ackermann;[10] or people rally around a common set of initiatives to revive the organization's ability to compete. When a firm realizes it may no longer be competitive can be attributed, in effect, to market isolationism, when the success of the organization hinders its ability to sense changes in the market, customers or competitive landscape. Senior managers in retail banks may not see the warning signs until it is too late. When people in the firm adopt an attitude of 'if it's not broken don't fix it', the organization is signalling its inability to embrace the pace of competition in a rapidly globalizing economy. In Champy's view, change is a relentless force that organizations must embrace, by incorporating change as a continuous process within the firm's business process structure:

> In the economic environment of the twenty-first century, where change is nearly continuous, Darwin's theory of survival applies to the world of business as well as it does to the world of biology. Undoubtedly, a company's capacity to respond quickly and adroitly to change will surely determine its long-term success or failure; hence managers must anticipate transitions, sometimes provoking them, and always embrace them with open arms.[11]

Therefore, changing business conditions are the catalyst for value proposition redefinition and, if change is indeed continuous, retail banks must periodically, for example annually, revisit their value proposition to customers in order to remain competitive. Organizations that do not anticipate changes to the way in which they operate risk having their business model become irrelevant as market demands present opportunities for competitors. Gunneson argues that firms must enable processes to be self-renewing, in which the people engaged in the activities review tasks and customer obligations daily to determine and make changes in the operating environment.[12] The combination of business process design coupled with the skills, competencies and structure of the organization provide the means to use technology in innovative ways to fulfil changing customer needs.

Retail banks must be cognizant of the fact that the long-term viability of the firm may rest not on technology, but on the structure of the organization and, as conditions change, the structure must be capable of changing to adapt to the new market conditions, as noted by Tushman et al.:

> As competitive conditions change, fundamentally different organization forms are required. However, due to organization inertia, many organizations either do not effectively attend to environmental change or, if the threat is registered, act to bolster the status quo.[13]

Tushman et al. make an important point in the identification of organizational inertia as a force that inhibits the firm's ability to adapt to changing business conditions. Countering organizational inertia must be taken into account when devising strategic initiatives because of its ability to retard the combined output of the firm. Here again, Gunneson observes that corporate cultures do not simply change; they must be transitioned. Managers must be coached and people must be given proper incentives.[14] The increased level of competition in retail banking requires that financial institutions should leverage technology by establishing processes that aggregate skills into corporate competencies. Retail banks, in order to remain competitive, must adopt a modular construction by establishing cross-functional cells of competencies, as Toffler explained:

> the best way to organize is not bureaucratically, but ad-hocratically, so that each organizational component is modular and disposable, each unit interacts with many units laterally, not just hierarchically, and decisions, like goods and services, are custom-made rather than standardized.[15]

Competencies must be developed not as a hierarchical structure, but as resources to be applied to the underlying business processes within the institution. The organization must leverage the diversity of skills within the workforce by engaging a cross-cultural, multinational pool of talent, using

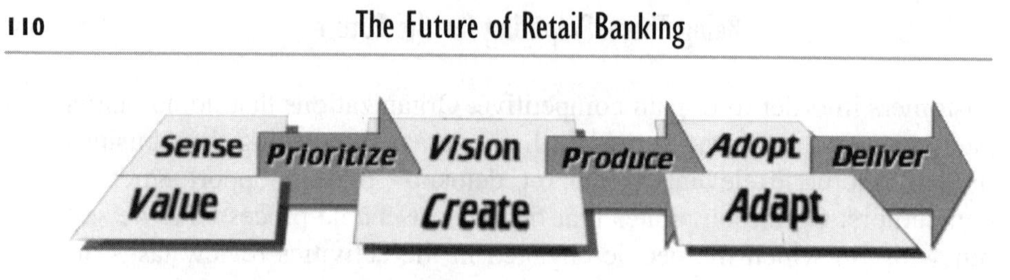

Figure 3.2 Management competencies for retail banking

technology and physical location as assets to be managed as part of the value proposition to customers. That said, retail banks must leverage their technological assets in whatever form and establish processes to aggregate skills into competencies that sense the market, prioritize opportunities, envision new business scenarios, adapt processes and adopt new ideas to deliver value to customers in increasingly new ways, as illustrated in Figure 3.2.

One of the first steps (and perhaps the easiest place to start) is to develop the competency of sensing the market and customers. Retail banks have learned that there is a renewed value in the face-to-face exchange between customers and branch personnel. This value is based on the creation of a shared tactile experience, establishing an informal bond between the customer and the brand identity of the firm such as 'my banker knows my name when I walk into the branch'. The physical meeting between customer and trusted advisor humanizes a relationship that can become sterile and semi-detached in a relationship based solely on technology. One lesson learned by business leaders who are separated by great distances in a transnational firm is that efficiency, productivity and higher morale is achieved by regular, predictable intervals of communications between subordinates and peers. For retail banking, this translates into increased communications between the customer and the trusted advisor or relationship manager.

The value of the branch is realized by organizations such as the Finance and Information Union in New Zealand, which notes that branches are a vital resource for the future of retail banking only if the nature of the work performed at the branch is significantly different from traditional retail banking activities. Retail banks are undergoing a transition from simply executing transactions to selling financial products and servicing a wider range of customer needs, demanding increased skills at the branch level, coupled with the increasing level of experimentation with different forms of physical presence, such as supermarket banking, mobile managers, kiosks and so on, and a highly skilled workforce is not a luxury but a necessity.[16]

The rapidly accumulating data from branch interaction with customers reveals that high levels of customer satisfaction are also a byproduct of a satisfied workforce, as Mark Story observes:

> Research from Citibank's annual customer and staff surveys claims a direct link between employee satisfaction and return on equity (ROE) – or profit generated as a percentage of shareholder funds.[17]

Citibank's research also reveals the link between customer dissatisfaction, poor customer satisfaction levels and the level of knowledge of branch relationship managers. Interestingly, Citibank's research brought to light the direct proportional relationship between the calibre of product knowledge by branch personnel and their comprehension of how to apply products to customer needs. The second interesting aspect of Citibank's research is that employee satisfaction is a key driver in increasing customer satisfaction.

Achieving higher levels of customer and employee satisfaction can be attained by improving three key aspects of the branch: the physical design; redefining the lines of business; and a rejuvenation of branch personnel through compensation and skills improvement schemes. The ANZ Grindlays Bank in Ahmedabad 'branch of the future' concept addresses the physical nature of the branch by incorporating three key functional components into its floor plan: a relationship manager, a service advisor module and an information module, in addition to the traditional teller, branch manager and strong room.[18]

The physical attributes of new age branch design are not solely for the satisfaction of customers. Innovative design fosters higher morale in branch personnel which, when coupled with redesigned compensation schemes and a programme for continuous skills improvement, acts as a powerful motivational incentive for branch personnel to excel at forging more intimate relationships with customers. In an operating environment of trusted advisors, retaining talent will be more important in the next few years. To maintain the high degree of customer touch that is the hallmark of a trusted advisor, retail banks must have a continuous influx of talent to remain competitive. As I have argued elsewhere, although it is counterintuitive, during times of economic downturn, financial institutions can gain a competitive advantage by taking action along two lines: the retention of highly talented personnel, and the recruitment of new talents.[19] Traditional retail banks now realize that, in the banking model of the future, people are the greatest asset and are integral in the differentiation of banking products and services with customers. Because any type of company can acquire technology and perform banking services, when employees leave the firm for whatever reason, the firm is not cutting costs, but losing an asset that makes it competitive. So what is the solution for retail banks and how will they rethink their lines of business to meet the new competition?

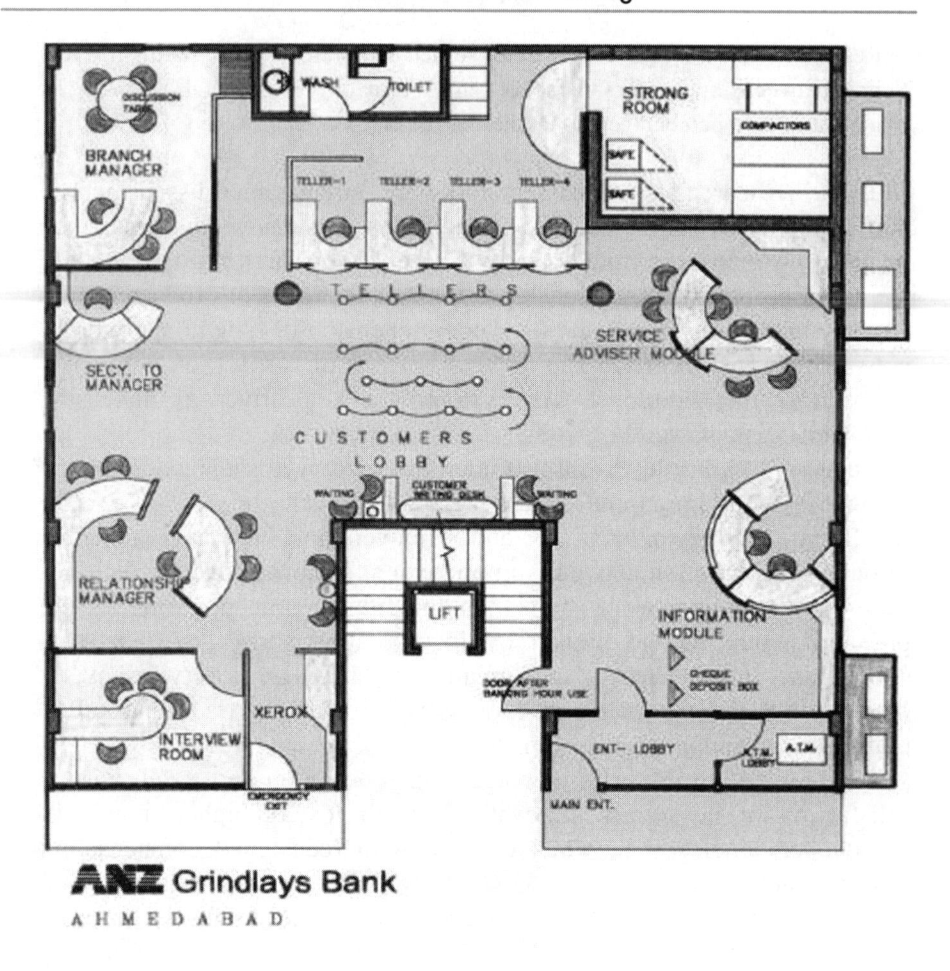

Figure 3.3 ANZ Grindlays Bank 'branch of the future'

Rethinking lines of business

Retail banks that are rethinking their traditional lines of business and associated products discover that the new globally competitive business must excel at providing the customer with service convenience and product clarity. Products must be divorced from the infrastructure that enables the delivery of the product because they are temporary. A product's life is determined by its perceived value to the customer, while the infrastructure, and its ability to facilitate the use of the products by customers, is valuable to the organization and its stockholders. The primary objective of infrastructure is to support the underlying business processes found within each line of business. Retail banking products are resources, means and mechanisms used by the processes within each line of business and, as customer demands change, they are introduced, used, refined and retired.

Rethinking its lines of business, Bradford & Bingley's advertising and media campaigns reinforce a 'marketplace' theme, which, from the perspective of branch design, incorporates an interior that brings in the outdoors. By utilizing canopies and floor finishes that reflect a real outdoor market, the branch design reflects a fundamental rethinking of the branch experience and the supporting lines of business. Realizing the appeal of the design to customers and staff, Bradford & Bingley engaged Claremont Business Environments to modularize the design, thus reducing the branch of the future's refitting cost, with innovations such as individual kiosk areas and a variety of standard units and furniture that can be combined to accommodate the needs of all branches.[20] The key to Bradford & Bingley's approach is to enable each branch to redesign the physical layout of their location using modular components, so catering to the needs of local customers while preserving the core brand identity, as reflected in Figure 3.4.

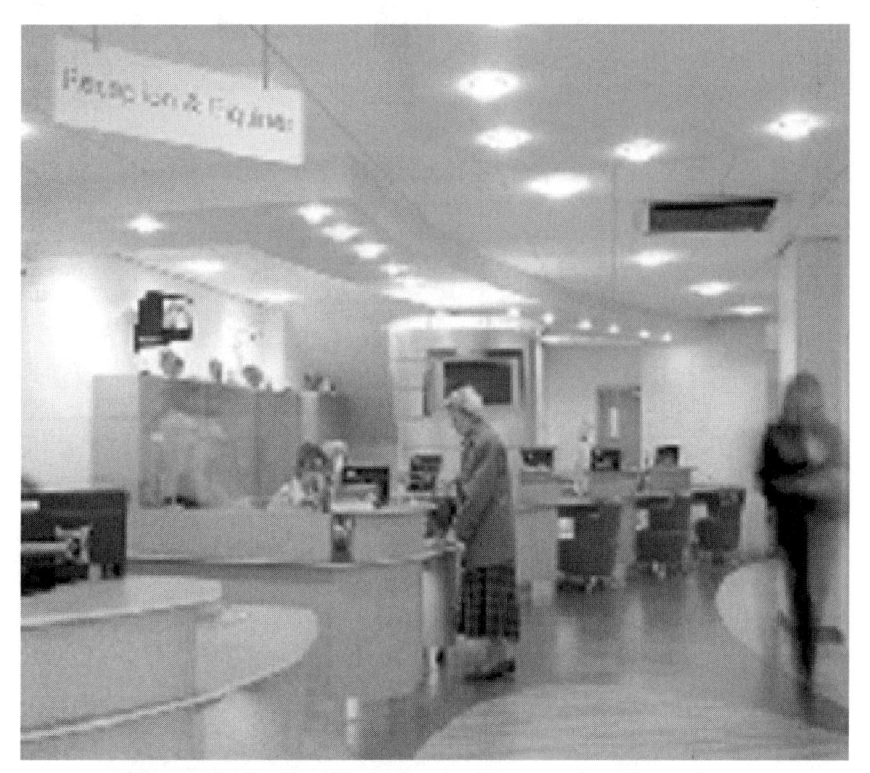

Figure 3.4 Bradford & Bingley's marketplace theme

Burgan Bank, Kuwait

Industrial and Commercial Bank, China

Wells Fargo Bank, USA

Banco Popular, Dominican Republic

Figure 3.5 Mobile banking vehicles

When we hear the term 'mobile banking' in the retail banking industry, visions of mobile phone applications, personal digital assistants (PDAs) and other electronic devices that cater to the mobility of the customer come to mind. Several banks have rethought the question of mobility by asking themselves: what if the customer was stationary but located in geographies not easily serviced by the existing branch network? Several banks, as illustrated in Figure 3.5, have discovered mobile banking in which the branch itself is mobile.[21] Primarily used for special events as movable ATMs or remote branch locations, the vehicles are self-contained and include power, security and wireless communication equipment.

The Citizens Banking Company of Sandusky, Ohio, extended this type of mobile banking even further when it began offering business customers a mobile banking courier service, providing businesses with convenient pick-up and delivery of banking products such as standard transactions and correspondence seven days a week, crediting most deposits on the same day. Transactions that originate via the mobile branch are insured against fire, theft, loss and are FDIC (Federal Deposit Insurance Corporation) insured at the time of pick-up from the customer's business.[22]

Other approaches to new banking models centre on a higher utilization of the Internet. I discussed elsewhere the evolution of eMarketplaces in the financial services industry as taking three distinct paths: a market maker, a market facilitator and a market integrator.[23] Venezuela's Banco Mercantil's personal portal provides an example of the emerging use of banking institutions as a market facilitator by linking banking activities to shopping. From the viewpoint of most customers, a bank is simply a place to store money until it is needed. When customers adopt this mindset, they commoditize the added value of the bank because the bank is considered a secondary intermediary. Banco Mercantil's approach moves the bank to the centre of the action, making purchases, paying for services, making plans and doing things. This is evident from the design of the website's features to the placement of the bank's logo at the centre of the customer's options, as shown in Figure 3.6.

Banco Mercantil's personal portal is a sterling example of how the Internet can be used to engage banking customers in non-banking activities.[24] The banking relationship is at the heart of the interaction, which is illustrated by the use of its brand identity on the initial webpage and throughout the website. The design centres on various aspects of your life, sprinkled with products designed to facilitate lifestyle choices. For example, selecting *mi casa* (my house) enables the customer to look for a new place to live, obtain a mortgage, purchase insurance, buy furnishings

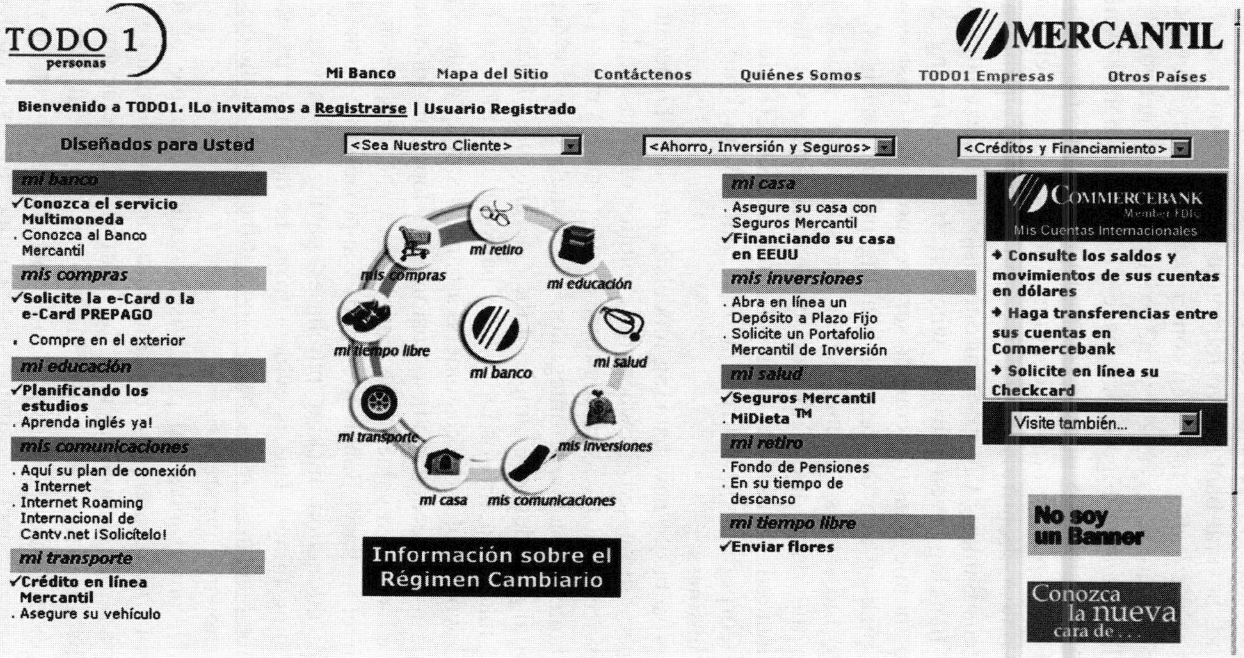

Figure 3.6 Banco Mercantil's personal portal

and other household goods, even the purchase of goods from the US to be shipped internationally. Selecting *mi salud* (my health) provides health information, health insurance, links to health-related products, medications and direct links to local chemists. In each category of lifestyle choice, there is either a link to Banco Mercantil's retail banking products or an affiliated service provider. Even *mi retiro* (my retirement) includes links to special events and restaurants to help you enjoy your retirement. This engagement of customers and lifestyles is reflected in the company's mission statement:

> To provide excellent financial products and services to meet individuals', companies, and the community's expectations, and to ensure that stockholders and clients receive appropriate return on investments.[25] (author's translation)

Banco Mercantil's approach uses the bank as the centre of the customer experience, with links to external banking and non-banking relationships that introduce ancillary products and services.

Ancillary lines of business

Ancillary services represent new opportunities for retail banks to expand their markets, establish new lines of business and engage customers new and old with additional touch points and transactions. However, when this happens, the branch is encroaching in other markets and becomes itself a new entrant into an existing market. Therefore, the value for service ratio must be clearly understood and deemed higher than profit margins within the existing lines of business. Retail banking institutions must assess their entry into mature markets because of the high degree of commoditization and low margins. Organizations mistakenly assume that by offering travel services, for example, throngs of new customers will magically appear just because they are providing a new service. It is true that a certain percentage of the market will naturally gravitate to the new service; however, the majority of customers will require a high degree of motivation to switch from incumbent providers. Therefore, they must be wooed away from their existing market channel. The cost of customer acquisition through these ancillary channels must be assessed and monitored as part of the portfolio of integrated market offerings. As Howcroft and Lavis pointed out, retail banks, seduced into providing ancillary services as a means to use up excess branch capacity, have learned, in many cases the hard way, that these services must be viable entities in their own right or risk reducing total operating profits.[26]

Developing revenue opportunities and fee income

Retail banking consumers and small businesses typically establish a relationship with an institution that is predicated on receiving good value for services over a long-term relationship. The majority of customers realize that changing banks has an inherent cost that is identifiable as inconvenient; it causes delays and, more importantly, loss of time that could be better spent on more productive pursuits. Therefore, to gain customers, a bank must motivate them to leave their existing banking relationship. Motivations come from two sources: the bank itself, typically the product of successive poor performance, or a change in the perception of value offset by increases in fees; or an external source, such as a traditional bank offering better value for money or a non-traditional entity providing an alternative means to link with another product or service. In many cases, a steady decline in service performance makes customers doubt the value for money of the retail banking service and they look elsewhere for better service. Once the seed of discontent is planted, the torrent of media-based marketing materials triggers customers to switch to a new perceived value source or they become so overwhelmed with choices that they will attempt to reconcile the existing relationship.

Having a long-term relationship with a retail banking customer is not a gift from the consumer or small business to the institution; it is the product of a process of customer service. This process, now identified as 'customer relationship management', consists of establishing the relationship, monitoring customers' use of services, measuring the effectiveness of the services from the customers' perspective and the profitability from the institution's perspective and finally analysing the relationship from a holistic value perspective. Providing service that enhances the customer relationship is not simply offering a plethora of banking products which give the customer a myriad of choices; customer relationships must be optimized so they are viable, profitable channels to market for the bank. As we can see in Figure 3.7, the optimization of a customer relationship occurs under two fundamental and deliberate sets of actions: those that increase revenues to the firm; and/or those that reduce the cost of maintaining the relationship.

Like a manufacturing production process, the customer relationship must have an aim in which deviation can be measured. Each option under the path of increasing revenues or reducing cost requires a deliberate action on the part of the organization that must be measured, monitored and reevaluated periodically, in order to optimize the total customer relationship relative to the underlying profitability of each market segment. Understanding the dynamic relationship between these factors is essential

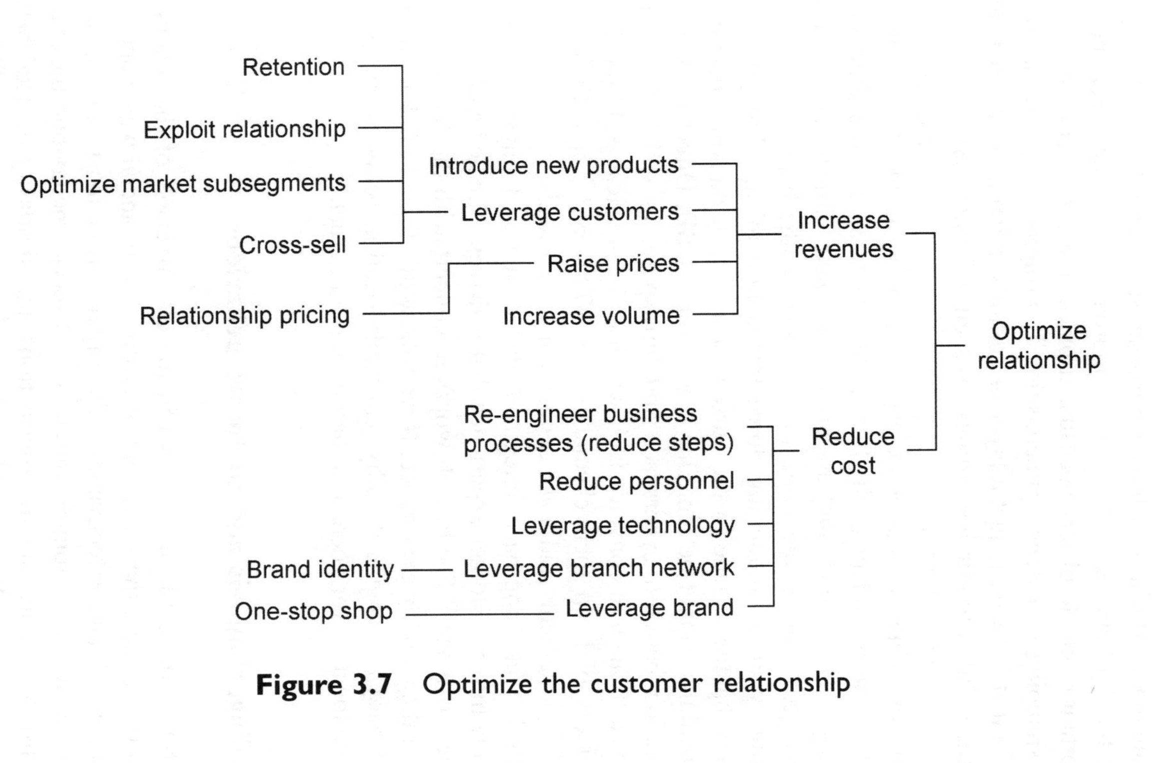

Figure 3.7 Optimize the customer relationship

input information in the formulation of marketing campaigns and other promotional activities, primarily because it demonstrates quantitatively and/or qualitatively the effectiveness of loss-leader products or services and ancillary offerings within each market subsegment.

In the Philippines, BPI Direct's approach to ancillary services is an important model to observe because it places the customer at the vanguard of a shopping experience, subconsciously bringing customers to the realization that banking is just a layer of administration between their money and their ability to purchase things (as seen in Figure 3.8).

Buying goods and services, paying bills and initiating transactions are all part of living in modern society, and banking is simply a means to an end but not an end in itself. In simple terms, people like shopping and buying material goods that are often associated with fun and memorable experiences, but, at the same time, people loathe banking, which often conjures visions of tracking down transaction mistakes in your current account balances. Due to the current structure of banking, people think that banking cannot be fun. One key feature of BPI Direct is its seamless integration between cyberspace and terraspace, in which the customer selects a 'branch of convenience', which is the physical BPI branch where customers pick up their cheque books, ATM cards, sign their account opening documents and make deposits or withdrawals.

BPI Direct's approach integrates the virtual and physical worlds of banking into a customer experience that is driven, directed and maintained by the customer.[27] The branch works in concert with the Internet component of the banking experience. If we follow this line of thinking further, it is not hard to imagine the physical bank location being expanded into a pick-up location for goods purchased on the Internet.

Branding, channels and customer behaviour

The future of retail banking lies in the effectiveness of the institution's brand to facilitate the fulfilment of customers' financial wants and needs. To achieve brand effectiveness, the organization must develop a deep understanding of customers' purchase and service behaviour, the channels they use to initiate banking transactions and similarity of need between customer groups. Retail banking customers have embraced with varying enthusiasm the use of increasingly different types of technology to perform basic banking and share trading transactions. As customers move beyond this initial interest in self-sufficient services, they will look towards retail banks to add value by being their trusted advisor on finan-

Figure 3.8 BPI Direct

cial matters. Customers perceive a trusted advisor as a source of counsel and as a conscience, not someone that is continually selling them a product. Trusted advisors counsel them on the right products and the right time to use banking and investment products to support their lifestyles.

Retail banks that evolve to be a customer's trusted advisor depend heavily on their brand identity and the use of their brand to reflect the values of the firm, such as stability, security, financial expertise, market awareness and a comprehensive approach to solving financial problems. However, like products, brands cannot be complacent, unchanging or perceived to be dated. Retail banking brands are dynamic, incorporating changes in the marketplace and quickly adapting to reflect changes in customers' lifestyle needs. Today's banks require a cohesive branding strategy to determine the limits of their global ambitions, the effective reach of their organizations and, most importantly, the perceived relative value of their products and services to the local customers they serve. One key thing to remember when developing brands, channels and customer product offerings is that all customers are now local.

Without a doubt, at first glance Sir Richard Branson's Virgin brand identity reflects a vibrant, youth-related market. In spite of this, under closer analysis, one realizes that it is more than just a cleverly crafted Internet presence; it is a present-day example of the future state of the customer experience, documenting the marriage between banking, retail and other lifestyle/life-stage services. Virgin's brand identity and value proposition is simple, clear and precise

Virgin's One Account[28] links financial products in a such a way that the value proposition to the customer sells the product, in contrast to most other banking products that have to sell the product and explain its value proposition. Virgin's banking model goes to the heart of a customer's banking dilemma: 'how do I juggle the five primary banking activities every month to get the best long-term return on my money without having to get a degree in economics from Harvard?' The Virgin One Account optimizes the movement of funds between a customer's use of debt instruments such as a mortgage, loans and credit cards against the individual's short- and long-term assets, for example savings and current accounts. The Virgin One Account benefits the customer in three ways: any direct interest is not paid to him or her, reducing income tax liability; actions are taken on a daily basis, so removing the need to guess and negating any direct customer action; and the customer controls the rate of repayments as life events (marriage, birth of a child, divorce, death in the family, relocation, amongst others) alter financial commitments. The elements in the value proposition to the customer are:

- telephone or online account information
- one balance representing the big picture
- an optional breakdown of the balance, giving the traditional view of individual mortgage, loans, savings and current account balances
- a monthly financial statement overview
- a repayment guide
- an annual review to promote awareness of the full potential of the account
- money management tools that enable the customer to analyse his or her savings and spending to create a monthly budget.

One of the key ingredients in Virgin's value proposition is typically overlooked when retail banks develop similar schemes: the educational aspect of the account. While the account has some traditional elements (makes the transition easier), the newer, educational elements of the repayment guide coupled with management tools allow customers to learn at their own pace and over time fine-tune their account relationship. Herein lies the clue that the Virgin model is not targeted primarily at the youth market; if it were, why would they need a traditional view? Perhaps to explain it to their parents. This sounds similar to the problem of how to set the clock on the VCR.

As more non-banking companies offer additional financial services products, brand identity and a clear value proposition are paramount to the success or failure of the organization. Taking advantage of the variety of banking products, niche market players, such as the UK's Black and White Mortgage Company, act as both a market aggregator and customer contact point. With a value proposition designed primarily to reduce the confusion between mortgage products and other options, the Black and White Mortgage Company clarifies industry jargon into language that is easily understood by all its customers and offers the same service for a variety of insurance needs.[29]

The examples of Virgin's One Account and the Black and White Mortgage Company illustrate the rising trend of aligning basic value propositions to customer behaviour. Within the retail banking experience, customer actions can be categorized into three basic behaviours: *transactions* which receive funds, exercise credit and pay bills; *precautionary actions* such as time deposits, savings accounts and insurance; and *speculative actions* such as share trading and other investment vehicles, as illustrated in Figure 3.9.

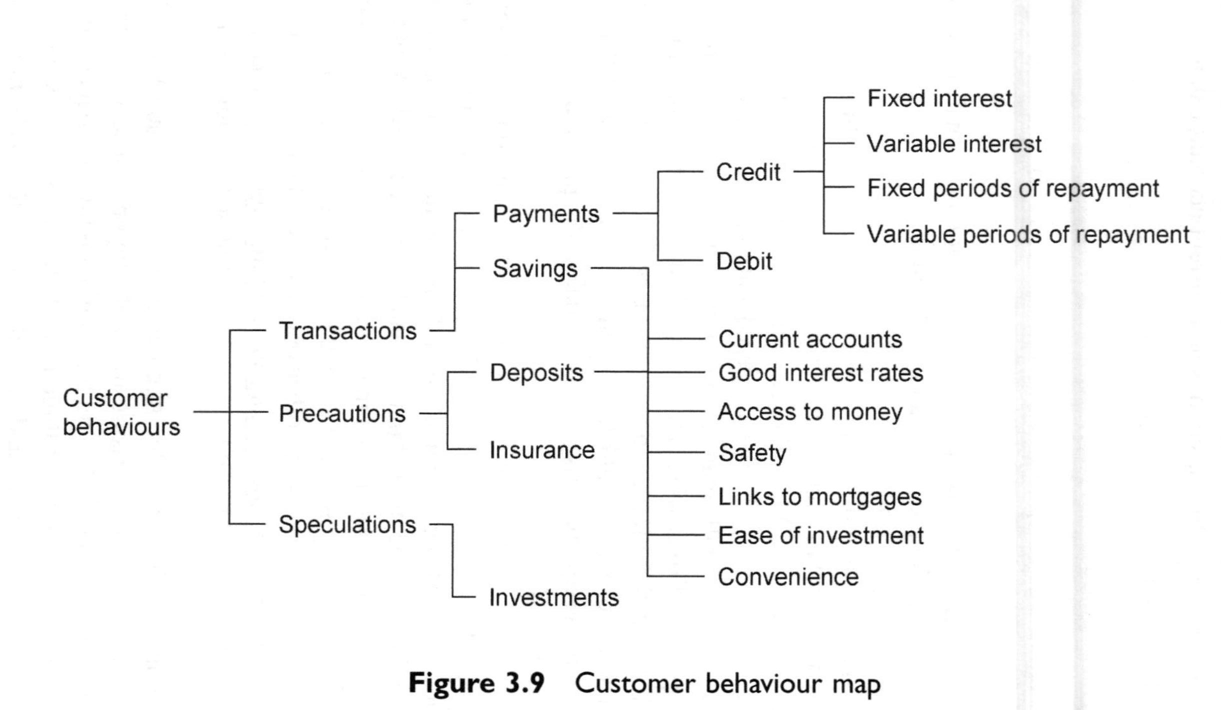

Figure 3.9 Customer behaviour map

According to Blythe, consumer behaviour is the result of a complex interaction of many factors, which will vary from customer to customer and change over time, due to fashion, social conditions and other influencing forces.[30] Blythe reminds us that there are very few absolute rules for behaviour that is repeatedly influenced by new ideas, approaches and products that are continually adopted. For retail banks, this means that the formula for market segmentation and the alignment of products to customer behaviours is a dynamically occurring process and must be re-evaluated periodically to ensure the highest yield per banking product.

One strategy to hedge the continuous customer movement between products is to change the focus from the products themselves and concentrate on achieving an end goal with the banking customer. This is seen at Singapore's DBS Bank and its Treasures Priority Banking product that is designed to enhance not just your wealth but your personal well-being too. DBS Bank's approach merges two key concepts: long and short-term, family-focused, financial goals, and the acquisition of services normally associated with achieving lifestyle privileges. Put simply, the bank's offering operates a philosophy that customers enjoy enhancing their wealth, and therefore the bank should help customers to enjoy doing it. DBS Bank also offers a variety of private events and access to specialists at Treasures Centres and Treasures Counters at selected DBS branches.[31] It takes a large degree of planning and execution to bring to the market many of these visions of the new banking environment and the increasing number of associated products, which is the subject of the next chapter.

Notes

1. J. B. Howcroft and J. Lavis, *Retail Banking: The New Revolution in Structure and Strategy*, Oxford: Basil Blackwell, 1986, p. 140.
2. H. Engler and J. Essinger, *The Future of Banking*, London: Pearson Education, 2000, p. xv.
3. *The Asian Banker*, 27 May 2003, available at http://www.theasianbanker.com/.
4. M. Sanchanta, 'Japan's first online-only bank opens', *Financial Times*, 12 October 2000, p. 37.
5. A. Rowley, 'New kid on the block', *The Banker Supplement*, London: Financial Times, March 2001, p. 11.
6. T. Burt, 'Carmakers eye route to twin track revenues', *Financial Times*, 28 February 2001, p. 1.
7. M. Dickie, 'Sars sends stay-at-home Chinese on to the net', *Financial Times*, 22 May 2003, p. 31.
8. J. DiVanna, *Synconomy: Adding Value in a World of Continuously Connected Business*, Basingstoke: Palgrave Macmillan, 2003, p. xi.
9. G. R. Bushe and A. B. Shani, *Parallel Learning Structures. Increasing Innovation in Bureaucracies*, Wokingham: Addison-Wesley, 1991, p. 3.

10 R. Brookes, 'Ackermann set to lead Deutsche Bank', SwissInfo, 20 May 2002, Swiss Radio International, available at http://www.swissinfo.org/.

11 J. Champy, *X-engineering the Corporation: Reinventing your Business in the Digital Age*, New York: Warner Books, 2002, p. 160.

12 A. Gunneson, *Transitioning to Agility*, Reading: Addison-Wesley, 1997, p. 224.

13 M. L. Tushman, B. Virany and E. Romanelli, 'Executive Succession, Strategic Reorientations, and Organization Evolution', in M. Horwitch (ed.) *Technology in the Modern Corporation: a Strategic Perspective*, Oxford: Pergamon Press, 1986, p. 215.

14 Gunneson, *Transitioning to Agility*, p. 174.

15 A.Toffler, *The Adaptive Corporation*, London: McGraw-Hill, 1985, p. 108.

16 Bank of the Future Briefing Papers, Briefing Paper 3: Branches, Finsec New Zealand, available at http://www.finsec.org.nz/future_branch.htm, May 2003.

17 M. Story, The Power of Happy Staff, *The New Zealand Herald*, 4 June 2003, available at http://www.nzherald.co.nz/employment/employmentstorydisplay.cfm?storyID=3450618&thesection=employment&thesubsection=management.

18 ANZ Grindlays Bank, Ahmedabad, The Branch of the Future Concept, Sudhir Gandhi Architects, available at http://www.sudhirgandhi.com/anz-ahmedabad.htm, April 2003.

19 DiVanna, *Synconomy*, p. 176.

20 Bradford & Bingley, Branch of the Future, Claremont Business Designs, Claremont-Europe.com, available at http://www.claremont-europe.com/, May 2003.

21 Mobile Branch Facilities, MBF Industries, Inc., available at http://www.mobileatm.net/, April 2003.

22 Mobile Banking Courier Service, The Citizens Banking Company, available at http://www.citizensbankco.com/mobilebanking.html, April 2003.

23 See DiVanna, *Redefining Financial Services: The New Renaissance in Value Propositions*, Basingstoke: Palgrave Macmillan, 2002.

24 MiBanco, Banco Mercantil, Tudo I Services, Inc., available at http://www.bancomercantil.com/mercprod/site/home, May 2003.

25 Banco Mercantil, Venuzuela, available at http://www.bancomercantil.com/actual/informacion/default.html?link=0-0-0.html, May 2003.

26 Howcroft and Lavis, *Retail Banking*, p. 165.

27 BPI Direct Savings Bank, e-shopping center, available at http://www.bpidirect.com/e-shopping/e_home.htm.

28 Virgin 'The one account', available at http://www.oneaccount.com, May 2003.

29 The Black and White Mortgage Company, available at https://www.blackwhitemortgageco.co.uk/index.htm, May 2003.

30 J. Blythe, *The Essence of Customer Behaviour*, London: Pearson Education, 1997, pp. 2–3.

31 Treasures Priority Banking, DBS Bank, Singapore, available at http://www.dbs.com.sg/treasures/, March 2003.

CHAPTER 4

Competing There: Competing with New Rules

> Technological innovations played a key role in rendering decades-old banking laws and regulations obsolete. The relaxation of these regulations has, in turn, further reduced barriers to competition and accelerated the modernization of our financial system. That evolution, however, must continue to occur in a manner that preserves the fundamental soundness of the financial system and, in particular, the nation's banks. History teaches us that a sound banking system, willing and able to take deposits and extend credit, is a prerequisite for the long-term health of the national economy. Securities markets alone will never be able to substitute for the extensive and detailed knowledge that bankers – especially community bankers – bring to the intermediation process.[1]

Unravelling the Gordian knot of retail banking is best expressed by this oversimplification of the underlying competitive problem: various components in the world of financial instruments require specific expertise. However, providing that expertise to all customers in all locations is not cost effective, efficient or necessary. Technology that can transport expertise across time and space provides a means in which expertise can be leveraged across the firm's product portfolio. However, even with the benefits which technology brings (real or imagined), competing retail banking companies armed with the same technology deliver astonishingly different financial results. Technology does not apply to all customer market segments and must be applied as a spectrum of solutions that each offer a specific value proposition to the target market segment.

The variation in corporate performance is due primarily to the skills, competencies, attitudes and culture of the organization, and not the capabilities made possible by technology. The approach to technology-based services and the development of new, closer relationships with customers by traditional retail banking companies has been entirely too conservative. Ironically, this is not due to a history of fiduciary responsibility or an inherent risk-averse philosophy. Rather, it is the result of a hierarchical organizational structure that over time has developed a myriad of functional silos. Banks need to rethink fundamentally their products, lines of business, organizational hierarchy, required skill sets, distribution channels and the relationship with customers and collaborators. Broadly, banks need to reassess their basic value propositions. Are they still merely an intermediary that facilitates transactions for customers, or do they actually offer a means to facilitate the way in which people live, influence their financial responsibilities and assist them in achieving their financial goals and objectives?

The first step is to develop an operating philosophy that communicates to the customer the value proposition, as can be seen at First Independent Bank in Vancouver, Washington:

> Philosophy:
>
> As a locally owned community bank we have a strong commitment to friendly, hometown service as well as leadership in providing innovative financial services to our customers. Below are our seven Corporate Philosophies that guide how we care for our customers and operate the Bank:
>
> - A hometown tradition since 1910.
> - No bureaucracy.
> - More value and excellent service.
> - Ensure that every customer likes doing business with us.
> - Focus on profitable banking relationships.
> - Big enough to serve you and small enough to know you.
> - Always conscious of the bottom line.[2]

However, this level of customer expectation setting may be substantially easier for small banks and becomes exponentially harder for large multiregional or transnational banks. The key for larger banks is to keep the underlying value proposition as simple and concise as possible. Firms that set expectations too high often find that they never live up to their customers' expectations, no matter how hard they try. Here again smaller financial institutions have a distinct advantage in their bureaucracy-light ability to mobilize resources to compete.

Larger organizations are repeatedly discovering how the sociocultural structure of the organization and the underlying incentive system to motivate performance works against the process of value proposition realignment, as experienced by the collective organizations operating under Sir

Richard Branson's Virgin brand identity. Branson's vision of an Internet portal – a central interaction point acting as a gateway to the growing portfolio of companies within the Virgin group – offers customers a clear value proposition, providing them with a starting point for the Virgin experience. Economies of scale for the Virgin companies can be achieved by pooling resources into a common infrastructure, while economies of scope are created by incorporating (seamlessly, from the customers' viewpoint) additional products, services and companies into the structure. Unfortunately, in early 2002, Virgin announced it was unable to make the Virgin.com portal the focal point of the marketing efforts, due to internal organizational squabbles between operating units over the allocation of profits resulting from additional sales.[3] Fortunately, to the management team's credit, customer use of Virgin.com as a gateway has not been adversely affected by the internal organizational misalignment from the value proposition, which links innovative financial offerings such as Virgin money, Virgin credit cards and the Virgin One Account, and personal loans.[4] What retail banking institutions can learn from Virgin's innovative approach is not the growing number of complementary companies that will ultimately reflect consumer choices and products for almost every lifestyle and life stage, but the cohesive unity of the brand identity which is facilitated by mechanisms such as the Virgin credit card and the Virgin ISP (Internet service provider) services. From the perspective of value generation, Virgin's strategic initiatives lay the foundation for a consumer experience of a multi-product, multi-brand, lifestyle support centre. It could be argued that the next step in Virgin's development will be to act as a market aggregator, in which non-Virgin products and services are co-branded, whereby, in essence, a collection of product partnerships could be viewed by customers as being equal to Virgin quality and receiving a seal of approval. This concept is important for retail banks to understand because of the implications for the delivery of traditional financial services, which tend to be based solely on a commoditized service model which will eventually be seen as non-value added. To compete in the emerging financial services marketplace and establish value, retail banks must develop strategic initiatives in one or more of the following categories:

Think global

- Economies of scale (reduce cost of service, consolidate operations, streamline operations, combine infrastructures, centralized infrastructure services)
- Brand strategy (reduce cost of sales, franchise products)

- Service aggregation (increase revenue, partnerships).

Act regional

- Tailored services (increase customer satisfaction, call centres, targeted market subsegment products)
- Compliance with regulations (control cost and/or expand when restrictions are relaxed)
- Co-opetition with partners (increase customers, economies of scope).

Look local

- Interoperation with partners (increase services and product offerings, interchange with consumers and merchants, more autonomy for branches)
- Talent (leverage local knowledge, optimize talent pools, capitalize on branch network)
- Merge brand/products (commoditize and optimize, increase customer touch points).

Think global

A classic mistake for a retail bank, regardless of size, is to interpret the concept of globalization as indistinguishable from 'standardization of financial product offerings' or, even more damaging, to think that globalization is simply providing a suite of generic financial products. The standardization of banking products enables the organization to reduce the overall cost of operations and minimizes the number of things people within the organization have to learn. However, companies entering the retail banking marketplace have a distinct competitive advantage because they can rapidly adapt their products and services to changing market conditions, in many cases because less corporate bureaucracy makes them more agile. Globalizing a retail bank by using a standard suite of technologies, such as centralized back-office systems and other core systems, means that from a standardized mechanism of interchange, the delivery components must be used as a foundation for developing offerings to niche market opportunities. Without access to the same volume of resources as big transnational banks, the competitive advantage for small local banks is brand recognition and their greater propensity to provide a higher degree of customer service.

Thinking globally, Saudi Arabia's National Commercial Bank has launched a strategic initiative to make Islamic investment products available globally to any Muslim investor. Phase One established a partnership with Deutsche Bank to launch an equity-based product called Islamic EquityBuilder, denominated in US dollars, sterling and euros. Phase two will introduce globally oriented products focused on markets outside the Gulf region, complete with Islamic insurance (*Takaful*) and the bank's existing shariah-compliant Islamic equity funds.[5]

Economies of scale are often a goal based on the hierarchical alignment of resources designed to codify activities in order to achieve an economy by centralizing core functions. Hammer argues that the notion of an economy of scale is limited and achieves a diseconomy of scale, that is, as the organization grows the multiple layers of bureaucracy retard the organization's ability to perform.[6] As Hammer suggests, this problem can be avoided if the retail bank divides core functions across smaller, multiple organizations. One element of the brand which is rising in importance is the perception of ethical, social and environmental behaviour. The Co-operative Bank noted that 30 per cent of its new customers indicated that the bank's ethical stance was a substantial contributory factor in switching to the bank's offerings.[7] Brands can reduce the cost of sales when they retain customers. We have seen several examples of service aggregation, in which the express goals are to give the customer a greater choice, and in actual practice, packaging services together presents an opportunity to cross-sell and engage the customer in more services that are based on fee income.

Act regional

The preservation of regional cultural values should be foremost in the minds of financial services firms. This is expressed, for example, in HSBC's marketing campaign as 'the world's local bank'. Within regional/local regulations, tailored services are rapidly changing within geographies to increase competition, making it easier for banks and non-banks to offer a wider range of services and increase customer satisfaction, as seen in the US with its proposed revisions that will result in non-banks providing services. A second aspect is the influence of national and regional regulations and legislation to protect economic activities, as can be seen in Europe in protectionist policies and new regulations such as Basel II.[8] The extent to which regulatory and legislative political decisions affect the operations of the retail bank must be assessed relative to the goal, objectives and the underlying value proposition for customers.

When retail banks establish brands, services and product offerings for specific regions, they often fail to incorporate the needs of ethnic groups within the population. In some regions it is cost prohibitive to develop products culturally. To overcome this problem, banks can use white-labelled services from a partnering bank that performs back-office processing, trading and clearing services for local financial institutions, thus extending the reach of the brand and customer base. Banks offering white-labelled services enable smaller retail banks to outsource basic banking services and focus on strategic initiatives such as brand development and management, improving customer service and introducing new products. Another option is to co-brand retail banking products with a larger institution for a wider market appeal and broker services via the aggregated infrastructure of the larger institution.

The ability to tailor services to cultural groups, lifestyles, life stages and other means of personalizing banking products clearly meets the growing demand of customers at the beginning of the third millennium. Empowering branch personnel to customize services and establish the role of a trusted advisor increases customer satisfaction and will ultimately lead to higher levels of sensing customer need. Economies of scale can be achieved to some degree at the regional level as more customers become able to self-customize their banking products. Cooperating with and competing for customers within the same regional geography will be based on clear definitions of customer market subsegments, targeted customers and the applicability of a product or service to that market. Not all products can be profitable within all sectors of a given market. Therefore, retail banking institutions will naturally collaborate under these conditions. Where there are overlaps in markets, customers and the applied use of specific products, banks will compete for a customer's total relationship or simply sell single banking products or ancillary products or services.

Look local

At the local level and from a customer's perspective, the retail banking marketplace appears fragmented as large banks move in and non-traditional banks establish new locations or appear in previously non-banking retail properties. Fragmentation also appears within a single bank, as customers frequently do not have a single point of contact to receive advice and compare retail banking products from providers and/or the bank's competitors. This temporary market confusion creates an opportunity for traditional retail banking institutions to reinvent themselves and realign services to meet the needs of their customers' lifestyles, beliefs, cultural preferences and financial sophistication. Interoperation with partners at the local level will be primarily to increase the geographic coverage and/or improve the quality of services. Local partnerships and cooperative ventures have been centring on the sale of ancillary products and services, such as establishing a coffee shop within a branch, which is simply an outsourcing partnership with a local provider.

Given that the new competitive environment forces financial institutions to take action globally, regionally and locally, banks must develop strategic initiatives which move them towards a future operating state, which is the topic of the next section.

Developing strategic initiatives

The biggest challenge that retail banking institutions face is developing a set of cohesive strategic initiatives to enable the efficient performance of the various financial functions required by their customers. Financial institutions establish strategic initiatives in several distinct areas: internal initiatives such as re-engineering, cultural change management and activities to streamline operations; external initiatives such as marketing campaigns and community service actions; and collaborative initiatives such as co-branding, joint marketing and participation in a network of value.

All strategic initiatives are composed of four essential elements: vision, capability, sustained refinement and continuous feedback. Although initially appearing to be a daunting task, creating a vision for the organization is only the first step in a complex process of managing incremental change within the organization. In order to realize the vision, the management team has to have a clear understanding of the organization's competencies – the combination of skills and tools with which individuals execute tasks to support primary business processes and specific banking products. Zurich Financial, for example, realized that a critical element of moving from vision to reality was an integrated, cross-organizational, secondary business process of collaboration and organizational learning, which, once established, would provide the means to refine the core process and tailor banking products using a continuous feedback loop. As a result, Zurich Financial have established nine practice boards linked horizontally across the organization, that act as an internal network of value synthesizing the changes in customer demand, while assessing the impact of business trends and cycles on the supporting organizations' ability to deliver. Within Zurich Financial, five practice boards focus on customer segments: consumer, corporate, commercial, small business and wholesale, while the other four practice boards centre on aggregated corporate capabilities such as communications, capabilities (human resources), finance and IT/eBusiness. This multidimensional process of continuous organizational alignment is illustrated in the 2001 annual report of Zurich Financial Services Group,[9] as shown in Figure 4.1.

Traditional retail banks and any organization that has offered financial services in the past now stand at a crossroads, in which operating in a globally competitive environment forces management teams to choose between reducing costs to increase shareholder value and making investments to satisfy a demanding new breed of customer. The management team faced with this dilemma realize that a series of continual tactical manoeuvres will be effective in the short term. However, to achieve significant long-term shareholder value and improvements in customer relations, a fundamental reinvention of retail banking must occur. Reinvention does not mean abandoning existing operations nor does it mean starting again. Reinvention, as described by Deloitte Research, is a series of changes that are designed, planned, coordinated and executed by business units to produce a fundamental shift in the business, resulting in a transformation. In Deloitte's view, there are six distinct types of transformations that financial institutions can capitalize:

1. the redesign of business processes
2. the creation of a customer-centric organization
3. the creation of a technology-enabled enterprise
4. establishing a rapid deployment capability
5. developing an extended enterprise
6. a basic recreation of the firm's business model.[10]

Therefore, a banking transformation does not have to be organizationally traumatic if planned as strategic initiatives which are coordinated by business units and timed to meet the expectations of shareholders, customers and employees.

Business processes redesign

Since Hammer and Champy's book *Reengineering the Corporation*, much has been written about re-engineering as a transformational process – the

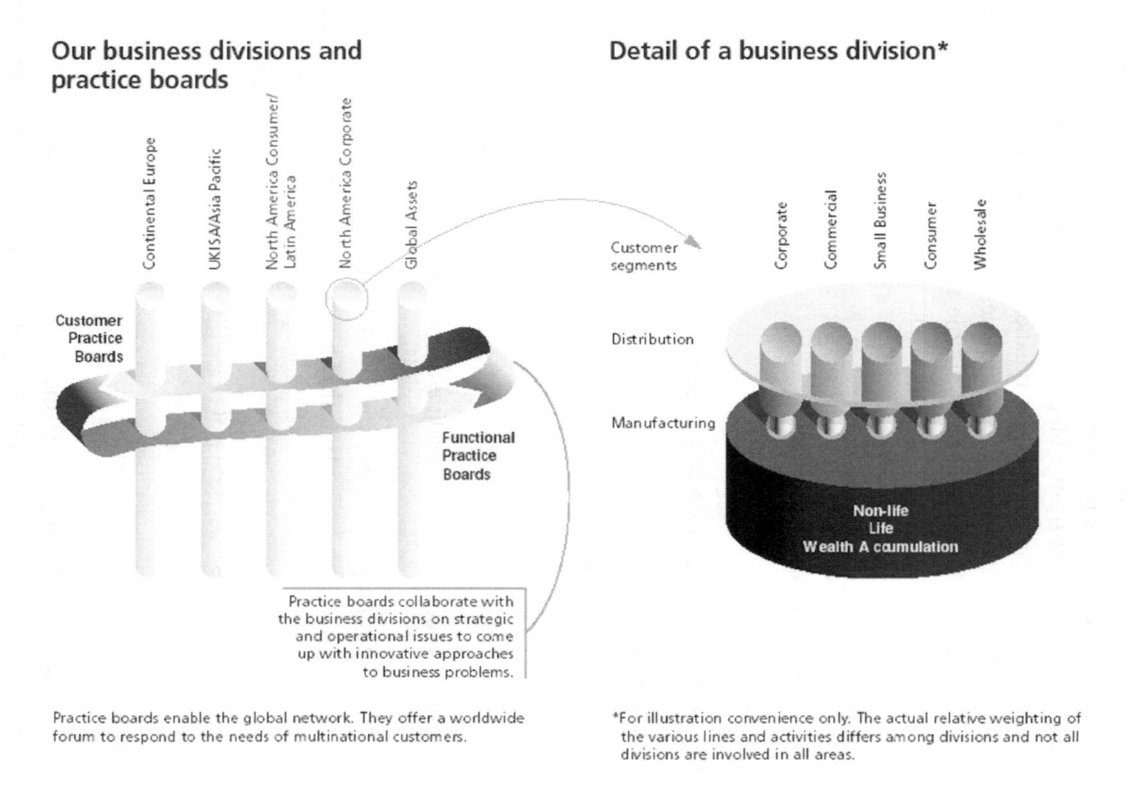

Our business divisions and practice boards
Continental Europe
UKISA/Asia Pacific
North America Consumer/ Latin America
North America Corporate
Global Assets
Customer Practice Boards
Functional Practice Boards
Practice boards collaborate with the business divisions on strategic and operational issues to come up with innovative approaches to business problems.
Practice boards enable the global network. They offer a worldwide forum to respond to the needs of multinational customers.
Detail of a business division*
Customer segments
Distribution
Manufacturing
Corporate
Commercial
Small Business
Consumer
Wholesale
Non-life
Life
Wealth A ccumulation
*For illustration convenience only. The actual relative weighting of the various lines and activities differs among divisions and not all divisions are involved in all areas.

Figure 4.1 Zurich Financial: practice boards

techniques, process of implementation and use of technology. What is clear from the popular discourse on re-engineering is that business transformation is the result of a process, not an event, or the implementation of technology. To remain competitive, retail banks must embark on a journey of transformation simply to survive. It is no longer a matter of if, but when. Business process redesigns either start from a blank sheet of paper or are a deliberate effort to streamline and rethink existing business processes. Hammer and Champy observed recurring themes in companies undergoing the redesign of their business processes, ranging from simple to complex interventions. Business process redesigns, according to Hammer and Champy:

- act to combine job functions
- empower workers to make decisions
- reorder process steps
- use or clone multiple versions of a process
- free work from the command and control structure of the organization
- reduce checks and controls
- minimize reconciliation
- create single points of contact between the process and the customer
- enable hybrid processes that centralize/decentralize operations.[11]

The key to redefining process steps is to ask why and how each process step was established. Often banks find that a process step was established to handle a historical exception that is no longer valid. The goal of business process redesign is to streamline the business process and increase its effectiveness in satisfying customer expectations.

The customer-centric organization

Traditionally, banks have organized themselves to maximize the efficiency of the organization by establishing a hierarchical structure and creating lines of business.

Fred Wiersema argues that to become customer-centric, an organization must develop an in-depth understanding of the customer's experience cycle and develop a hierarchy of customer needs, anticipate those needs and develop mechanisms that communicate them back to the organization.[12] For many retail banks, this translates into buying customer relationship management technology, which in many cases is a mistake. Before organizations rush out to buy technology, they must first leverage their knowledge of the daily interactions with customers to define the customer's experience cycle.

Customer-centricity is an understanding of the customer's experience with the retail bank, from the perspective of the customer. In the process of the exchange of value between customers and the entities they trade with (the things they buy and bills they pay), the value the bank adds in executing the process step must be transparent to customers. Process designers must answer several fundamental questions: how does our service offering add value to the exchange? Can we use technology to improve the performance, increase customer satisfaction and lower operating cost or expand the range of products? The adoption of customer-centric banking processes is not just an American trend, even though the majority of initiatives have come from North America. Evidence of global customer-centric behaviour can be seen by the increase in the establishment of more personalized banking front-ends, with websites such as Jacksboro National Bank's MyBank[13] in Texas, Singapore's OCBC Bank's mybank@ocbc.com and for private or premier customers me@ocbc.com,[14] Maryland's First United Bank & Trust's mybankfirstunited,[15] and initiatives like Citibank's MyCiti.[16] The essential component in moving to a customer-centric design is not the applied use of technology when developing service offerings; it is, however, asking the simple question: what intrinsic value does each business process step add to a transaction and is it perceived as valuable to the customer?

The technology-enabled enterprise

Retail bankers today have realized that simply buying technology to automate a business process or to use advanced technology as a delivery mechanism does not differentiate them in the marketplace. Technology has become less costly and easier to obtain by competitors and new market entrants. Technology is also turning out to be more complex in construction, less difficult to interface and more difficult to integrate. This combination of factors means that technology which can be applied with equal vigour by any organization is no longer a market differentiator. Michael Hammer reinforces the view that it is *how* a company applies a technology, coupled with the process design and the skills of their people, that generates market differentiation.[17] Market differentiation based on technology alone is rare and in most cases temporary. Creating market differentiation by the next generation of retail banks will stem from an understanding of the ways in which the organization applies technology in product delivery and the achievement of higher levels of customer service. As I argued elsewhere, the new business paradigm shifts the focus of technological innovation from the creation of new technologies to the applied use of technology to a company's value proposition.[18] Technology cannot just be applied; it must be leveraged to provide long-term value to retail banking operations.

Establishing a rapid deployment capability

Implementing technology, organizational change initiatives and other transformational programmes all have one common weakness – in most cases they fail to deliver significant value to the business. We can argue that technology is now so integral to business that a banking institution can no longer function manually and must view the acquisition and application of technology as a continual process, not a periodic capital expense. In many firms, participating in an implementation project is considered added work, often without any additional incentive or compensation. When organizations treat the implementation of technology and other business process improvement initiatives as temporary events with a beginning and an end, they fail to realize that projects never end unless the world ends. Therefore, as counterintuitive as it appears to be, executing strategic initiatives and implementing technology projects demand that the organization adopts a process that regularly, predictably and consistently delivers change, at a rate at which the people within the organization can absorb it, typically in 90-day cycles. The implementation of technology, improvements to the process and other efforts to optimize the performance of the organization should not come as interruptions to the business, they *are* the business, and therefore the core competency that the firm must develop is the ability to deploy capabilities in a manner that continually adds value to the underlying business process.

Developing an extended enterprise

Corporations engaged in banking activities acknowledge that few organizations today can compete locally or globally by operating as a solely independent entity; they are, as Michael Porter defined, part of a value chain of discrete activities.[19] More descriptively, as Hines et al. described, businesses are a part of a set of activities linked functionally, forming a value stream in which the functions of design, customer specification, production and distribution are the product of bidirectional sharing between firms.[20] To effectively extend the reach of the bank, the organization must operate within a synergic network of value, interoperating with external resources, suppliers, competitors and customers. Operating in a cooperative, co-mingled and inter-networked state presents the retail bank with the challenge of striking a balance between competition and collaboration. Long-term viability in the retail banking marketplace requires a comprehensive and holistic approach to managing the execution and performance of disparate, globally focused activities leveraged by technology. Extending the enterprise to include partners, joint ventures, strategic alliances, affiliations and associates demands that banks develop and manage a portfolio of added-value relationships.

Recreating the bank's business model

Throughout this book, you have been exposed to a worldwide variety of new banking business models. It would be naive, even foolhardy to decide suddenly to change the nature of your bank and embrace a new business model without carefully examining its applicability to your local operating environment. The effectiveness of a business model is relative to the environment in which it operates, greatly influenced by culture, religion, politics, regulations and many other factors. That said, new business models offer fresh perspectives on how to enhance significantly the existing banking offerings and introduce new services.

As retail banks establish strategic initiatives to reshape the organization, redesign their products and realign technology to provide higher levels of service to their customers and a greater return to shareholders, they must remember the fundamental characteristics of successful transformation:

- leaders must embody the transformation ethic
- the management team must be emotionally united
- employees need a rallying cry to action
- hierarchical organizational structures must be minimized
- simple performance measures must be established to report on the effectiveness of the initiatives
- at least one core competency must set the firm apart from its competitors.[21]

The key to generating long-term value with strategic initiatives is for senior management teams to create mechanisms to push decisions down to the lowest level within the organization that can effectively handle the problem.[22] A strategic initiative must be a definition of an expressed goal of the management team, encapsulated in measurements that disseminate the mechanisms of control to the business process. Effective strategic initiatives place the management as a resource in the organization, not a control point in the process.

The purpose of a strategic initiative falls into one or both of two distinct categories of corporate activities: increase revenue or decrease cost. Measurements do not need to be complex in order to be effective. One approach to measuring a strategic initiative is to break it down in to three definable components, each with a measurement that demonstrates relative motion towards the end goal. Measurements can be both quantitative and/or qualitative, being essential to the establishment of a mechanism for understanding the behaviour of process components. In order to develop an understanding of the integral role which process components play in each line of business, we must examine innovation in financial services, which is the topic of the next section.

Innovating new products and technology

When financial institutions implement technology or employ technology in a new way, they often make the same two fundamental mistakes found in other industries: they use new advanced technologies merely to do the same thing, and/or they put the wrong people in charge of the application of innovation. The first mistake assumes that acquiring new advanced technology and innovation are synonymous. Firstly, to most companies the benefits of the Internet have yet to be realized, simply because the expectations of how Internet and eCommerce technology can transform business is reduced when these technologies are simply applied to existing business processes and practices. A quantum change in the cost of business cannot be achieved by using technology to do the same thing but faster. At best, any company or financial institution can expect an incremental improvement in costs such as a lower cost per transaction. Secondly, the inherent gap between the lines of business and the technology organization leads to a technologist becoming responsible for the implementation and later operation of a technological solution, such as IT people becoming the corporate webmaster. Although there are exceptions, technology managers typically focus on the technical aspects of websites, such as programming, without an in-depth knowledge of customers or customer buying behaviour. Webmasters manage a channel to market, a brand image, and are the first point of contact with the firm for many new customers. Webmasters do need a technical counterpart who brings a deep understanding of how to implement current technology and, more importantly, the potential capabilities of new emerging technology.

There is a clear difference between implementing new banking products and true banking innovation. Today, most banking products come from software vendors and are associated with traditional lines of business, such as call centre telephone banking, mortgages, private banking, retail banking, stock brokerage, customer relationship management (CRM), annuity administration, payment systems, cheque processing and Internet banking. As vendors add new features and products, they provide an equal opportunity for all providers of banking services to utilize their technology to add value in similar ways. Unable to modify the physical software without incurring tremendous expense, retail banks must turn to applying the technology to the structure of the organization, increasingly depending on the skills of their people and the competencies they create as their differentiation in the marketplace.

Market innovation comes from combining resources to do old things in different ways, new things using old ways, or fundamentally new things in new ways, as exemplified in the case of Virgin's One Account, the Intelligent Finance's offsetting accounts,[23] and the Barclays Open Plan.[24] The premise behind these innovations is a fundamental rethinking of why customers have so many accounts that work at cross-purposes. The concept offers customers a range of services not based on different banking products, but on the customers' total personal balance sheet. These account schemes allow customers to offset their assets (such as balance in current and savings accounts) against liabilities such as mortgages and car loans. Offsetting reduces the amount of interest paid on loans by giving the customer a choice not to receive interest paid to them on deposits and applying these assets against the total amount borrowed, with the customer only being charged for the remaining loan difference. Other banking innovations occur in faraway places such as the Bank of East Asia's Cyberbanking offering, which is designed to place the individual customer at the heart of the relationship, with features such as MyCyberWorld personal banking, which allows access to up to 12 related accounts using a single account number. Other customer-driven services include MyPortfolio, MyAccounts and MyStock, which is an aggregated profile of accounts and assets held within the bank and with external sources. MyProperties keeps abreast of specified property valuations, MyLoans sums up loan profiles and assists in managing the customer's liquidity, whereas MyCreditCards manages credit card payments to avoid overdue interest. MyBills schedules payment instructions for up to a year for specific bills, including telecommunications, insurance, credit card, public utilities and government institutions, with a bill presentment option to view electronic bills over the Internet. These individually focused services, coupled with Cybertrading, CyberFund, CyberMortgage, CyberConsumerLoans, CyberCreditCards and CyberInsurance, enable the customer to access his or her accounts via an assortment of channels and offer frequently used functions and a switch to move easily between the instruction languages.[25]

Along a similar line is HSBC's rolling average total relationship balance, which determines the level of bonus interest on Hong Kong dollar savings accounts and monthly fee on HSBC Premier, PowerVantage and Super Ease accounts from which you can benefit. The total relationship balance aggregates deposits (both Hong Kong dollar and foreign currencies) with utilized lending facilities (excluding mortgages and amounts outstanding on credit cards), the savings component on life insurance, investments including securities, unit trusts, bonds and monthly investment plans, as depicted in Figure 4.3.[26]

This type of technology-intensive offering is no longer limited to larger banking institutions; even smaller banks can offer a variation of this type of service, with techniques like sweeping accounts found at the Farmers & Merchants Bank,[27] and WesBanco.[28] According to Mark Daubert, Northwest Bank & Trust Company, a community bank in Davenport, Iowa, has been offering sweep accounts since 1982 when it developed a product called the Bank Sweep Manager.[29] The same sweeping technology can be applied to investments such as Agiletics' fund sweep software, which automatically invests commercial and retail customers' available demand deposits into money market mutual funds and performs all shareholders' accounting on an in-house computer.[30]

Sweeping technology has a clear value proposition of improving the cash flows in the SME market subsegment, such as with the products offered by banks such as First Independent Bank[31] and Consumers National Bank.[32] The utilization of the sweeping technology from First Independent Bank can help to optimize a company's cash when a sweep account automatically transfers money between a business account and an investment account or business money market account. The transfers are fully automated based on your cash flow needs; therefore, small businesses can earn the maximum possible on their daily cash balances, avoiding overdrafts. The sweep concept can also be applied to local governments, such as the United Trust's offering, which sweeps accounts for local government

Figure 4.2 Bank of East Asia's Cyberbanking

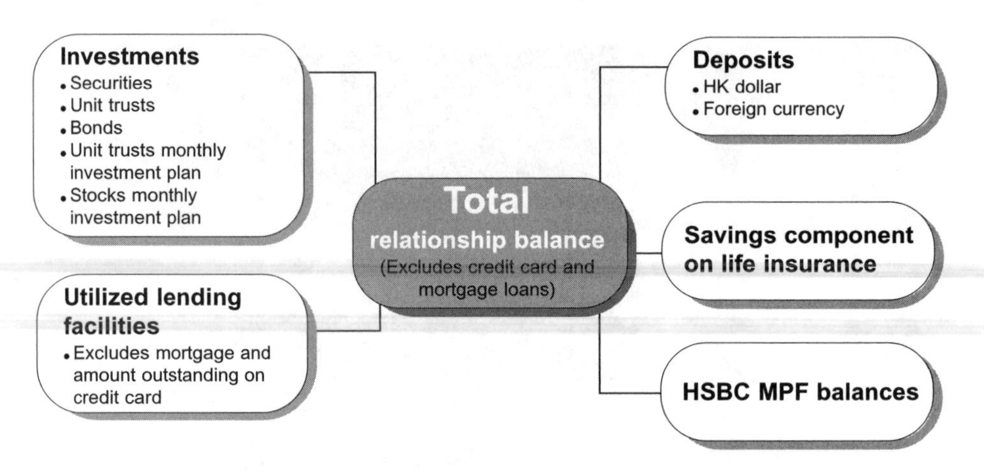

Figure 4.3 HSBC total relationship balance

municipalities to maximize effective returns on excess funds, increasing the efficiency of the local government.[33]

Retail banks realize that their technology is an important component in their value proposition to customers; however, they are also aware that technology is no longer the prime differentiator. Market differentiation based on technology alone is rare and in many cases only exists for a short time. The challenge will be to establish market differentiation as a product of how the organization applies the technology for better delivery of banking products or to achieve higher levels of customer service. What has been observed is a shift in the focus of technological innovation from the *creation* of new technologies to the *application* of technology to a bank's value proposition. Traditional and non-traditional retail banks must establish a process of innovation, using the existing technology and infrastructure of the firm and incorporating new technologies to enhance their banking product offerings, customer service levels or operating efficiencies. Ultimately, this will become the market differentiation.

Another innovation worth noting is the next generation, person-to-person email money transfer system called Yahoo PayDirect, which is the product of a collaborative partnership between HSBC and Yahoo in Hong Kong. This system permits individuals to send money or donations and request payments, or collect money from anyone in Hong Kong, requiring only an email address, as shown in Figure 4.4.

Once again, we find PayDirect's value proposition to be simple, clear and easily understandable to customers, regardless of their technological sophistication. The process begins with the individual registering and receiving a Yahoo ID and security key and a verification of their email

YAHOO! PayDirect from HSBC
Yahoo! HK - Help
Welcome to Yahoo! PayDirect
Already Enrolled?
Getting Started
To get started, just click below and give us your name, address and bank information.
It's as easy as 1-2-3!
get started now!
View Tour!
View Flash Demo!
(Flash plug-in required)
Already Enrolled?
Sign In Here
Email money to anyone.
(for any reason.)
send & receive money instantly
click & it's on its way!
collect money
send out an email bill to collect funds.
private & secure
our policy guarantees your money arrives safely.
"Sending money by email is so convenient"
1 Tell us the email address of the person you want to send money to or receive money from.
2 Tell us how much money you would like to send or receive.
3 We'll move the money and send you a confirmation email!

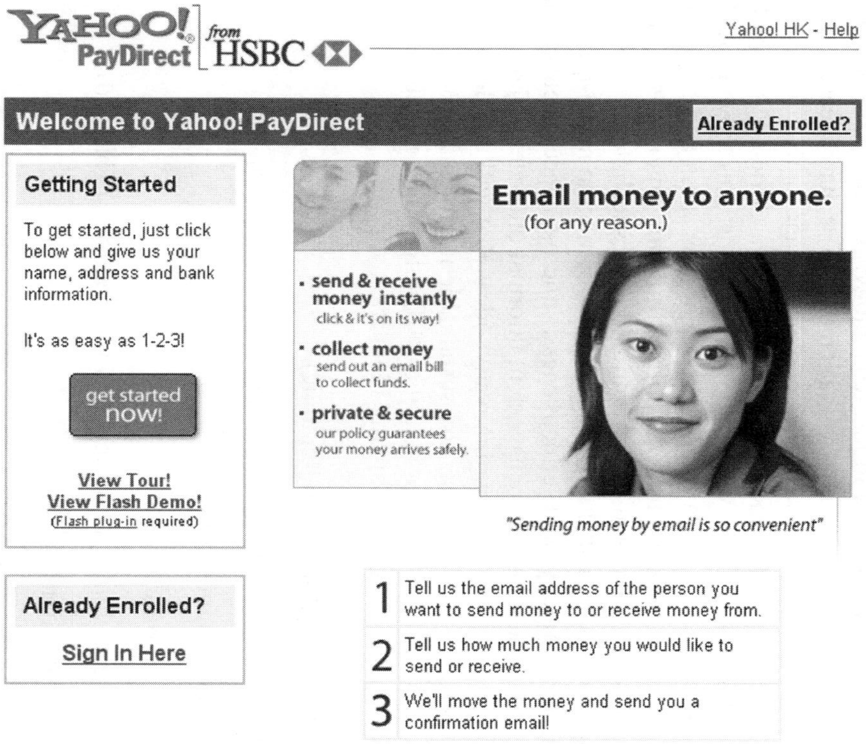

Figure 4.4 Yahoo PayDirect: HSBC Hong Kong

address; next, the user assigns the method of funding for the account and is able to execute transactions. Transactions are simple: enter your email address and the amount you wish to transfer or collect, PayDirect makes the transfer and then PayDirect sends you an email confirmation.[34] Two key features are that money requests and request for donations can be sent to an individual or a group, and customers can use this service as an alternative to placing their credit card information over the Internet.

Innovation is never limited to just technology: banking professionals in the Global Network for Banking Innovation (GNBI)[35] share ideas, concepts and best practices in a network of regulated financial institutions from Latin America, Asia, Europe, North America and Africa. As a part of Women's World Banking (WWB), GNBI demonstrates how providing financial services to the poor can be both good business and a means to change the world, one community at a time. Imparting innovative concepts to the network of affiliates, the organization provides technical services and training tailored to each affiliate's stage of development in micro-financing, organizational strategy and effectiveness, micro-finance products and processes, loan tracking and management information systems. The goal of the organization is to propagate innovative ideas that will enable affiliates to develop responsive, efficient, and sustainable micro-finance services in many of the world's poorer communities.[36] The founding members of the WWB's Global Network for Banking Innovation are:

- Banco ADEMI (Dominican Republic)
- Bandesarrollo Microempresas (Chile)
- Banefe Banco Santander (Chile)
- Bank Dagang Bali (Indonesia)
- Bank for Agriculture and Agricultural Cooperatives (Thailand)
- Bank Rakyat Indonesia (Indonesia)
- BlueOrchard Fund (Switzerland)
- Citigroup Foundation (USA)
- Delta Life Insurance (Bangladesh)
- Deutsche Bank Microcredit Development Fund (USA)
- Equity Building Society (Kenya)
- F.F.P.F.I.E. (Bolivia)

- Financiera Grupo Interfisa (Paraguay)
- FinComún (Mexico)
- Government Savings Bank (Thailand)
- Mibanco (Peru)
- National Development Bank (Sri Lanka)
- Kenya Post Office Savings Bank (Kenya)
- SEWA Bank (India)
- Shorebank (USA)
- Triodos Bank (The Netherlands)
- World Council of Credit Unions (USA).

The Internet has acted as a catalyst for innovation in the banking industry, producing new product ideas, new service offerings, redesigns of branches and back offices and the re-engineering of traditional lines of business. Technological innovation is heading the industry towards the next evolutionary step in banking services, with its anticipatory products and a greater focus on customer-centricity. One opportunity for retail banks is to develop service offerings which are proactive to customers' needs, such as when customers come to the bank for a debt consolidation loan after they are already experiencing credit trouble. Proactive banking provides consumers with tools based on the data collected about their banking behaviour that will guide them to avoid such actions. Anticipatory technologies permit new levels of customization, where the customer can tailor financial services products to his or her lifestyle, and also provide advice on impending transactions, offering preventive solution sets to meet life events. A customer's behaviour can be analysed against other customers in similar circumstances in order to develop perspectives on anticipatory actions. The behavioural aspects of these forms of transactions is that they provide market intelligence for the institution on trends that transcend customer groups, such as developing an understanding of how to untangle the finances of a couple going through a divorce.

From an innovation point of view, technology represents an ever-changing state of capabilities that can be combined with the human resources and intellectual capital of the bank to form core and non-core competencies. Technologies are truly innovative when they add value to a business process, customer need or solve a specific problem. Unfortunately, sometimes innovation is cloaked in the guise of a technology capability without assessing its relevance to the value proposition, as was seen when WAP technologies, designed for share trading by high net worth investors, failed to generate interest beyond a few small groups. It is clear that technology's innovativeness is determined by two factors that are sometimes out of synch with each other: the organization's ability to apply the technology to add a distinct element of benefit to the firm's value proposition, and the rate at which the technology appeals to and is adopted by particular groups of people. Often innovations that spring from technology face a time-lag between their introduction into the marketplace and their acceptance by the majority of a population. This effect was observed by Richard Buckminster Fuller in the early 1980s.[37] Later, Clayton Christensen observed a similar delay when studying the effects of a disruptive technology's ability to unseat incumbent technologies.[38]

The time-lag represents the time required to educate the population on the explicit and implicit benefits of the innovation. In retail banking, these technologies, such as new infrastructure, may appear to deliver great benefit to the bank with little added value to the customer. Nevertheless, even infrastructure, if packaged correctly, can present benefits to customers, such as lower operating cost, the ability to offer a greater number of services and higher levels of customer service. Therefore, from a retail banking perspective, technological innovations that are implemented and not readily embraced by customers indicate that although there may not be anything wrong with the technology or its implementation, there is something wrong with the way it was packaged or targeted to a specific market subsegment.

The trusted advisor

In Chapter 2, we examined the technology that supports bots, finbots and valagents. Here we shall discuss their practical application for retail banks to add value to customers. I have discussed elsewhere the merits of an emerging technology called 'valagents.'[39] Because valagents are an emerging technological capability in the aforementioned time-lag, it is appropriate to visit briefly their applicability to retail banking. Valagents or value exchange agents are intelligent agent technologies that bridge the gap between advice and action in financial services, representing to some degree a virtual trusted advisor. When employed directly to the bank's customer value proposition, valagent technology enhances the customer relationship by performing functions such as a consolidated portfolio view, portfolio rebalancing, asset allocation recommendations, risk mitigation and trade execution optimization. Although still not in widespread use, valagent-based technologies, such as IBM 's Virtual Private Banker[40] and German-based Financialbot.com's finbot,[41] provide mechanisms for financial services firms that extend the reach of an investor. These are some further examples:

- The JAM Project, in collaboration with the Financial Services Consortium including Chase, First Union and Citibank, Columbia University and Florida Tech, uses local classifier agents and meta-learning agents, allowing financial institutions to inspect, classify and label each incoming secured electronic transaction.[42]
- Agent Builder: Agents for Electronic Commerce is an application integration toolkit that enables the creation of intelligent agents quickly and easily, consisting of three interacting agents: one buyer agent and two store agents.[43]
- Agentis: Pioneered by the Australian Artificial Intelligence Institute and now available through Agentis International, applies artificial intelligence to business process management and can be applied to self-service call centre operations, real-time simulation and monitoring, and online compliance and detection.[44]
- The New York-based Artificial Life Inc. agent technology engages a user in natural language conversations, reducing the complexity of navigational schemes that often confuse users in many websites.
- ALife-PortfolioManager assists individual investors in selecting securities that match their investment objectives, presenting performance-related information in a visually simple format. Investors select sources of their choice to keep abreast of the market and are constantly updated with news. Ashton, the portfolio bot, educates the user and also serves as an alert system.[45]
- ALife-WealthManager is designed for goal-oriented financial planning, educating a user in investment concepts and assisting in calculations by identifying variables and statistical information, such as average costs, which are essential to managing investments. Using natural language, the conversation allows the user to interrogate options with personified agents Kubera and Ashton about retirement planning or planning for your child's education.[46]

- Botizen provides customizable customer service agents that enable rapid service response to a website 24 hours a day, seven days a week using natural language two-way conversations.[47]
- NativeMinds features virtual representatives (vReps) that can answer any questions you have about NativeMinds and its virtual representative technology, with facial expressions that match their responses. vReps such as Nicole provide a best-fit response in conversational language.[48]

However, for any retail banking institution that wants to become more familiar with this technology, the French website Agentland.com demonstrates the potential of agent technology, where agents have been aggregated and made available to individuals for use in various activities, such as shopping and active website searching.

Becoming customer intimate

Fred Wiersema provides us with the best definition of customer intimacy when he describes it as not simply increasing customer satisfaction, but taking responsibility for the customer's results.[49] To differentiate a traditional retail bank to a customer amidst the myriad of competitors, ultimately, banking customers will measure their relationship with the bank based on its ability to generate and maintain their wealth, contrary to the current view of the relationship as a generator of fee income. Soon customers will hold retail banks accountable for their ability to increase the quality of their lifestyle, and not view them simply as a place to hold money temporarily. The latest banking mantra is to get closer to the customer and embrace relationship banking. In 1992, Violano and Van Collie made a key observation that must not be discounted by today's retail banking institutions when developing their customers' banking experience:

> 'Relationship banking' is the buzz phrase by which retail bankers define their wildly diverse strategies. However, customers probably have a better relationship with their butcher or baker than they do with their banker. In fact, in numerous consumer surveys, banking scored second only to insurance as the industry perceived as least responsive to customers.[50]

To develop an understanding of customer intimacy within the firm, banking organizations must answer several key questions: who are our customers? How do we segment them in order to target our products and services efficiently? Are there some customer segments that we do not service or elect not to service? In the portfolio of retail banking service offerings, it is vital to understand which products are used by which customers and at what volume. Understanding the ratio between customer behaviour and volume is essential in establishing fees and allocating costs. Few retail banking companies categorize products by number of customers and transaction volumes. The channels to market most used by customers, ranked by profitability, raises another important question: can customers be motivated to use the most profitable channels? Another seemingly straightforward question is: why do customers use a specific product or service and what event or condition will trigger them to move to another institution? Put simply, under what circumstances do the product or service offerings lose customers and/or volume? Using a lifestyle/life-stage approach, at what point in the customer's life should the product be used and how does the bank assist in any required transition from one product to another during a change in the customer's lifestyle or life stage? Finally, can the customer's historical use of financial service products and services be used by the bank to help to educate the customer to be more self-sufficient?

Wealth management for everyone can become a reality at any retail bank by leveraging the right suite of technologies. However, on the other hand, wealth preservation is generated by combining technology with know-how and financial discipline, a market that has been traditionally associated with Swiss private banking institutions.

Becoming customer intimate does not necessarily mean that the retail bank must go it alone; outsourcing and partnering offer opportunities to optimize the cost of the relationship while expanding the reach and quality of service. An organization such as LINK Interchange Limited provides a fundamental service called MutualPlus that extends the channels to existing customer relationships. This service includes basic outsourcing such as the management of ATMs, and provides a gateway for credit/debit card services by acting as a connection to the Mastercard/Europay international network and to VISA via a VISA access point (VAP).[51] The most significant service offered by Link Interchange is the concept of branch sharing, in which two collaborating institutions do not simply share a common infrastructure but act as a platform for services in areas not covered by the other partner, as seen in the arrangement between the Britannia and Yorkshire building societies.[52] An agreement to share branches effectively provides the building societies' four million plus customers with alternative places to bank, enabling any of their customers in a part of the country without a branch of their own society to use the facilities of a sharing branch of the other society.[53]

This concept of sharing central resources is not unheard of within the financial services community, as five private banks operating in Switzerland have been utilizing a similar cooperative structure since the 1930s.[54] Geneva's private bankers operate as one entity for relations with government agencies, keeping member banks abreast of regulatory developments and coordinating information to the press and public via regular newsletters. This example of co-opetition reveals that these banks have achieved an operating synergy due to their common backgrounds and distinct value propositions to customers. Each bank addresses a unique market niche and offers customers a varying degree of customer intimacy similar to a client–attorney relationship. The motivation for this cooperative is simply to focus the resources of each firm on its core competencies – preserving and enhancing their clients' wealth.

Rethinking the branch from the perspective of a total customer experience, the Bank of Western Australia's (BankWest) branch of the future combines a service ethos of the 'over-the-counter era' with an open, retail plan and the latest in online and customer service technology. The customer experience can vary from face-to-face service for traditional day-to-day banking, the use of touch screens to investigate products and services offerings and an opportunity to learn more about online banking. Employing touch screen technology to reduce queuing, customers choose the type of service they require on arrival at the branch. Although the fundamentals of the branch's value proposition are convenience, ease of use and fast access for all customers, the goal is to use the branch to educate customers by providing them with the means to interact technologically and/or with highly trained staff.[55]

A variation on the theme of a more self-reliant customer, the Alliance & Leicester branch of the future's design has points-of-service and self-service zones within the branch equipped with staff to provide consultations, seating areas replacing formal counters, coffee for customers and a play area for children.[56] Similarly, the branch of the future at the Halifax (Figure 4.5) offers education, speed and convenience by fundamentally rethinking the basic misconceptions surrounding products such as loans and mortgages. Halifax is altering customers' perceptions of the branch by creating an environment where they can call in and obtain information on how much they can borrow, often receiving assessments of their mortgage limits within 15 minutes.[57]

However, branch of the future projects do not have to be overly elaborated to achieve a new level of customer intimacy. At the Venezuelan Banco Mercantil, the branch of the future provides an electronic identification to reduce the time customers must wait for teller windows, issuance of cheque books, cashiers' cheques and Abra 24 ATM cards.[58] This initiative focuses

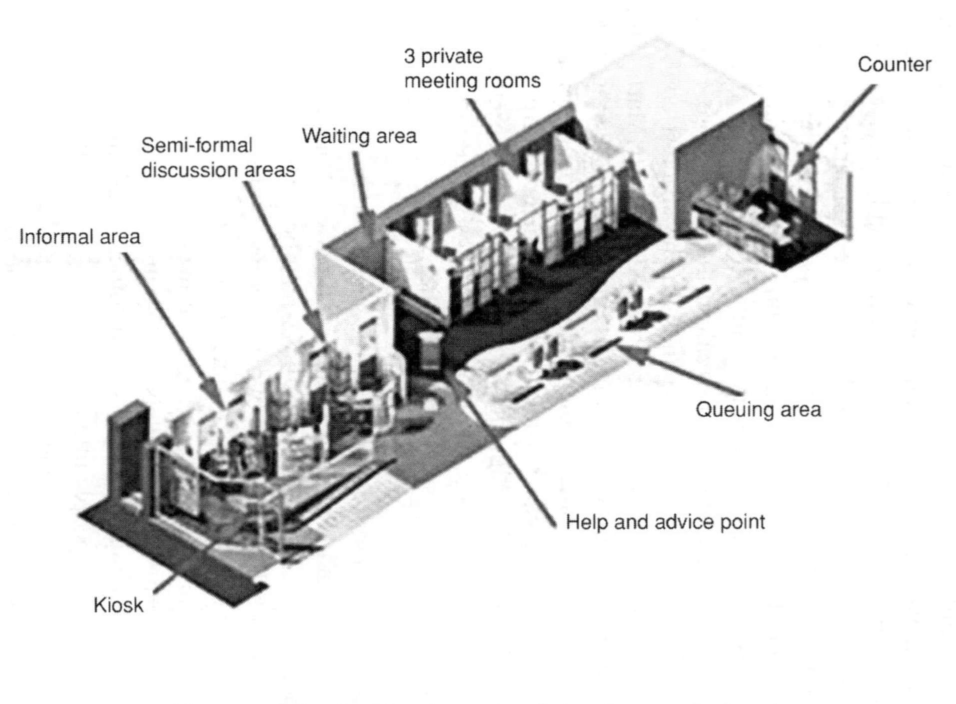

Figure 4.5 Halifax branch of the future design

on one element of their value proposition. Banco Mercantil's approach is simple and straightforward: identify the elements of your value proposition and address each one with highly focused technology projects.

Maris Strategies Ltd in Cambridge, England, has developed the Global Banking Survey,[59] a diagnostic instrument for financial services companies to self-assess their capabilities against the framework of Treacy and Wiersema's 'value disciplines'.[60] The survey/diagnostic, which is taken by individuals at various levels within the organization, asks questions to ascertain the organization's views, attitudes, and understanding of the firm's vision, goals and objectives. Survey questions are organized to gain information from the participant on business process, the applied use of technology and the structure of the organization. Banks and other financial institutions use this diagnostic to investigate gaps in their performance and identify opportunities to realign the firm's core competencies along one of the three value disciplines. In the strictest confidence, the results of all diagnostic/surveys are relayed back to Maris Strategies, where the data is synthesized into global and regional averages. An institution's relative performance is then compared to global averages and fed back to the firm so it can review its performance objectives relative to the global playing field. Although no institution can see the individual scores of another institution, the global averages gauge measures such as performance, technology spending and other strategic factors against an industry benchmark.

One interesting factor identified by the survey's data during the past two years is the dichotomy between a bank's expressed strategic goals and the tactical actions it takes relative to those intentions. For example, Figure 4.6 overlays global averages of two key areas of the survey – strategic intentions and tactical actions. Financial institutions indicated that their highest strategic priority was to be more intimate with their customers and focus on improving service levels, enhancing the customer experience, implement wealth management and customer relationship management systems and develop people into the role of a trusted advisor.

However, what Figure 4.6 also reveals is that their actions and spending habits indicate that their true focus during the last two years has been to reduce cost, with little attention to the expressed goal of customer intimacy. Banks have learned from the survey that they have either not been answering survey questions honestly or they have been lying to themselves about their ability to achieve the strategic initiative of customer intimacy. In reviewing their results, financial institutions have realized that achieving customer intimacy is more than making a declaration in the corporate mission statement; customer intimacy is a product of a deliberate process to

Figure 4.6 Global banking survey data

improve performance in managing customers' expectations over the lifespan of the relationship. Several banks have now begun to use the survey twice a year to measure progress towards objectives and keep abreast of changes in their performance relative to the global average. The survey is available to any banking services organization by contacting Maris Strategies.

Operational process excellence

Martin Dolan of Misys International describes the underlying problem with achieving operational excellence in traditional retail banks:

> All banks have a latent potential to generate value which in most cases is not understood. Retail banks begin to realize that they have this potential, typically, after competitive forces have suddenly captured a significant portion of their market share. It is at that time when competitive pressures force a bank to rethink their competitive strategy do they discover the unused capabilities of the firm, in many cases, having already missed the market opportunity.[61]

Dolan's point is that traditional retail banks are so busy implementing technology that they rarely look at the applied use of technology in the context of the business processes used to deliver a suite of banking services. This condition creates operational latency, which manifests itself in the technology organization's inability to serve the needs of the firm. In many cases, no matter how hard technology groups try to deliver value-added technological components to the business, they always appear to the rest of the firm as habitually delivering too little, too late, being viewed as unresponsive to the needs of the individual lines of business. The technology organizations and the lines of business must work together to deliver one thing – a process that consistently and predictably delivers technological components at regular intervals. After nearly fifty years of technology projects being viewed as something that interrupts the 'real' work of the business, companies are beginning to realize that technology implementations are part of the business and must not be considered extra work; these projects are the work that keeps the firm competitive. When financial institutions strive to achieve operational excellence, they often overlook this process of continual technological enhancement that reinvigorates the individual business processes within the firm.

Fortunately, there are many ways in which to achieve operational excellence within a financial services firm and, more specifically, within the retail banking services that it provides. The Industrial and Commercial Bank of China (ICBC) has approached the problem by acquiring a joint Midas and Trade Innovation solution from Misys Wholesale Banking Systems. By centralizing 15 international branch operations into a single overseas data centre hub, ICBC achieves economies of scale and scope while creating an opportunity to re-engineer its core and non-core processes.[62]

Another approach to achieve one aspect of operational excellence can be found in the utilization of software to manage operational risk. In Cambridge, England, Tactical Networks developed the RiskNetwork product to perform corporate arbitrage on risks that can be directly and indirectly associated with the business activities of the company. Tactical Networks methodology assigns risk directly to an organizational unit, a business process component or a product or service performed by the organization, the risk is then profiled against risk events and possible mitigators of the risk. As the business processes within the organization operate normally, risk is continually assessed against a list of probable causes or contributing factors and compared to mitigators or safeguards; the result is a risk profile for each individual operation in the organization. Individuals managing operational risk can alter the severity, likelihood and impact associated with each risk (Figure 4.7) in order to rank the relativity of each risk based on predetermined criteria.[63]

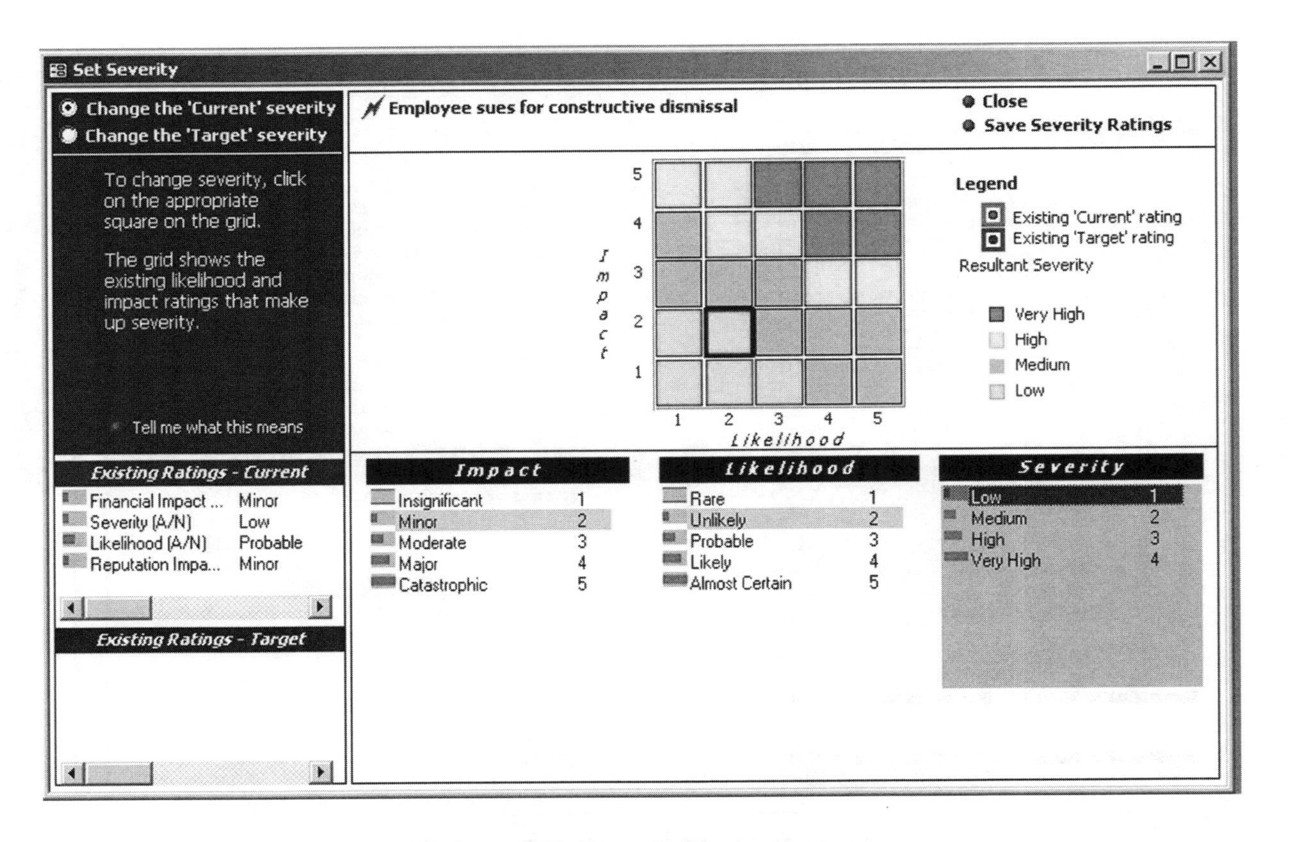

Figure 4.7 Managing operational risk

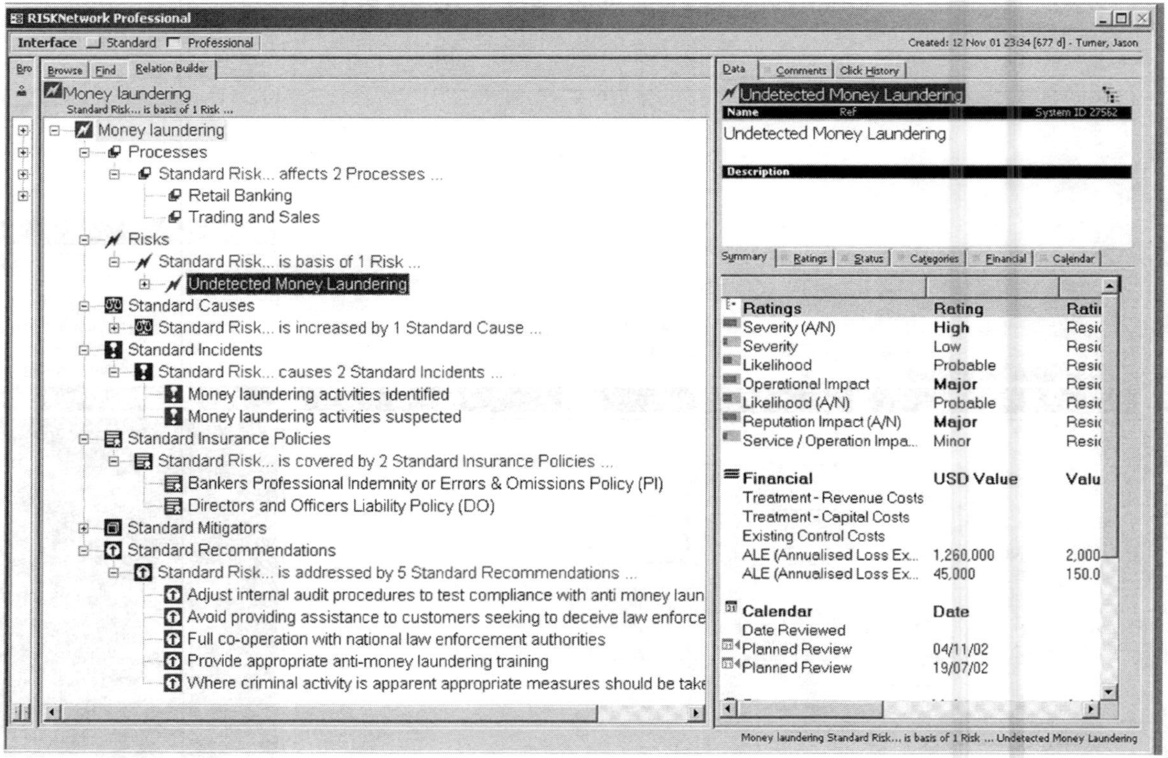

Figure 4.8 Assessing money laundering risk

The approach used by Tactical Networks can be used by companies to link actions that occur within the firm directly with the work flow of each underlying business process. This approach places risks associated with the activities of the institution into an operational context, allowing risk managers to act proactively instead of reactively. Specific risks such as money laundering (see Figure 4.8) can be managed within a set of operational parameters, which are monitored moment by moment, evaluating the individual risk against the total risk exposure of the firm.

Operational excellence can be achieved by viewing the lines of business as interoperating business processes, each linked via infrastructure and associated degrees of risk. Assessing the variables that control each process relative to the work flow of the retail bank reveals process steps that are not optimized and organizational groups lacking appropriate skills to perform all associated activities within a given process component. Even technological shortfalls can be identified and linked as an associative risk. In order to simplify this complex subject, tools of this nature allow managers to calculate rapidly what parts of the business are broken and ascertain the impact on other parts of the business.

Strategic sourcing and engaging co-opetition partners

The mistake that many financial institutions make is to assume that almost everything can be outsourced, broken up and reduced to a commodity. Banks, like any business organization, must continually combine corporate functions that provide various services in a cost-effective manner. In the act of combining functional services, the end product is ultimately twofold; a greater diversity in product offering to the customer and an increase in the efficiency of a co-mingled organization, whose output is more cost effective than that of both organizations if taken separately.

During the 1990s, these efficiencies were thought to come from two distinct sources: technology and outsourcing. However, in the post-dot-com era, organizations are quickly realizing that the key to delivering a comprehensive portfolio of products is in leveraging combinations of competencies composed of people and technology, and less on technology alone or wholesale outsourcing to a technology or service provider (Figure 4.9).

The Halifax's strategic 'branch of the future' modernization programme contains two key concepts and two technologies that retail banks should consider in developing a branch strategy, that of targeted innovation and strategic sourcing. The strategy uses a multimedia kiosk to direct customers

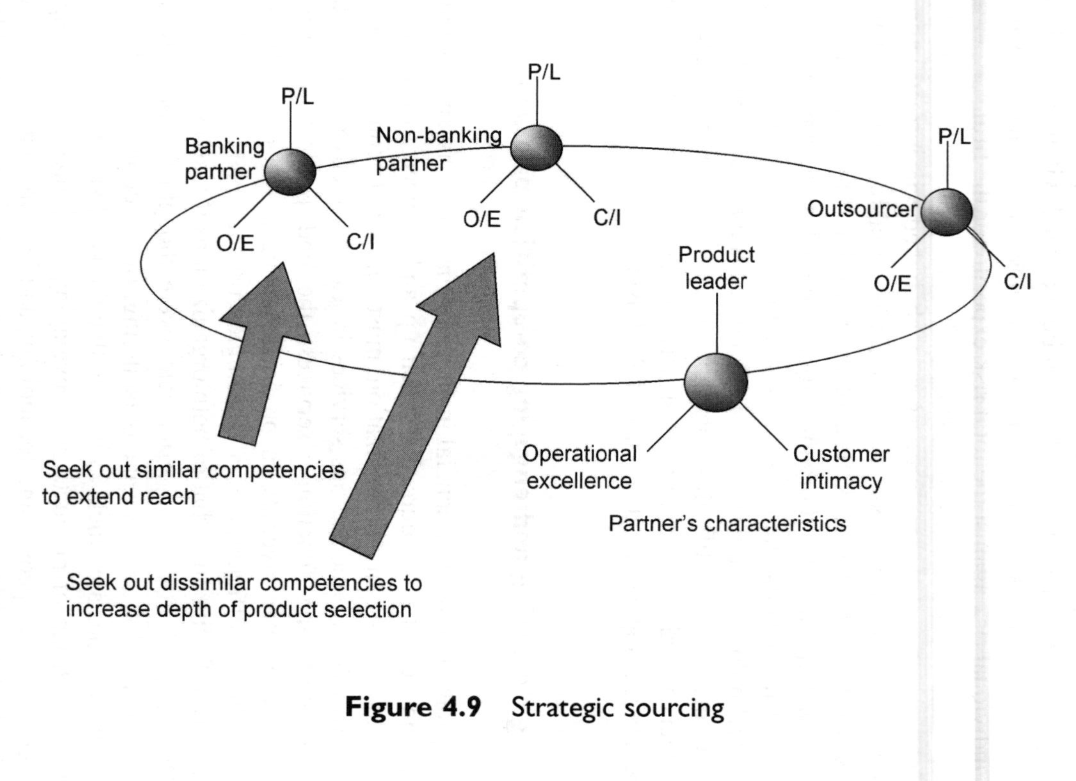

Figure 4.9 Strategic sourcing

Figure 4.10 Halifax plasma kiosk

to various areas of the branch and perform inquiry services, while plasma displays engage passing customers with narrowcast broadcast (the Halifax channel) content, containing a scheduled mix of video advertisements, animated customer messages and news (Figure 4.10).

These messages are adjusted to reflect the daily cycle of branch activity, designed with 'queue-busting' tips and messages to reduce busy lunchtime queues.[64] From a strategic sourcing perspective, the kiosks, loaded with interlinked applications, and the plasma displays operate on an in-branch network linked to a private extranet that is remotely administrated by the media company Tui Interactive. Content for the Halifax channel is controlled centrally, administered remotely and tailored for each branch.[65] Retail banks are using a smart sourcing approach to address three primary business concerns: customer attraction, customer retention and profitability.

Notes

1 A. Greenspan, 'Remarks by Chairman Alan Greenspan', Structural changes in the economy and financial markets, at the America's Community Bankers Conference, Business Strategies for Bottom Line Results, New York, 5 December 2000, available at the Federal Reserve Board, http://www.federalreserve.gov/boarddocs/speeches/2000/20001205.htm, May 2003.

2 First Independent Bank, Vancouver, Washington, available at http://www.firstindy.com/au_philosophy.html, April 2003.

3 J. Mackintosh, 'Virgin switches strategy with card launch', *Financial Times*, January 17, 2002, p. 22.

4 Virgin financial services, London: Virgin Management Ltd, available at http://www.virgin.com/, May 2003.

5 Mushtak Parker, 'NCB Aims to Take Islamic Investment Globally', *Arab News*, April 7, 2003 available at http://www.arabnews.com/.

6 M. Hammer, *Beyond Reengineering: How the Process-Centred Organization is Changing Our Work and Our Lives*, London: HarperCollins, 1998, p. 189.

7 C. Pretzlik, 'Co-op Bank reports 10th consecutive year of growth', *Financial Times*, 24 April 2002, p. 31.

8 *Banking Survey 2000.* Berlin: Bundesuerbank Deutschen Banken, July 2000, p. 156.

9 Practice Boards, Zurich Financial Services Group Annual Report 2001, Zurich: Zurich Financial Services Group, 2001, p. 13.

10 A. Tirabasso, F. Woosley, J. Witlin, K. Hayley, P. Strause and H. Lovel, Deloitte Research white paper, *Reinventing Financial Services: Succeeding with Corporate transformation*, Deloitte Consulting and Deloitte & Touche, 2001, pp. 6–9.

11 M. Hammer and J. Champy, *Reengineering the Corporation: A Manifesto for Business Revolution*, New York: HarperCollins, 1993, pp. 53–68.

12 F. Wiersema, *Customer Intimacy: Pick your Partners, Shape your Culture, Win Together*, London: HarperCollins Business, 1997, pp. 50–9.

13 MyBank, Jacksboro National Bank, Jacksboro Texas, available at http://www.jnb-mybank.com/, April 2003.

14 OCBC Bank, Consumer Banking, available at http://www.ocbc.com.sg/info/abt_OCBC/biz_act.shtm, April 2003.

15 MyBankFirstUnited, First United Bank & Trust, Oakland, Maryland, available at http://www.mybankfirstunited.com/, April 2003.

16 MyCiti, Citibank, N.A., New York, available at http://www.citibank.com/us/index.htm.

17 Hammer, *Beyond Reengineering*, pp. 101–7.

18 J. DiVanna, *Thinking Beyond Technology: Creating New Value in Business*, Basingstoke: Palgrave Macmillan, 2003, pp. 14–15.

19 M. Porter, *Competitive Advantage*, New York: Free Press, 1985, pp. 11–15.

20 P. Hines, R. Lamming, D. Jones, P. Cousins and N. Rich, *Value Stream Management: Strategy and Excellence in the Supply Chain*, Harlow: Pearson Education, 2000, p. 5.

21 R. Koch, *Strategy: How to Create and Deliver a Useful Strategy*, London: Pearson Education, 2000, p. 269.

22 J. DiVanna, *Synconomy: Ading Value in a World of Continuously Connected Business*, Basingstoke: Palgrave Macmillan, 2003, p. 109.

23 Intelligent Finance, Division of Halifax plc, available at www.if.com, February 2003.

24 Open Plan, Barclays, available at http://www.barclays.co.uk, May 2003.

25 MyCyberWorld, Bank of East Asia, available at http://www.hkbea-cyberbanking.com/index.htm, April 2003.

26 Total relationship balance, part of the HSBC PowerVantage, HSBC Hong Kong, available at http://hsbc.com.hk/hk/personal/bank/power/, April 2003.

27 Farmers & Merchants Bank, available at http://www.fmfbank.com/p_sweep.cfm, April 2003.

28 WesBanco Inc., Wheeling, West Virginia, available at http://www.wesbanco.com/wesbanco/bank/buscashmng.htm#sweep, April 2003.

29 M. Daubert, The Bank Sweep Manager, Northwest Bank & Trust Company, available at http://www.theformsgroup.com/wizard/webs/banksweepmanager/index.html, April 2003.

30 Fund Sweep, Agiletics Inc., available at http://www.agiletics.com/fundsweep.html, April 2003.

31 Business Banking Sweep Accounts, First Independent Bank, available at http://www.firstindy.com/bb_sweep_accounts.html, April 2003.

32 Consumers National Bank, available at http://www.consumersbank.com/sweepaccounts.htm, April 2003.

33 Government Sweeps, United Trust, subsidiary of United National Bancorp, available at http://www.vistabancorp.com/government/sweep/index.asp, April 2003.

34 Yahoo PayDirect with HSBC Hong Kong, available at http://www.hsbc.com.hk/hk/personal/payment/yahoo.htm, April 2003.

35 Global Network for Banking Innovation, available at http://www.swwb.org/English/1000/gnbi/index.htm, May 2003.

36 Woman's World Banking, available at http://www.swwb.org/INDEX.HTM, May 2003.

37 R. Buckminster Fuller, *Critical Path*, New York: St Martin's Press, 1981, p. 148.

38 See C. Christensen, *The Innovator's Dilemma: How Disruptive Technologies can Destroy Established Markets*, Cambridge: Harvard University Press, 1997.

39 J. DiVanna, *Redefining Financial Services: The New Renaissance in Value Propositions*, Basingstoke: Palgrave Macmillan, 2002, pp. 190–6.

40 Virtual Private Banker is a concept of IBM's Financial Services, available at http://www.ibm.com/industries/financialservices.

41 financialbot.com is a subsidiary of the Incam group, a stock market information service which specializes in the asset management of shares and investment fund deposits as well as the marketing of investment products.

42 S. J. Stolfo, JAM Project, Columbia University, available at http://www.cs.columbia.edu/~sal/JAM/PROJECT.

43 AgentBuilder, Reticular Systems Inc., available at http://www.agentbuilder.com.

44 Agentis, available at http://www.agentisinternational.com/.

45 PortfolioManager, Artificial Life Inc., available at http://www.artificial-life.com/products/portfoliomgr.asp.

46 WealthManager, Artificial Life Inc., available at http://www.artificial-life.com/products/wealthmgr.asp.

47 Botizen, VQ Interactive Sdn Bhd, available at http://www.botizen.com/product.html.

48 vRep, NativeMinds, available at http://www.nativeminds.com.

49 Wiersema, *Customer Intimacy*, p. 6.

50 M. Violano and S. Van Collie, *Retail Banking Technology: Strategies and Resources that Seize the Competitive Advantage*, Chichester: John Wiley & Sons, 1992, p. 9.

51 Link Interchange Network Ltd, available at http://www.link.co.uk/, April 2003.

52 Branch sharing, Link Interchange Network Ltd, available at http://www.link.co.uk/services/mn_services_branchsharing.html, April 2003 and more details can be found at the Yorkshire Building Society at http://www.yorkshirebuildingsociety.co.uk/about_us/mutuality/mutualplus/index.jsp.

53 Cambridge News Online, Cambridge: Cambridge Newspapers Ltd, 21 August 2000, available at http://www.cambridge-news.co.uk/archives/2000/08/21/business.html.

54 M. Dérobert, Geneva Private Bankers – The founders of a tradition, Geneva: Groupement Des Banquiers Privés Genevois, available at http://www.genevaprivatebankers.com/en/gbpg_profile.pdf, March 2003, p. 1.

55 Bank of Western Australia Ltd, BankWest launches branch of the future at Garden City, available at http://www.bankwest.com.au/newsroom/media/media_releases/2000/ 20001123_01 _ BankWest_launches_branch_of_the_future_at_Garden_City.asp.

56 Alliance & Leicester, Step into the Future, NCR Corporation, available at http://www.ncr-teradata.net/repository/case_studies/self-service/alliance_and_leicester.htm, May 2003.

57 R. Lindsay, Banking Technology Online, March 1999, available at http://www.bankingtech.com/online/features/1999/march.html, April 2003.

58 Branch of the future project, Banco Mercantil, Venezuela, available at http://www.bacomercantil. com/actual/informacion/reportes/quarter_report3/301099_b.html, May 2003.

59 Global Banking Survey, Maris Strategies Ltd, Cambridge, England, available at http://www.marisstrategies.com, May 2003.

60 M. Treacy and F. Wiersema, *The Discipline of Market Leaders*, Reading, MA: Perseus Books, 1997, p. 45.

61 M. Dolan, Misys International Banking Systems, Dubai, Telephone Interview, 29 May 2003.

62 The Asian Banker Interactive, 30 May 2003, available at http://www.theasianbanker.com.

63 RiskNetwork Walkthrough Document – Doc: AN1002-02, Tactical Networks, Cambridge, UK, June 2003.

64 Sun Micro Systems, Halifax Scoops a further two awards for innovative technology, 12 November 1998, available at http://java.sun.com/industry/news/story/8306.do, April 2003.

65 Halifax Branch of the Future Kiosk, London: Tui Interactive Media, available at http://www.tui.co.uk/pages/halifax01.html, April 2003.

CHAPTER 5

Conclusion: Synergistic Banking

This book has identified a number of opportunities for organizations engaged in providing retail banking services to prepare for the future. The future is not about doing any one specific thing; rather it is about doing many things right at varying times. The challenge for retail bankers is to balance continually the resources of the firm with the opportunities presented by the marketplace. From a theoretical perspective, resource balancing sounds easy. However, in reality, maintaining a judicious balance is extremely difficult, not because resources are limited, but because market conditions are changing at a dynamic rate, which means that sometimes products must be abandoned before their full return on investment is realized. These conditions create a new problem for bankers, that is, to understand the relationship between the product's life cycle and the waxing and waning of consumer and SME demand.

In order to capitalize on this relationship between product life cycle and customer demand, retail banking institutions must develop two critical skills: market sensing and rapid product commercialization. Sensing the market is not the duty of a group of individuals within the firm, but a process that must be established within the organization to assess continually market conditions, customer behaviour and competitors' actions. The process must employ people from all parts of the organization to identify new opportunities continually and, more importantly, rapidly assess the relativity of those opportunities to the resources of the firm. Therefore, the process occurs in three steps:

1. the ability to sense conditions in the competitive marketplace
2. the aptitude to rank these opportunities quickly and assess the firm's ability to capitalize on them

3. the ability to take these opportunities and implement them when favourable market conditions prevail.

In the past, an organization's ability to commercialize a product was proportional to the resources that were held in-house. In today's environment, the more important skill set is the ability to collaborate with external entities and business partnerships to bring retail products and services to market in the shortest possible time, while maintaining a high-quality service and preserving brand identity. Where financial institutions often make mistakes is in confusing the processes of commercialization with those of implementation. These two distinctly different activities are contained within a single process. Implementation can be achieved in one of three ways:

1. solely within the confines of the organization
2. through a series of connected partnerships between the organization and other firms already providing a complete product/service or portions of the product/service
3. outsourcing the delivery of the product or service completely to a third party.

Only with the balance of these three implementation options can a financial institution achieve varying degrees of operational synergy between divisions within its internal organization or between the internal organization and external companies, or a combination of both. In the case of outsourcing, the external synergy is not achieved by the coordination of resources only, but also by monitoring the input and output of the process in total. The resulting process input and output measurements must be viewed in the context of the firm's goals and other corporate objectives. These measurements are important for two reasons: they provide a means to measure and manage the relationship between organizations; and they establish benchmarks to which future performance can be calibrated. The key lesson is that the internal organization's ability to rapidly construct products and get them to the market is not the only skill needed by financial institutions.

The ability to negotiate and partner with external organizations is the fundamental skill that is leverageable in the long term, because it increases not only the capability and depth of the organization in the marketplace but also enables the institution to leverage the outsourcing provider or partner to gain access to new markets. The second fundamental difference is that in the future of retail banking, technology itself does not play the central role in attracting and retaining customers. The ability of a firm's products and services to generate overall wealth or an increasingly better financial condition for an individual is the key. Technology has been effective with customer segments that desire to optimize their relationship with a financial services firm based primarily on convenience and price. However, using technology within these segments has a hidden consequence: as the market segments of early adopter or convenience seekers become saturated, they will realize that the cost per transaction is not as important as total wealth optimization.

Developing synergistic behaviour

Retail banks can develop synergistic behaviour in three steps:

1. focus on a single product or group of existing products
2. optimize the internal business process and infrastructure that support the product
3. develop external relationships with supplier, outsourcers and distributors to provide or acquire a service or competency that supports or complements the product.

Synergistic behaviour is not simply coupling retail banking products together because they share a common potential to be purchased due to similar consumer behaviours. Retail banks can achieve synergies within a network of partners by looking for products and services that are interdependent and share requirements for a common infrastructure, thereby optimizing the cost structure of both organizations. For example, a bank has 20,000 Internet banking customers paying a single utility company for their water bill. The opportunity for synergy is that the bank can extend its service to customers and act as a buying group for the customers to get the best price for water. In addition, the bank can act as the outsourcer for the water company's accounts receivable, thereby improving the water company's cash flow and receivables ratio. When firms offering retail banking products alter their focus to external business capabilities this realignment of purpose demands a proactive change from the traditional inwardly focused measurement criteria.

Today, the retail banking market sits at the threshold of an era in which the industry will undergo three distinct changes: a move towards a value proposition that is transparent, that is, clearly understood by customers; the establishment of corporate competencies that enable dynamic adaptations to the needs of consumers and SMEs; and a proactive consultative approach, because the nature of retail banking is shifting from a product orientation to a customer-centric model which must anticipate changes in lifestyles and provide advice to maximize an individual's wealth. This fundamental realignment of the industry is taking place in three phases. The first phase, born during the dot-com frenzy, raised the competitive bar for many institutions and resulted in the realization that any organization could become a competitor for retail banking services. Phase two, the present, is slowly fostering a competitive landscape in which retail banking institutions understand that unless they have access to huge resources, a competitive strategy must include a set of partnerships. The third phase, and by no means the last phase retail banking will ever go through, is shaping up to be a period in which retail banks will develop co-mingled services that are the product of a network of transient relationships which ebb and flow with social preferences and are fundamentally shaped by global cultures.

To achieve greater synergies with partnering organizations, personnel within each organization must fully engage in a process of collaborative strategic thinking in order to continually improve the competencies of each firm, while keeping pace with changes in the marketplace and new demands from customers. A key lesson from companies that have already moved into this area of synergistic behaviour is that buying technology to establish a learning organization is vastly different from developing an organization that learns. Both organizations must learn from each other and from external sources to remain competitive during and after the collaborative partnership. Collaboration occurs within the banking industry and increasingly with non-banking entities such as supermarkets, retail stores and other merchants. In most cases, synergistic behaviour begins by sharing resources, information, expertise or data on the behaviours of customers, as Howcroft and Lavis note: 'Point-of-sale electronic funds transfer (EFT/POS) dramatically illustrates the need and preference for competition within a co-operative framework.'[1] Evidence of synergistic behaviour can be seen in the First National Bank of Central Florida's value proposition of 'Tomorrow's bank today', which is designed for one-stop convenience, with branches located inside the chemist Save Rite, the grocery store Winn Dixie and the retailer Wal-Mart.[2]

Another aspect of synergistic banking is the relationship between the institution and the community it serves. In many cases, this is more than just providing public trust as a third-party intermediary or a safe haven for

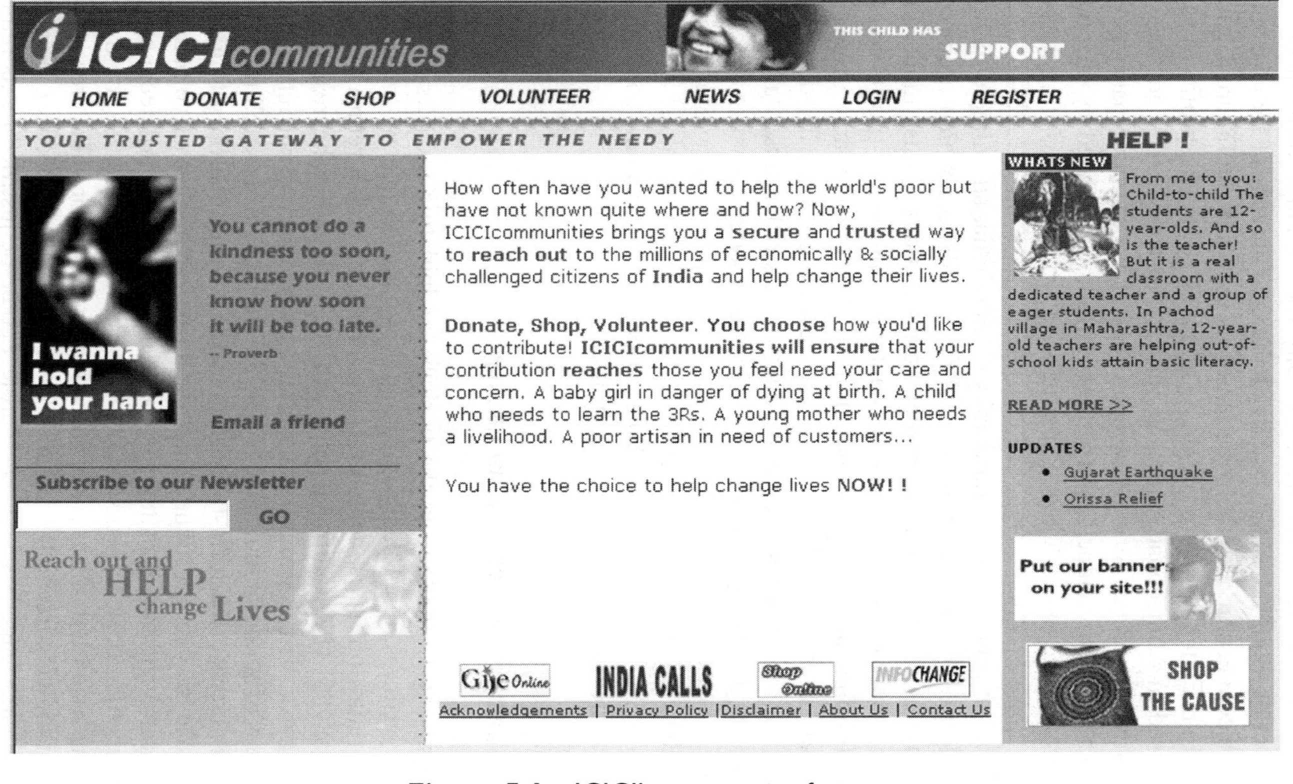

Figure 5.1 ICICI's community focus

deposits; it requires a degree of engagement with the community. ICICI's vision to be the trusted worldwide gateway for the empowerment of the 'millions of economically and socially challenged citizens of India' exemplifies this connection with the community, as shown in the Figure 5.1.[3]

The GIVE Foundation, a professionally managed not-for-profit organization based in Ahmedabad, India, in partnership with ICICI Ltd, one of India's largest financial services companies, follows a unique partnership model, where each 'channel' on its Internet portal is managed by different partner organizations or 'channel partners'. Partners in this community bring a value-added expertise and/or a special passion to each channel. One important aspect of this community is GiveIndia, an online donation channel owned and managed by the GIVE Foundation, which promotes acts of 'giving' to help non-governmental organizations to raise funds, and promotes greater transparency and accountability in the non-profit sector.[4] The GIVE Foundation operates with an interesting model that treats every donor as an 'investor' looking for 'impact returns' on his or her donation. A second tier of important community links is 'Shop the cause', a channel that offers high-quality handicrafts produced by poor artisans, which is managed by Craftsbridge, an organization dedicated to promoting traditional Indian art and artisans.[5] IndiaCalls, the volunteering channel, is managed by MITRA Technology Foundation, an organization committed to promote the cause of volunteering in India.[6]

Adopt a return on process mentality

When applying technology to the business or initiating projects to revitalize the business, retail banks have an opportunity to jettison traditional views of return on investment (ROI) and move towards a return on total process (ROP). The traditional approach of ROI views the result of a project's associated resources and labour as a one-time event rather than the product of a continuous process. In the current business climate, the use of the Internet, the infrastructure to support it and interoperating core banking systems are not luxury channels to market or alternative paths to the customer, but prerequisites for conducting business. All technology projects should consider two simple methods for the reconciliation of the use of corporate funds: ROI for justification and ROP for value creation.

In the following example (Figure 5.2) of technology projects needed to support the mortgage business, each project could be justified by its return on investment. However, projects rarely consider the incremental investments necessary to maintain the complete process of mortgage processing.

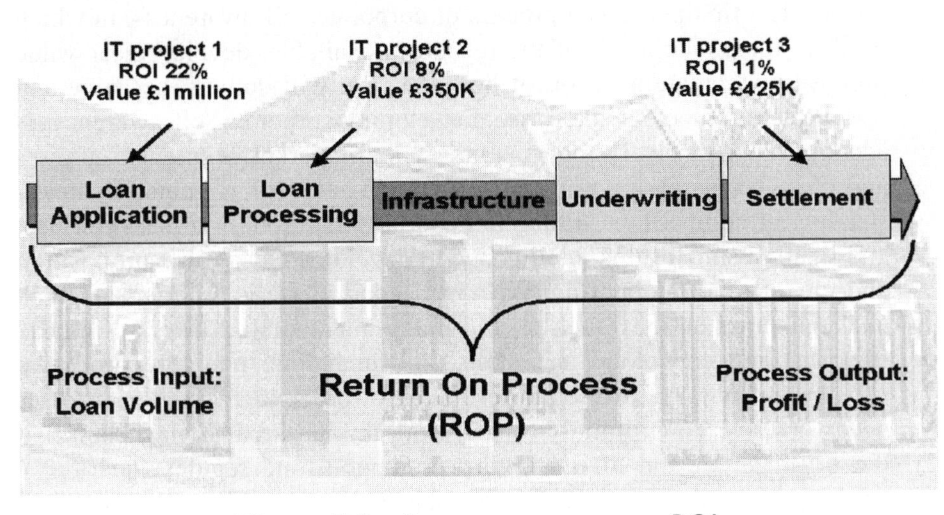

Figure 5.2 Return on process vs ROI

Repeated investments in infrastructure require a holistic approach to anticipate changes in business processes. Investment in infrastructure must be made strategically before any rise in demand to avoid playing a continual game of catch-up. Put simply, when considering the projects illustrated in Figure 5.2, investments in infrastructure must be made based on the incremental improvement to the entire mortgage processing capability of the firm. Adopting a return on process perspective dictates that technology investments must always result in an improvement in one or both sides of an equation of value, either by providing capacity for an increase in the loan volume or a direct reduction in the cost of mortgage operations.

Because of the increased levels of competition made possible by technological advances, retail banks can ill afford the view that technologies used in the delivery of service offerings are one-time investments that can be justified by the reduction in costs or labour that they bring. The business reality of the global marketplace is that in retail banks, technology is such an integral part of the business that it must be justified on the direct or indirect value it creates for customers.

Three steps to synergy

Achieving operational synergy within a network of value-added partnerships is not as daunting a task as it may appear at first. Organizations that have recently made the transition have found that it occurs in three phases. The first phase is a process of corporate self-awareness, in which the firm must take stock of the resources available, develop clear value propositions, create a vision of how the firm will deliver the value and operate as a competent enterprise. Developing corporate self-awareness is accomplished by analysing customers, their market segments, cultures and lifestyles, assessing the competition and developing a detailed understanding of competitors' traditional and non-traditional service offerings, and finally using all this intelligence to develop a clear value proposition and identify target opportunities. The second phase is a period of quick and deliberate actions such as the realignment of the firm's products, organization, technology and skills, at which time non-core processes may be outsourced to free up resources in order to focus on customer needs or drive down initial costs. During this phase, it is important that the organization and all its initiatives demonstrate regular (quarterly), predictable results towards the end objectives. The third phase delivers the firm closer to a new operating state in which options such as outsourcing core processes and establishing cells of competencies can be exercised. It is during this final phase that organizations must quickly achieve synchronization with partners in the network of value, linking products, co-branding, white labelling and other activities that establish an inherent bond between the capabilities of the firms to deliver value to customers. Lastly, but by no means least, a firm must optimize costs and mitigate risks.

A final note

Retail banking is undergoing tremendous changes, with amazing advances in technology enhancing the customer experience and providing banking personnel with ever-increasing real banking knowledge. Changes in how a bank works, how banks adds value to the customer and serve the communities in which they operate will be revolutionary, as the processes of globalization and disintermediation reshape the economic and political structures of the world. People within the retail banking community stand at the vanguard of this next evolutionary step in banking and world economics; they are the standard bearers for change as customers from all parts of the world look to retail banks to be the pinnacle of ethical and moral behaviour and provide a measure of stability in an increasingly uncertain world. It was my intention when writing this book to expose the reader to the global cornucopia of banking services that are not simply making money for shareholders but, as we have seen, enhancing the lives of their customers, regardless of culture, religion, race, sex, politics or economic standing. It is hard to imagine a more vibrant and exciting place to be than in financial services during the next 20 years.

Notes

1. J. B. Howcroft and J. Lavis, *Retail Banking: The New Revolution in Structure and Strategy*, Oxford: Basil Blackwell, 1986, p. 67.
2. Tomorrow's Bank Today, First National Bank of Central Florida, available at http://www.tomorrowsbanktoday.com/index.htm, May 2003.
3. ICICIcommunities.org, managed by the GIVE Foundation and supported by ICICI Limited, India, available at http://www.icicicommunities.org/communities/index.asp, May, 2003.
4. GiveIndia, the GIVE Foundation, available at http://www.givefoundation.org, May 2003.
5. Craftsbridge, available at http://www.craftsbridge.com, May 2003.
6. IndiaCalls, Mitra Technology Foundation, available at http://www.mitra.org.in, May 2003.

REFERENCES

J. Blythe, *The Essence of Customer Behaviour*, London: Pearson Education Ltd, 1997.

F. Braudel, *Civilization and Capitalism 15th–18th Century, volume II: The Wheels of Commerce*, London: William Collins & Sons, 1982.

C. Brown-Humes, 'Competition pushes Iceland's bank to form new alliances', *Financial Times*, 28 May 2003.

R. Buckminster Fuller, *Critical Path*. New York: St Martin's Press, 1981.

T. Burt, 'Carmakers eye route to twin track revenues', *Financial Times*, 28 February 2001.

G. R. Bushe and A. B. Shani, *Parallel Learning Structures. Increasing Innovation in Bureaucracies*, Addison-Wesley, 1991.

J. Champy, *X-engineering the Corporation: Reinventing your Business in the Digital Age*, New York: Warner Books, 2002.

C. Christensen, *The Innovator's Dilemma: How Disruptive Technologies can Destroy Established Markets*, Cambridge: Harvard University Press, 1997.

Consumer Acceptance of Banking Technology, ABA Banking Journal Supplement, American Bankers Association, November 1997.

G. Davies, *A History of Money from Ancient Times to the Present Day*, Cardiff: University of Wales Press, 1996.

H. Davies, *Averaging in a Framework of Zero Reserve Requirements: Implications for the Operations of Monetary Policy*, London: Bank of England, 1998.

M. Dickie, 'Sars sends stay-at-home Chinese on to the net', *Financial Times*, 22 May 2003.

J. DiVanna, *Redefining Financial Services: The New Renaissance in Value Propositions*, Basingstoke: Palgrave Macmillan, 2002.

J. DiVanna, *Thinking Beyond Technology: Creating New Value in Business*, Basingstoke: Palgrave Macmillan, 2003.

J. DiVanna, *Synconomy: Adding Value in a World of Continuously Connected Business*, Basingstoke: Palgrave Macmillan, 2003.

H. Engler and J. Essinger, *The Future of Banking*, London: Pearson Education, 2000.

H. Engler and J. Essinger, 'Sir John Bond Interview', *The Future of Banking*, Harlow: Pearson Education, 2000.

J. Essinger, *The Virtual banking Revolution: The Customer, the Bank and the Future*, London: International Thompson Business Press, 1999.

A. Fifield, 'Kiwibank can afford to hold critics to account', *Financial Times*, 24 April 2003.

A. Greenspan, 'Remarks by Chairman Alan Greenspan', Structural changes in the economy and financial markets. At the America's Community Bankers Conference, Business Strategies for Bottom Line Results, New York, 5 December 2000.

T. E. Gregory, *The Westminster Bank: Through a Century*, London: Westminster Bank, 1936.

A. Gunneson, *Transitioning to Agility*, Reading: Addison-Wesley, 1997.

M. Hammer, *Beyond Reengineering: How the Process-centred Organization is Changing our Work and our Lives*, London: HarperCollins, 1996.

M. Hammer and J. Champy, *Reengineering the Corporation: A Manifesto for Business Revolution*, New York: HarperCollins, 1993.

D. Hargreaves, 'Where do you think you're going?', *Financial Times*, 13–14 July 2002.

P. Hines, R. Lamming, D. Jones, P. Cousins and N. Rich, *Value Stream Management: Strategy and Excellence in the Supply Chain*, Harlow: Pearson Education, 2000.

P. Hollis, 'Sandler Seminar Speech', Department of Work and Pensions, 9 October 2002.

J. B. Howcroft and J. Lavis, *Retail Banking: The New Revolution in Structure and Strategy*, Oxford: Basil Blackwell, 1986.

E. Hunt and J. Murray, *A History of Business in Medieval Europe 1200–1550,* Cambridge: Cambridge University Press, 1999.

J. Jordan, *The Functions and Future of Retail Banking*, Cleveland: Federal Reserve Bank of Cleveland, 1996.

J. M. Keynes, *The General Theory of Employment, Interest and Money.* London: Macmillan, 1946.

R. Koch, *Strategy: How to Create and Deliver a Useful Strategy*, London: Pearson Education, 2000.

J. Le Goff, 'The Usurer and Purgatory', in Fredi Chiappelli (ed.), *The Dawn of Modern Banking,* New Haven: Yale University Press, 1979.

R. Lopez, 'The Dawn of Medieval Banking', in Fredi Chiappelli (ed.), *The Dawn of Modern Banking*. New Haven: Yale University Press, 1979.

J. Mackintosh, 'Virgin switches strategy with card launch', *Financial Times*, 17 January 2002.

N. Negroponte, *Being Digital*, London: Hodder & Stoughton, 1995.

C. Pass, B. Lowes and L. Davis, *Unwin Hyman Dictionary of Economics*, Leicester: Unwin Hyman, 1999.

H. Pirenne, *Economic & Social History of Medieval Europe*, London: Kegan Paul/ Trench, Trubner, 1937.

M. Porter, *Competitive Advantage*, New York: Free Press, 1985.

M. Prestwich, 'Italian Merchants in Late Thirteenth and Early Fourteenth Century England', in Fredi Chiappelli (ed.), *The Dawn of Modern Banking*. New Haven: Yale University Press, 1979.

C. Pretzlik, 'Co-op Bank reports 10th consecutive year of growth', *Financial Times*, 24 April 2002.

C. Pretzlik and W. Hall, 'Alps provide no shelter for Switzerland's private banks', *Financial Times*, 24 April 2003.

J. Rossier, 'Ethics and Money: What is required of the banking professional', *La Lettre*, Geneva: Geneva Private Bankers Association, No. 23, March 2003.

A. Rowley, 'New kid on the block', The Banker Supplement, London: *Financial Times*, March 2001.

M. Sanchanta, 'Japan's first online-only bank opens', *Financial Times*, 12 October 2000.

C. P. Smith, *Retail Banking Rethink: Strategic Marketing in Action*, Dunblane: Doica, 1990.

E. Solomon, *Virtual Money: Understanding the Power and Risks of Money's High-Speed Journey into Electronic Space*, Oxford: Oxford University Press, 1997.

J. Teplitz and C. Mills, 'Filling the value gap in mergers', The Banker Supplement, London: *Financial Times*, March 2001.

A. Toffler, *The Adaptive Corporation*, London: McGraw-Hill, 1985.

M. Treacy and F. Wiersema, *The Discipline of Market Leaders*, Reading, MA, Perseus Books, 1997.

M. L. Tushman, B. Virany and E. Romanelli, 'Executive succession, strategic reorientations, and organization evolution', in M. Horwitch (ed.) *Technology in the Modern Corporation: a Strategic Perspective*, Oxford: Pergamon Press, 1986.

V. Vijayshanker Bhatt, *Financial Systems, Innovation and Development*, London: Sage, 1995.

M. Violano and S. Van Collie, *Retail Banking Technology: Strategies and Resources that Seize the Competitive Advantage*, Chichester: John Wiley, 1992.

W. Waldron, 'Banking on Tomorrow', *Fast Company*, Issue 51, October 2001.

F. Wiersema, *Customer Intimacy: Pick your Partners, Shape your Culture, Win Together*, London: HarperCollins Business, 1997.

J. Williams (ed), *Money: a History*, New York: St Martin's Press, 1997.

R. Wirtz, 'Breaching the buckskin curtain', *The Region: Banking and Policy Issues Magazine*, Minneapolis: Federal Reserve Bank of Minneapolis, September 2000.

INDEX